Philosophy of Law

Fundamentals of Philosophy

Series Editor: A. P. Martinich, University of Texas at Austin

Each volume in the *Fundamentals of Philosophy* series covers a key area of study in philosophy. Written with verve and clarity by leading philosophers, these authoritative volumes look to reveal the fundamental issues and care problems that drive interest the field.

Philosophy of Law

Mark C. Murphy

Blackwell Publishing

BLACKWELL PUBLISHING
350 Main Street, Malden, MA 02148-5020, USA
9600 Garsington Road, Oxford OX4 2DQ, UK
550 Swanston Street, Carlton, Victoria 3053, Australia

The right of Mark C. Murphy to be identified as the Author of this Work has been asserted in accordance with the UK Copyright, Designs, and Patents Act 1988.

First published 2007 by Blackwell Publishing Ltd

3   2009

Library of Congress Cataloging-in-Publication Data

Murphy, Mark C.
Philosophy of law : the fundamentals / Mark C. Murphy.
   p. cm. — (Blackwell fundamentals of philosophy ; 2)
Includes bibliographical references and index.
ISBN 978-1-4051-2946-6 (hardcover : alk. paper)
ISBN 978-1-4051-2960-2 (pbk. : alk. paper)
1. Law—Philosophy. I. Title. II. Series.

K230.A3M87 2007
340′.1—dc22

2005031980

A catalogue record for this title is available from the British Library.

For further information on
Blackwell Publishing, visit our website:
www.blackwellpublishing.com

for Finnian Thomas

Contents

Contents

Contents

Acknowledgments

It is unlikely that the idea of writing an introduction to the philosophy of law would have occurred to me had it not been suggested by the general editor of Blackwell's Fundamentals of Philosophy series, Al Martinich. I am grateful to him for putting me up to this as well as for his criticisms and comments on drafts of the text. I also owe thanks to the editorial staff at Blackwell, particularly Jeff Dean and Danielle Descoteaux, for their help in improving the book and moving it along. At important points in the book's writing – at the proposal stage, after a complete first draft, and near completion – they solicited the help of referees whose contributions were very valuable to me. While it is customary in academia for these referees to remain anonymous, I hope that they know how grateful I am that they were willing to undertake this service. I am extremely grateful also to Jenny Roberts, the project manager, who showed extraordinary care and good sense in seeing the manuscript through production.

To the extent that this book manages to engage the reader and to help him or her see the main contours of the topography of legal philosophy, I owe a great deal to the students in my philosophy of law classes at Georgetown University, who are very forthright about letting me know which ways of presenting arguments are perspicuous and which are not. I owe a special debt to the students in my fall 2004 class, who were subjected to the first drafts of these chapters as part of their course reading, and provided me with useful feedback. (I am particularly indebted to Brian Griffin, Matt Middleton, and Beth Mueller, whose comments led to substantial rewrites.) During that semester I was also privileged to sit in on my colleague Robin West's Torts class at Georgetown Law Center. I am certain that my way of seeing the philosophy of tort law is heavily influenced by Robin's framing of tort doctrine, and I owe her thanks for suffering a philosopher's presence.

As always, the greatest debt incurred in writing this book is to my wife, Jeanette. During the semester in which the first draft was written, my schedule was extraordinarily hectic. While this made for an intellectually exciting time for me, as a result she bore a massively

Acknowledgments

disproportionate share of the burdens of our family's life, burdens that she shouldered with her characteristic humor and grace. While forbearance is only one of her many excellences, it is the virtue that stands in relief in this case.

Mark C. Murphy

Herndon, Virginia

September 30, 2005

Introduction

It is owing to their wonder that men both now begin and at first began
to philosophize.

(Aristotle, Metaphysics, 982b15)

The most natural way of doing this is to start from the things which are
more knowable and obvious to us.

(Aristotle, Physics, 184a17)

0.1 Philosophy, the Familiar, and the Unfamiliar

Aristotle says that philosophy begins in wonder, but that the starting
point of systematic investigation is what is "more knowable and obvious to us" – what is most familiar. One might think that these two ideas
don't fit very well together, for it would seem that by affirming both we
could reach the conclusion that what is familiar is a cause of wonder.
But isn't what is wondrous the *unfamiliar*? We don't experience wonder
at amusement parks by doing laundry but by going on roller coasters,
and we don't experience wonder at movie theatres by watching films
filled with the trivia of everyday life but by seeing Spider-Man swing
between skyscrapers. It turns out, though, that Aristotle's two remarks
together express an important truth about all fields of philosophy,
including our field, the philosophy of law: while the starting points in
philosophy are extraordinarily familiar, these familiar starting points
generate issues and ideas that are far from ordinary.

All fields in philosophy begin with what is familiar and proceed to the
unfamiliar. Consider, to take just one example, the philosophical area of
epistemology. Epistemology is the study of knowledge and belief. When
one begins to investigate matters in the field of epistemology, one
characteristically begins not with bizarre puzzles ("How do I know
that what I'm experiencing isn't all a dream?" "How do I know that
I am not being deceived by an evil demon?" "How do I know that the
world didn't come into existence five minutes ago?" – that sort of thing)

1

but with rather ordinary, down-to-earth points that all of us accept about belief. We accept that we believe some things and disbelieve others, and that there are yet other things that we neither believe nor disbelieve. We accept that sometimes we believe what is false, or disbelieve what is true. We accept that some beliefs are better than others – some beliefs are silly, others sober; some irrational, others rational; some foolish, others wise – and that some beliefs, though not all, are so good that they qualify as knowledge. We accept that our beliefs can be supported in a variety of ways – through sense-experience, through testimony of others, through memory, through logic. One comes to epistemology not empty-handed but with a stock of common truths about belief that all of us seem to endorse, and which are so uncontroversial as to rarely require comment. We can call these enormously uncontroversial claims *commonplaces*, and we can summarize by saying that the starting point of epistemology are the *commonplaces about belief*.

Now, if the commonplaces about belief were not only the starting point but also the middle and ending points, epistemology would be an intensely boring enterprise. But it is not. For the commonplaces generate questions of their own. What is it for a belief to be "supported" by evidence? (Can you, right now, explain it to your own satisfaction?) Do all beliefs require support? (Can you provide evidence for every belief you hold?) How exactly is it that different sorts of evidence serve to support belief? (We all know that our senses, and testimony, and memories, can deceive, after all.) What exactly is the difference between knowledge and mere belief? (Not everything believed is known: if a Flat-Earther and a Round-Earther face off, each believes that his or her view is correct, but at least one of them doesn't have knowledge.) Furthermore, there are tensions among the various commonplaces about belief. For example: we all accept that people can be praised or blamed for their beliefs. But we also accept that beliefs are not the sort of thing that can be summoned up at will – they are not directly under our control. How can people be praised or blamed for their beliefs, if their beliefs are not directly under their control?

The questions that can arise from reflection on our commonplaces about belief are of two sorts. One type of question we can call *analytical*, or *conceptual*. These are questions that concern the concepts involved in our commonplaces about belief: what is *belief* ? What is *knowledge?* What is *support* for belief? What is *evidence*? What is *rationality* in belief? These questions are about *our own ideas* – they are about what we mean, about how the various concepts about belief hook up with each other. A second type of question we can call *substantive*. These are questions, not about our ideas, but about how reality matches up to our ideas. We have the concept of knowledge – but what things do we *really* know? We have the concept of evidence – but what methods *genuinely* provide evidence for different sorts of belief? We have the idea of rationality – but what standards must one *in fact* satisfy in order to count as rational?

The two points that I have made, using epistemology as an example, are that philosophy begins with commonplaces and that the interesting questions in philosophy, whether conceptual or substantive, aim at getting clearer about or resolving conflicts among these commonplaces. The third point that I want to make is that there are no advance guarantees, whether positive or negative, in any philosophical field. We cannot say for sure that our philosophical investigations will lead to the enrichment of our understanding of a field or to the conclusion that our commonplaces are vacuous or muddled or otherwise irretrievable. Staying for the moment with the case of epistemology, we cannot say in advance that epistemology will lead to the result that all of our commonplaces about belief are consistent with each other, and when spelled out in greater detail can lead to our setting our belief lives in proper order. But neither can we say in advance that epistemology will lead to skeptical conclusions, that our commonplaces about belief are contradictory, or too hazy to admit of interesting elaboration, or that we are doomed to fall disastrously short of any ideals of rationality in thought that epistemology happens upon. To begin with our everyday thoughts about belief is not to assume that our everyday thoughts are just fine as they are or that they are ripe for undermining. It is simply to acknowledge that they are our everyday thoughts, and that they initially mark out the subject matter to be investigated.

We cannot assume that our houses are in order, and proceed with blithe confidence that all will work out; and we cannot assume that we are simply muddled, and that we need to reject the commonplaces as mere confusion and start afresh. Neither the conservative nor the radical can assume that in philosophy things will turn out in his or her favor. We must simply dive in and start identifying and thinking through the issues as cleanly and honestly as we can, not knowing where our investigations will ultimately lead us.

0.2　What Are Our Commonplaces About Law?

The starting point in each philosophical field is the set of everyday truths, the commonplaces, about a given subject matter. These commonplaces anchor philosophical investigation in our common experience, providing us a shared subject matter for inquiry. Philosophical investigation is investigation, both conceptual and substantive, of these commonplaces. What, then, are the commonplaces about law that serve as our starting points for the philosophy of law?

I will identify three commonplaces about law to focus the analytical and substantive investigations that make up this book. I have two aims here. First, I must be able to tell you clearly what these commonplaces are – we need to be clear about the *content* of these commonplaces. Second, I must convince you that these are in fact commonplaces about law, that they are not simply my private opinion about law, or an opinion about law that you and I happen to share, but rather the *common* understanding of law that all of us potential inquirers bring to the table.

The three commonplaces about law around which philosophy of law revolves are these: law is a social phenomenon, law is authoritative, and law is for the common good.

0.2.1　Law is a social phenomenon

When I say that it is a commonplace that law is a social phenomenon, I mean that whatever else we want to say about law, its existence is, at least in part, always *a matter of social fact*. When we say that a legal system exists, or that a certain law is valid, or that the law in a certain case is such-and-such, what makes those claims true is always, at least in part, a matter of social fact.

In order to make it both plausible that it is commonplace that law is always a matter of social fact, it is necessary to say something about what makes a fact a social fact, and what distinguishes social facts from other sorts of facts. To speak roughly, we can divide the world of facts into two sorts – evaluative facts and nonevaluative facts. On the evaluative side, there are facts like *murder is wrong, beets are good for you,* and so forth. On the nonevaluative side, there are facts like *there is a murder a day committed in Washington, DC, beets are red,* and so forth.

4

On the nonevaluative side, we can distinguish between what we might call *objective* and *subjective* facts: objective facts are those that do not involve the existence of subjects, that is, beings with beliefs, desires, points of view, and so forth (e.g., *Mount Everest is 29,000 feet high, grass is green,* etc.); subjective facts are those that involve the existence of subjects (e.g., *some people think that the stock market is about to go up, one-half of the citizenry is in favor of some legal restraints on abortion,* etc.). Social facts, as I mean "social facts," are to be found on the subjective side. In particular, social facts are those subjective facts that concern *interaction between subjects* – facts about subjects, their beliefs, desires, objectives, aims, choices, points of view, insofar as those beliefs, desires, and so forth make reference to other subjects. So *the Discovery Channel Team is trying to get Armstrong to the winner's podium* is a social fact, a fact about the coordinated aims and actions of the members of the Discovery Team. *Armstrong was in pain during much of July of 2005* is a subjective fact, but a nonsocial one. The distinction can be hard to draw in some cases, but there is no doubt that there is a distinction between these types of fact.

Social facts are nonevaluative, subjective facts involving interaction between subjects. While it is difficult to make the notion precise, the idea of a social fact is a familiar one, and I am claiming that it is among our familiar truths about law that law is, at least in part, a matter of social fact. When we take our first crack at describing law, we begin by talking about people, and how they are interacting with each other. We begin our characterization of law, that is, by mentioning social facts that obtain wherever there is law.

One clear way to recognize the truth of the claim that law is a matter of social fact – indeed, the obvious, banal truth of this claim – is through a couple of thought experiments. Here is the first. Imagine two societies, Society X and Society Y, that are *duplicates* of each other with respect to the nonsocial facts that hold within them – that is, the same evaluative facts hold, and the same nonsocial, nonevaluative facts hold. I take it that, under this assumption, it is possible for Society X and Society Y both to have law, or for them both to lack law, or for one of them to have law and the other to lack it. You could have two societies, existing in similar environments, one of which lacks law and the other has it. But now imagine further that Society X and Society Y are also duplicates in every matter of detail with respect to the practices that characterize that society, the nature of the interactions among their members, the beliefs and attitudes that the populations of each society has, and so forth. Now, if I were to say to you that Society X has law, but Society Y does not, you would balk at this suggestion. You would say that I am being inconsistent ("How can one have law and the other not? They're social duplicates of each other!") or that I am taking back what I said about their being alike in every social detail ("Oh, you mean they are not really *entirely* copies of each other; they do differ in that one society has law, and the other does not."). If this is indeed your reaction, then you are treating social facts as very important with respect to the existence of law. You are acknowledging that nonsocial facts are not sufficient all by themselves to make for law; social facts must be part of the story.

Here is a second, more direct thought experiment. Imagine a society that is not under law. Now reflect on this problem: what would have to change about the conditions there in order for that society to be under law? Certain facts about the conditions in that society would have to change, and it seems obvious to us all that the facts that would have to change would include social facts. For a society without law to become a society with law, people in that society would have to interact differently with each other. That conviction is the commonplace that law is, at least in part, a matter of social fact.

How central is law's status as a social fact to our understanding of law? In describing what makes something a law, or what makes an institution a legal system, do we need to refer *only* to social facts? Or do we need to refer to other sorts of facts – evaluative facts, for example – as well? Here we move from the familiar to the unfamiliar: whether law is entirely a matter of social fact is a disputed question of the philosophy of law; it is not settled simply by the commonplace that law is a social phenomenon.

0.2.2 Law is authoritative

To say that "law is authoritative" is a commonplace is to say that we include among the criteria for law that it serve a certain role, that of decider of certain questions within a certain domain. While I will say a great deal more about authority in Chapter 1, we need to get clearer on the notion of authority now in order to see both what the claim that law is authoritative means and why it is obviously a commonplace that the law has authority.

6

Introduction

We sometimes speak of authorities on the properties of plutonium-239, or on the history of architecture, or on formal logic. To be an authority in one of these areas is to be someone who is in the know about these areas, and thus whose say-so gives people reason to believe what they claim to be true. If an authority on plutonium-239 says that its half-life is about 24,000 years, then that gives the rest of us reason to believe that the half-life of plutonium-239 is about 24,000 years. If an authority on the history of architecture tells us that the oldest known use of flying buttresses is to be found in Roman architecture, then that gives the rest of us reason to believe that the oldest known use of flying buttresses is to be found in Roman architecture. This sort of authority is sometimes called "theoretical" authority, and it is the authority of expertise. To acknowledge another's theoretical authority over one is to acknowledge that one's beliefs are properly molded by that other's assertions, that his or her telling you that something is true is reason for you to believe that it is true.

Now, it is true that law is sometimes drafted by experts: either the bills themselves are written by experts, which are then sponsored and voted on by assuredly nonexpert legislators; or the law contains provisions that allow the details of its implementation to be worked out by experts working in government bureaucracy. But the authority that we commonsensically ascribe to the law is not theoretical authority. Law, we all know, is not first and foremost interested in molding belief; it is interested in guiding action. The kind of authority that is ascribed to law is thus not authority over belief, what we called "theoretical" authority; it is authority over action, what is sometimes called "practical" authority.

We said that for someone to have genuine theoretical authority over you in some area is for that person's assertions in that area to give you reasons to believe what is asserted. In a parallel way, for someone to have genuine practical authority over you in some area is for that person's orders, commands, dictates, and so forth in that area to give you reasons to act in the way that you have been ordered to act. If my parents have authority over me in household matters, then when they tell me to do the dishes, then I have a reason to do the dishes. If my teachers have authority over me with respect to class assignments, then when they tell me to write a course paper, then I have a reason to write a course paper.

We can say more. When someone has practical authority, his or her commands are not simply good reasons to comply. Their commands are not like requests from a friend, which one may take seriously and then decide against satisfying. Ordinarily someone who makes a request has no basis for complaint if the request is seriously considered, but decided against. But an authority's command is not just to be considered seriously; it is to be obeyed. If an authority is operating within its proper domain, its commands are the final deciders of the issues that it chooses to issue orders about. Its commands give decisive reasons for compliance.

Now, it is important to distinguish between genuine authority and de facto authority. A real expert is someone who knows what he or she is talking about, and whose (sincere) assertions nonexperts have reasons to believe – such experts have genuine theoretical authority. But sometimes people pass themselves off as experts who are really not, and sometimes these people manage to convince others that they are really experts. We might find it useful to have a term to describe those who are *treated as* genuinely authoritative, regardless of whether are not they in fact are genuinely authoritative. We can call all folks who are held to be genuine theoretical authorities "de facto theoretical authorities" – meaning that their assertions are *taken to be* reasons for accepting what they assert. We can make a parallel distinction with respect to practical authority. I might convince some people that I have been sent by God to be their ruler, even though I know this to be false and want nothing more than power for myself. These people may take me to be an authority over their actions, though of course they really have no good reason to do what I tell them to do. We can call my authority "de facto practical authority": while my dictates do not genuinely give these folks reasons for compliance, they take my dictates to give such reasons, and act as if my dictates were such reasons.

The case that I just described shows that one does not need to be a genuine practical authority in order to be a de facto practical authority. People can accept another's authority even when that other fails genuinely to have it. But it works the other way around as well. One does not need to be a de facto practical authority in order to be a genuine practical authority. A parent might be genuinely an authority over his or her children without the children recognizing the parent's authority, for example. God might be genuinely an authority over all human beings, even without human recognition of divine authority.

It is a commonplace that law is, in some sense, authoritative. The law does not request; it commands. Its norms are *rules*; its dictates are deemed *obligatory*; those that violate those norms are deemed *guilty*. Judges render *decisions* and *orders*, they don't beseech or advise. Those in charge of making and applying law call themselves, and are called by those subject to their rulings, *authorities*. It would be very strange indeed for one to hold that he or she had discovered a system of law in which the laws were mere pieces of advice, not obligatory but optional. We would respond that what was discovered was no system of law at all, but some alternative to law.

Law's status as authoritative is, then, a commonplace. But we have distinguished between de facto and genuine authority. When we say that law is in some sense authoritative, do we mean that law is de facto practically authoritative or that it is genuinely practically authoritative, or both? Again, to raise this question is to move from the familiar ground of commonplaces about law into the philosophy of law, for it is in fact one of the most fundamental questions about the nature of law what sort of authority is essential to it.

0.2.3 Law is for the common good

The commonplace that law is for the common good is supposed to give some sense of the common opinion about the *aims* of law. As is perhaps obvious, we cannot say very much in this area before we find ourselves outside of the area of basic agreement and into disputed questions, questions that are controverted over dinner tables and on editorial pages as much as in philosophy seminars. But we can say at least the following as a matter of explication of this commonplace about law.

To say that law is for the common good is to say that law – understood broadly to include legal systems generally, individual legal rules, particular decisions in cases – is supposed to be justifiable not just from the point of view of some privileged or unprivileged class, but to all those living under it. Law is not supposed to be something that benefits some class of persons, but is at best a nuisance and at worst a burden or awful affliction to the rest. Law is not supposed to be like a particular class's system of etiquette, which can be properly learned and judged only by some in-class, and which can be used to oppress the rest. No: law is for the *common* good.

Introduction

It is important to understand rightly the claim that law is for the common good. The commonplace that law is for the common good is a commonplace about whom law is to benefit, or to whom law is supposed to be justifiable; it is not supposed to be a claim about, say, the proper form of legislative authority. One might think, for example, that to say that law is for the common good must commit one to certain view about the way law is made – that, perhaps, law must be made democratically. But that would be to prejudge difficult philosophical questions about the best regimes, for example, whether monarchy, or aristocracy, or democracy is the best form of governance. Whether the many or the few should rule is a question that is distinct from that of the orientation of law to the common good. When writers in the classical tradition argued against democracy, the claim was typically that the many were not *fit* to rule; the common good is better served by the rule of the wise few rather than of that of the ignorant many. Regardless of the quality of this argument, it is clear that it rests, correctly, on a distinction between who should rule and who is to benefit, or to whom must law be justifiable. It holds that the rule of the few is justified because it is a benefit to the many.

The idea that law is for the common good is a relatively thin one. That it is a commonplace is perhaps most eloquently affirmed by those most interested in evading its apparent implications: for example, those who wanted to affirm that slavery was not an affront to the integrity of the law found themselves denying either that enslaved persons were genuinely among the "all persons" to whom the law must be justified, or that it was somehow to the slaves' good to be kept in legal bondage. More positively, we can note the prevalence of appeals to the common good in the law's self-image: just as legal systems affirm their own status as authoritative, they affirm their orientation toward the common good. Sometimes this is explicit, as in the United States Constitution, the Preamble to which affirms that the system of law and government aims at seeking the general welfare. Sometimes this is implicit. Note, for example, the way that officials in legal systems defend their decisions in a way that aims to be rationally justifiable to all those subject to those decisions.

That law is for the common good is indeed a thin commonplace, but its very thinness is what makes it such a fertile area for philosophical exploration. How should we interpret this vague notion of the common good? What are the values included within it that are the appropriate objectives of legal systems? What are the constraints that law must honor in pursuit of these objectives? And how can the features of the ordinary legal systems with which we are familiar be assessed in terms of the common good?

0.3 The Course of Our Inquiry

Law is social, authoritative, and oriented to the common good. The aim of this book is to introduce you to the richness of philosophical inquiry into law by considering questions that arise from these commonplaces both individually and in relation to one another.

In Chapter 1 – "Analytical Fundamentals: The Concept of Law" – our aim is to get clear on some of the perplexing analytical questions arising from the interaction of the three commonplaces. How is law's sociality to be spelled out and reconciled with law's authority and orientation to the common good? As we will see, the more strongly one interprets the claim about law's sociality, the more weakly one must interpret the claims about law's authority and law's orientation to the common good, and the more strongly one interprets the claim about law's authority and orientation to the common good, the more weakly one must interpret the claim about law's sociality.

In Chapter 2 – "Normative Fundamentals: The Basic Roles of Paradigmatic Legal Systems" – we consider some substantive questions about the demands of the various roles that appear in paradigmatic legal systems. These three roles are *subject* (those who are bound by authoritative legal norms), *legislator* (those who have the power to make authoritative legal norms), and *judge* (those who have the power to interpret and apply authoritative legal norms). Our aim is to get clearer on the problems of authority and the common good that arise with respect to these roles. What explains why subjects are in fact bound to adhere to the law's dictates – and in what cases is the law so poorly oriented to the common good that it lacks genuine authority over subjects? What are the virtues of legislators, and of legislative activity, that make possible the creation of good law, law that is both authoritative and for the common good? And what are the duties of judges with respect to the interpretation and application of law: how far must they rely on their own judgments of the requirements of the common good in applying legal norms?

In Chapter 3 – "The Aims of Law" – we are primarily concerned to understand the scope of the common good in light of law's status as an authoritative institution. While we can agree that the end to which it ought to impose those standards is the common good, there is a great deal of disagreement about how we ought to interpret the ideal of "the common good," and there is a great deal of disagreement about whether law should be concerned with each and every aspect of the common good. Among the most famous, and among the most plausible, suggestions for the limitation of law's scope is John Stuart Mill's "harm principle": restrictions of a subject's liberty, such as the restrictions imposed by law, are justified only for the sake of preventing harm to those other than the subject. Others go further, claiming that the exercise of legal authority is justifiable even for the sake of protecting the subject from performing actions that will lead to losses of his or her own well-being, or for the sake of protecting others from the profound offense that one's actions might cause, or simply for the sake of the prevention of moral wrongdoing. We will ask whether these further goals are worthwhile goals, and if so, whether law should or should not be concerned to realize them.

In the first three chapters, we consider what it is for legal norms to be in place, and by what general criteria legal norms should be put into place. In the fourth and fifth chapters, we consider the responses available to the violation of these norms. One sort of response is *violator-centered*: the law authoritatively responds *to the violator*. In Chapter 4 – "The Nature and Aims of the Criminal Law" – we consider the characteristic violator-centered mode of response, *punishment*. After dealing with analytical questions about the notion of punishment, we will inquire into the substantive question of what is the best normative account of criminal law. Another sort of response to the violation of legal norms is victim-centered: the law provides the victim with an authoritative means of redress. In Chapter 5 – "The Nature and Aims of Tort Law" – we will deal with this sort of response. Here the focus will be, again, on what normative views offer the best justification of the salient features of tort law. In what cases is compensation merited, and to what degree? What justifies the victim–violator model, in which the violator pays his or her or its victim damages, rather than other models, for example, schemes in which violators contribute to a common fund out of which victims can make claims?

In the concluding chapter – "Challenging the Law" – we will consider a variety of views that are unified by the idea that all is not well with the law and/or the philosophy of law – that our commonplaces are not in order, that they require substantive revision or rejection. If it is one of our commonplaces about law that it bears a certain connection to authority, and if it is one of our commonplaces about law that it bears a certain connection to the common good, then any view that held that, for example, practical authority is in principle incoherent or that, for example, the notion of a common good, as opposed to the good of some dominant class, is illusory, must call into question our ordinary understanding of the legal order. We will conclude, then, by considering both limited and more radical versions of such critiques.

For Further Reading

For a discussion of law's social character, see Joseph Raz, "Legal Positivism and the Sources of Law," in *The Authority of Law* (Oxford: Clarendon Press, 1979), pp. 37–52. For a discussion of the nature of authority and law's authoritative character, see Raz, "The Claims of Law," in *The Authority of Law*, pp. 28–33. Further considerations on the nature of authority can be found in Scott Shapiro, "Authority," in Jules Coleman and Scott Shapiro (eds.), *The Oxford Handbook of Jurisprudence and the Philosophy of Law* (New York: Oxford University Press, 2002), pp. 382–439 and in Mark C. Murphy, "Authority," in Donald Borchert et al. (eds.), *The Encyclopedia of Philosophy*, 2nd edn. (New York: Macmillan, forthcoming 2005). For a discussion of law's orientation to the common good, see, for example, Robert Alexy, *The Argument from Injustice*, trans. Bonnie Litschewski Paulson and Stanley L. Paulson (Oxford: Clarendon Press, 2002).

Chapter 1

Analytical
Fundamentals:
The Concept of Law

1.1 The Question, and its Importance

The basic question of the philosophy of law is about the analysis of its own subject matter: what is law? Law is a concept that is deployed in explaining behavior (e.g., *Consumption of alcohol in the United States decreased after 1921, because it became* illegal *to make or import alcoholic beverages*), justifying action (e.g., *You shouldn't cross the street here, because jaywalking is against the* law), and in self-understanding (e.g., *Our government is one "of laws not men"*). Surely it is, at least in those societies in which this book is likely to be read, one of the most important and frequently employed descriptive, justificatory, and interpretive concepts in use. But it is not as easy as one might think to provide an informative and sufficiently accurate explication of the concept. The concept of law, we might say, is not self-explicating – it is not perfectly obvious what law is. If you are not convinced of this, take a break from reading this and try to state what distinguishes law from all other things in the world.

Concepts that are both important (that is, in terms of description, justification, and/or interpretation) and intransigent (that is, hard to get at) are grist for the philosopher's mill. The concept of *knowledge* is central for the epistemologists, *cause* for the metaphysicians, *good* for the moral philosophers, and so forth. *Law* is the central concept of concern for the philosophers of law. Now, when philosophers offer an analysis of a concept – whether that concept is *law*, or *knowledge*, or *cause*, or *good* – there are two sources of information that they have to rely on, both for inspiration in offering their analyses and for correction if those analyses go wrong. We have already encountered one of these sources of information: our *commonplaces* about that subject matter. When one offers an analysis of a concept, it should be faithful to, and in some way incorporate and organize, our commonplaces about that subject matter.

Consider our concept of knowledge, for example. It is among our commonplaces about knowledge (1) that if one knows something, then one *believes* it; (2) that if one knows something, then one is *justified* in believing it; and (3) that if one knows something, then what is known is *true*. Any analysis of knowledge must respect these commonplaces. If I said, for example, that in my analysis knowledge is merely belief, you would rightly respond that this analysis cannot be right, for it fails to acknowledge the importance of justification and truth in our concept of belief. I might then revise my analysis to say that knowledge is justified, true belief. While there may still be problems with this analysis, it does seem closer to, more faithful to, our commonplaces about knowledge than the analysis that knowledge is simply belief.

There is another source of information in providing analyses of concepts. This source of information is our set of *clear cases* associated with a certain concept. By "clear cases" I mean instances to which a concept clearly does, or clearly does not, apply. Consider, for example, the following clear cases associated with the concept of knowledge. I know that I exist. I know that I am, at this moment, typing a book manuscript. I know that my name is Mark Murphy. And so forth. I do not know how many particles there are in the universe. I do not know where my children are at this very moment. And so forth. There may be some issues about which it is not clear whether I have knowledge. Do I know that God exists? Do I know that it is morally permissible to eat cows? I am unsure whether my beliefs in these cases add up to knowledge; and I am sure that there is disagreement among competent, well-informed users of the concept of knowledge whether these cases are instances of knowledge. So, regardless of whether I know these things, they do not count as clear cases, and so are not the material that I have in mind for providing analyses.

Clear cases are important because they can be used to shape and to test analyses. Consider the proposed analysis of knowledge as justified true belief. There is a powerful argument – one that relies on a clear case – that this is an inadequate analysis.[1] Suppose that you are looking at a clock in the center of town, one that has always been reliable, and is well-known for its reliability. (Indeed, the townsfolk call it "Old Reliable.") It says that the time is 1:32 p.m. You look at the clock, and as a result form the belief that it is 1:32 p.m., and on account of its well-known reliability you are justified in doing so. Suppose that it is in fact true that it is 1:32 p.m. So you have a justified, true belief that it is 1:32 p.m., and according to our analysis this means that you have knowledge. But unbeknownst to you, Old Reliable is broken, stuck at 1:32: it is a mere *accident* that you happened to gaze upon it at just the right time. There seems to be a strong consensus that in this case you don't have knowledge, because it is just *lucky* that your justified belief happened to be true. So there must be *something more* to the analysis of knowledge besides justified, true belief – that is, that the truth of belief is not merely lucky or accidental. (What counts as a belief's not being just lucky or accidental is a further, and it turns out very difficult, question.)

There are important questions about the identification of commonplaces and clear cases that one might raise (What sort of consensus is required for a commonplace to be commonplace, or a clear case to be clear? Is it possible for such consensuses to be in error?) but we will put them to the side here. You might still be wondering about the point of this exercise. Who cares, you might reasonably ask, about the concept of law, or any other concept? Why should we worry so much about the defining of our words and the unpacking of our ideas?

The reason for being concerned about the meanings of our words is that confusion in our words and their meanings cannot but generate confusion in our ideas. (Had any ideas lately that were not formulated in words?) And the reason for being concerned about confusion in our ideas is that we care about getting things right in our descriptions and explanations, in our justifications, and in our interpretations. Clarity in our words and thoughts makes possible clarity of understanding of things that matter to us.

So we have seen a way to proceed in asking questions about the proper analysis of the notion *law*. We have at hand a stock of commonplaces about law (including, but not limited to, the commonplaces identified in the Introduction – those concerning sociality, authority, and orientation to the common good), and we have a stock of cases that we recognize as clear instances of legal systems and individual laws or clear noninstances of legal systems and individual laws. Given these guideposts, how should we answer the question: what is law?

1.2 Basic Austinianism

The theory of law offered by John Austin serves as the reference point for a large proportion of contemporary accounts of the nature of law. Austin's lectures on jurisprudence were not much of a hit at the time of their delivery (he held a chair of jurisprudence at London University from 1826 to 1832, when he resigned because of the low numbers of students at his university lectures), but once published as *The Province of Jurisprudence Determined*, they were tremendously influential in the course of nineteenth- and twentieth-century philosophy of law.[2] What makes Austin's work so important is both the exactness with which he lays out his position and contrasts it to rival views and the fruitfulness of the very few ideas out of which he reconstructs what he takes to be our concept of law.

One way to follow the course of Austin's account of law is to conceive it as a search for those commonplaces about law that can fill out, made vivid and precise, the very general commonplace that law is a matter of social fact. When reminded that law is a matter of social fact, we would surely want to know what sorts of social facts are involved in the existence of law. We might suggest, as Austin does, that where there is law, there are patterns of commanding and obeying. That is to say: if you don't have a situation in which people are telling other people what to do and the other people are going along with it, you do not have law. So the most obvious place to look to provide an account of the social facts involved in law is the pattern of commanding and obeying that is essential for the existence of law.

It is not much of an exaggeration to treat Austin's general theory of the nature of law as an extended commentary on the nature of the command and the nature of the obedience that makes for law. Law is, on Austin's view, a kind of command, one that is *general* (imagine a statute that says "Always drive on the right") rather than specific to a given occasion (imagine a police officer directing traffic who points to the left and says "Drive on this side").[3] *Command* itself calls for conceptual analysis, and on Austin's view, command is to be analyzed as an expression of one's wish or intention that another act a certain way. (If I command you to write a paper, I am expressing my intention that you write a paper.) But not just any expression of an intention counts as a command: it is only the expressed intention of a *superior* who has the capacity and the willingness to inflict some evil (Austin calls it a "sanction") in the absence of compliance that constitutes a command.[4] (Perhaps I will threaten you with failure in the course if you fail to write the paper.) When these conditions for commanding are met, then when one has been given a command one is *obliged*, or *duty-bound*, to comply with it.

Let us take a break for a moment from this barrage of definitions in order to appreciate the way that the analyses that Austin provides fit with our ordinary experience and understanding of the law. It seems right that we encounter law typically in the commanding mode (we describe law as telling us what to do, as making demands on us, and so forth). Law characteristically comes down from a class of legal superiors who are able to generate these rules. And not only is it plainly obvious that we describe the demands of law as constituting legal obligations or legal duties, it is clear that failure to comply with them is accompanied by a variety of evils (execution, imprisonment, fines, etc.) that we would really rather not incur. So it seems that Austin is finding an elegant way to tie together a variety of commonplaces about legal experience.

On the side of obedience, Austin is clear that it is not sufficient for law that the compliance be a one-time occurrence, or a random set of coincidences. Rather, there must be a *habit* of compliance to the superior who gives the commands.[5] Now, this would not be enough to distinguish law from, say, the rules that parents lay down for children: even if children have a habit of compliance with parents' wishes, and parents lay down general rules backed by sanctions ("Clean your room every week or else . . . "), we would want to distinguish parental rules from the phenomenon of law. Austin's way of making this distinction is by taking note of the fact that while parents are superiors over their children, they are themselves inferior to others, who can give them commands. So Austin says that law is given by those with respect to whom others have a general habit of compliance, but who do not themselves have a general habit of compliance with respect to anyone else. Such folks are superior in the sense relevant to law and legal philosophy, and Austin calls such persons *sovereigns*; the persons in a society the bulk of which has the habit of compliance with respect to the sovereign we can call the sovereign's *subjects*. We can summarize Austin's view, then, as the position that law consists in general commands issued by sovereigns to their subjects.

Austin's views seem to be a very promising account of the nature of law. We have been focusing so far entirely on the way that his view constitutes a spelling-out of the sociality commonplace. What should we say about the way that it accommodates the commonplaces concerned with authority and the orientation to the common good?

With respect to the authority commonplace: recall that in the Introduction (0.2.2) we distinguished between two sorts of authority: genuine and de facto. Genuine authority in a given domain exists when one's dictates with respect to that domain give another decisive reasons for compliance. De facto authority exists only when the one's dictates are believed to give such reasons, are accepted as such. We did not decide there whether the authority that law must possess is genuine or de facto or both. But it seemed clear enough that law must have authority *in some sense* in order for the commonplace to be satisfied. Can Austin's view of law meet that desideratum?

Later I will argue that it cannot, but we should first appreciate the case that can be made on Austin's behalf. Notice that, on Austin's view, for there to be law it is necessary that subjects have a habit of compliance with respect to the sovereign. The source of this habit of compliance seems to be, on Austin's view, the superiority of the sovereign with respect to the infliction of sanctions for failure to comply. The superiority of the sovereign is, as Austin puts it, a superiority of might, that is, power, and the power in question is the power to impose sanctions. So we might say that the sovereign has a certain sort of authority in virtue of its sanction-imposing power: folks have reason to act in accordance with the law's dictates because of the sanctions that accompany noncompliance.

What about the commonplace that law is oriented to the common good? Austin is insistent – indeed, this is the aspect of Austin's jurisprudence that has been taken up and defended with the greatest gusto by later legal theorists – that the notion that law is for the common good cannot be understood as the claim that wherever law is to be found, it is ultimately for the good of all those subject to it. It is extraordinarily common, Austin notes, to find law that is imprudent, stupid, pointless, outdated. As he vividly remarks, taking as an example human laws that are contrary to the law of God,

To say that human laws which conflict with the Divine law are not binding, that is to say, are not laws, is to talk stark nonsense. The most pernicious laws, and therefore those which are most opposed to the will of God, have been and are continually enforced as laws by judicial tribunals. Suppose an act...be prohibited by the sovereign under the penalty of death; if I commit this act, and I object to the sentence, that it is contrary to the law of God...the court of justice will demonstrate the inconclusiveness of my reasoning, by hanging me up, in pursuance of the law of which I have impugned the validity.[6]

Austin thinks that it is a plain matter of social fact that there can be laws the existence and following of which do not serve the common good.

How, then, can Austin accommodate the commonplace that law is for the common good? He does not accommodate it by saying that there has never been a law that is contrary to the common good. He accommodates it by treating it just as a straightforward moral thesis about how law *ought* to be. *What law is* is entirely a matter of social fact, depending on who has power and who has issued what commands. *What law ought to be* is, Austin insists, a different question. On Austin's view, the appropriate standard that law ought to aspire to is that laid down by the divine law,[7] and the proximate standard for this aspiration – that is, the measuring stick that we ought to use to determine whether law is achieving its aspiration – is the *principle of utility*, the thesis that morality demands that we act in a way that maximizes overall societal well-being.[8] According to the principle of utility, then, law should be made and remade in whatever way maximizes overall societal well-being. That law should maximize overall societal well-being does seem to match up rather nicely with the commonplace that law is for the common good, and that is how the Austinian accommodates that commonplace. (Austin's theory of law is very similar to that of the famous utilitarian philosopher Jeremy Bentham, whose writings aimed to demystify the law, to remove its aura of grandeur, so that people could clearly recognize its shortcomings and be willing to reform it in a direction that better serves social well-being.)

But despite the obvious power and appeal of Austin's view, there are serious difficulties that preclude its acceptance as an adequate account of the concept of law. We will first consider a set of difficulties for Austin's view that result entirely from his emphasis on the notion of sovereignty as being essential to the analysis of law. We will then consider a couple of objections that are directed toward the Austinian's ultimate inability to respect the commonplaces that law is authoritative and that law is oriented to the common good.

The notion that law consists in commands issued by a sovereign is perhaps natural once we conceive of law as consisting in commands. For if we conceive of law as consisting in commands, then it is natural to suppose that we must identify some party as the commander, the one who issues the commands. So we are led to the idea that there must be some party, the sovereign, whose ability and willingness to lay down commands and back them with sanctions makes law possible. It may be, though, that this appeal to commands is a wrong turn, and it leads Austin to distort some features of clear cases of law and legal systems and to ignore others. (This is the extended line of criticism proposed by H. L. A. Hart, to whose account of law we will turn below.[9]) The point is that while some laws seem on their face to be a lot like commands – those laws that require one to perform or refrain from some course of action come immediately to mind (do not commit theft; pay your federal taxes by April 15) – a number of laws do not fit the model of orders backed by threats at all. Indeed, in most cases the lawmaking authority is itself a product of law, and cannot be plausibly viewed as a product of commands.

Consider, for example, laws that enable one to make a valid will. Such laws tell one what one must do in order to state one's wishes in a way that will be legally effective – that is, which will be enforced by the courts upon one's death. These do not look like *commands*; what they look like are *instructions* of a certain sort. Nor are they backed by threats to get one to comply with them.[10]

Consider, even more importantly, the power to make law itself. When the United States Congress votes positively on a bill that is then signed by the President, it becomes law. But what makes it the case that Congress's passing the bill and the President's signing it makes that bill law is, itself, another law. The power to issue rules that bear the force of law is itself characteristically the result of law, law that declares what must be done to make further law.[11]

Austin's view obscures these facts, and the way that he constructs his view around a sovereign whose status as such is not due to law but due to a habit of compliance that can be characterized in nonlegal terms generates puzzles that his view seems powerless to solve. Consider, for example, the persistence of law. Suppose that a society is ruled by a simple monarch, and that this monarch lays down a series of laws. The monarch later dies, and is succeeded (as the law provides) by her daughter. How are we to explain this? For if Austin is right, the succession cannot be a matter of law; for the original monarch is dead, and thus is powerless to give rules or impose sanctions. There cannot be law again until the members in that society have established a new pattern of compliance. But this seems to fly in the face of our ordinary experience of law: we know that lawmaking power can move from party to party without the gaps that would have to be involved in waiting for a new pattern of compliance to be established.[12]

The sovereign–subject model of law is a myth, suitable for only (if at all) a very specific form of society: one in which all allegiance to authority is personal allegiance, where the only law within the society is of the "you must do this" or "you must not do that" variety. But there are further troubles for Austin's view: it clearly fails to satisfy the authority commonplace and arguably fails to satisfy the common good commonplace.

We saw above that the best case that can be made that Austin's view satisfies the authority commonplace is that subjects have reason, because of the existence of sanctions, to comply with the sovereign's commands. But we can raise two objections here. The first is that even if we grant that the sovereign's sanctions can give reason for compliance, it is far from clear that they give *decisive* reasons for compliance. As Austin says, what matters is not the size of the sanction but that it exists; that is sufficient for there to be a law and a legal obligation ("Where there is the smallest chance of incurring the smallest evil, the expression of a wish amounts to a command, and therefore, imposes a duty."[13]) But the sovereign's commands being backed by a small punishment that one is unlikely to have imposed on one might not give anything like a strong reason, let alone a decisive reason, for complying with the sovereign's commands. So it seems that the reasons for compliance that Austin cites are *too weak* to make for the law's authority.

But there is another problem about authority, as well. It is not just that the reasons for compliance are *too weak*, it is that they are *of the wrong kind*. Austin says that it is the threat of sanctions that makes for a duty and obligation to comply. But this is a deeply implausible analysis of what makes for a duty. A gunman on the street may have the ability to threaten you with unpleasantness if you refuse to give him your money. But we would hardly say that you have an obligation or a duty to pay it, and we would certainly not say that the gunman had authority over you.[14] Threats of sanctions are not the right kind of reason for compliance with one's wishes to make one an authority.

Here is the source of the difficulty. Recall our earlier analysis of authority (0.2.2): when one has authority over another, one's say-so is a decisive reason for that other to comply. But the gunman's say-so is not the decisive reason for you to comply with his wishes; it is the threat that the gunman makes that is your reason to go along. There is a difference between doing what someone tells you to do because he or she has told you to do so and doing what someone tells you to do because he or she will make things unpleasant for you otherwise. For example: a parent may give two children the same order, to clean their rooms. One child may comply because the parent told him or her to do so, while the other may comply simply because he or she fears punishment if he or she fails to comply. There is an important difference between these children: the former child is treating the parent's authority as the reason to clean the room; the latter child is treating only the threat that the parent poses as the reason to clean the room. This is an important difference, and it is why we do not recognize the gunman as an authority even if his threats are severe and imminent.

Austin's view fails to get at the law's authority, treating the law as merely a very effective threat-maker. No doubt this captures something of our ordinary experience of law. But it fails to get at the fact that we think of law as something more than a threat-maker, and that is why it is a commonplace that law is in some sense authoritative.

We can also raise questions about Austin's treatment of the commonplace that law is for the common good. Austin treats this as simply a moral claim about how the law ought to be made and revised, because he sees no real alternative: it is not as if we can say that there is never immoral law, law that is blatantly contrary to the common good, for that there is such law appears to be a given. The Fugitive Slave Act of 1850 was passed in order to provide for the more efficient capture of runaway slaves, requiring people to refrain from hindering and even in some instances to assist in their capture. Few would argue now that this is for the common good. But it would be flying in the face of social facts about law – it was passed, signed, judicially enforced, socially recognized – to deny that the Fugitive Slave

Act was the law of the United States. So Austin seems to suppose that if there is some immoral law, then the commonplace that law is for the common good must be understood as simply a moral thesis about how legislators ought to fashion the law.

I want to raise a question to which we will return in a bit more detail later in this chapter. The question is: are Austin's possibilities the only two ways to handle the common good commonplace? That is, do we have to say that it means *either* that all law is desirable, genuinely serving the common good, *or* merely that legislators ought to make law as much for the common good as it can be? The former seems false, we must admit. But the latter seems insufficiently strong to capture what we mean when we say that law is for the common good.

Let me try to get this point across in a couple of ways. The first is to take note of, and expand upon, a point made by Robert Alexy.[15] We would find very peculiar, in a way self-contradictory, a bill passed whose explicit purpose was "unjust discrimination." Or compare the actual Preamble to the United States Constitution with an alternative. Here is the actual Preamble:

> We, the People, in order to form a more perfect union, establish justice, ensure domestic tranquility, provide for the common defense, promote the general welfare, and secure the blessings of liberty to ourselves and our posterity, do ordain and establish this Constitution for the United States of America.

Here is the alternative:

> We, the richest one percent, in order to line our own pockets, utilize injustice to our own advantage, secure our own tranquility regardless of the suffering it causes to others, provide for our mutual defense against the great unwashed, promote our specific welfare, and secure the blessings of liberty for ourselves, and ourselves only, do ordain and establish this Constitution for the United States of America.

Such a preamble – in intent, if not in words – might be the basis for a particularly ruthless organized crime syndicate. But as the basis for a system of law it does not seem merely evil, as it would also seem in the case of an organized crime syndicate. It seems, rather, to border on *incoherence*. There is something contradictory, something out-of-whack, about a system of law that purports to be not for the common good but for some partial and private good. We will need to examine this in more detail later. But let it suffice to say for now that there is nothing in Austin's view that goes anywhere toward explaining this internal incoherence of a legal system's declaring that it is not for the common good. A sufficiently powerful Austinian sovereign could, after all, simply declare that it is ruling for its own interests, and that those that do not fall in line will be severely sanctioned.

1.3 Positivist Lessons

Austin's is not a viable theory of the nature of law. But for all that, Austin has been tremendously influential in the history of the philosophy of law – and not just as an example of what mistakes should be avoided! The reason is that, regardless of the errors in Austin's account, there are two central theses embodied in Austin's view that have been taken to be largely right and which any more fully adequate theory of the nature of law would have to endorse.

The first is Austin's insistence on the primacy of the commonplace that law is a matter of social fact. In providing an account of the nature of law, we are doing a certain kind of high-level social science, providing an abstract characterization of a social practice.

The second is Austin's insistence on the distinction between what law is and what law ought to be. "Law's existence is one thing," Austin writes, "and its merits or demerits another."[16] Cold-blooded realism requires us not to romanticize law, not to provide it with a halo that makes it more angelic than it is. While law can realize noble aspirations and conquer injustice, it can also realize base corruption and act as an instrument of injustice. If we say that it is a commonplace that law has authority, then we need to realize that, however we interpret this, we cannot interpret it so that it means that, morally speaking, we ought always to do what the law tells us to do. If we say that it is a commonplace that law is for the common good, then we need to realize that, however we interpret this, we cannot interpret it so that it means that, morally speaking, law is always for the best interests of the people, justifiable to all who live under its constraints.

The two theses are related. The thesis that the existence of law is a matter of social fact implies, together with some uncontroversial additional premises, the thesis that there are no necessary moral constraints on the existence of legal systems or legal norms. These claims about the source of all law in social facts and the absence of a necessary connection between law's existence and its moral qualities is called "legal positivism." (The name "positivism" may seem strange and uninformative, but the idea is that it is of the nature of law to be *posited* – that is, to be put into place by us.)

Austin's sovereign–subject account of the nature of law is inadequate, but the inadequacy of Austin's view does not show that legal positivism is false – indeed, one can easily see why it is attractive. The question, then, is what a more adequate positivism, one that distances itself from Austin's sovereign–subject picture, would look like.

1.4 Hartian Positivism

H. L. A. Hart's work *The Concept of Law* is perhaps the most important work of legal philosophy of the twentieth century. Its transforming effect on the discipline was massive and immediate. Hart's view is unabashedly a positivist one: law is a social matter, an artifact of human sociality, and as a result there are no necessary constraints of morality on what can count as law. But, using Austin's and others' views as foils, he articulated a conception of the nature of law that has been subjected to numerous lines of criticism but still seems to be fundamentally sound.

For Hart, the key to providing an adequate account of the nature of law is to understand law not in terms of commands but in terms of *rules*. Commands have a much more limited scope than rules. We can command others to perform actions, but we cannot (literally) command ourselves. We can command the performance or the nonperformance of actions, but we cannot command that something be the case, or that someone have the authority to do something. We need a notion with a wider scope than that provided by a command: that of a *rule*. Law is, on Hart's view, a certain sort of social rule, or, better, a certain sort of system of social rules. In order to make this analysis of the nature of law perspicuous, Hart has to explain what social rules are in general and what makes law distinctive as a kind of social rule.

One important feature of the social rules that Hart has in mind is that they have an internal aspect.[17] We should distinguish, Hart notes, between what we might call "descriptive social rules" and "normative social rules." A descriptive social rule is in place simply when there is a persistent pattern of social behavior, when members of some group do something "as a rule." I might notice that when I teach in a classroom the entrance to which is on my left, most of the students in the class sit on the left side of the room; when I teach in a classroom the entrance to which is on my right, most of the students sit on the right side of the room. I might say that it is a descriptive social rule that students tend to sit on the side of the room that they enter. But this is no more than a description of the situation, no more than a statement of a fact about students' seating habits. There is no suggestion that students have ever explicitly formed thoughts like "Hmm, I'd better sit on the side of the room I entered" or "Look at Mike, sitting down on the side of the room opposite to the entrance . . . What could he be thinking? Who does he think he is, doing that?" There is no suggestion that the correlation between side of entrance and side of seating has been used by people as a guide to their conduct or as a basis for criticism of others' conduct.

Thoughts like "I'd better do that" or "Who does he think he is, doing that?" are the sort of thoughts associated with normative social rules rather than merely descriptive ones. Descriptive social rules have only an external aspect: they describe patterns of behavior, and that alone. Normative social rules have, however, an internal aspect. To say that there is a normative social rule in place is to say that (at least some significant portion of) a group uses that rule in the guidance and justification of its own behavior and in the praise and criticism of others' behavior.[18] Such rules do not describe the behavior of members of the social group; they provide a norm by which members of the group measure their own actions.

It is clear that there need not be a commander for there to be normative social rules. The rules of tic-tac-toe are one instance of social rule, as are the rules of etiquette. Neither of these is laid down by anything like a commander. And it is clear that rules can be about more than just the prescribing or proscribing of actions. There can be social rules about what counts as something else (it is a rule in chess that a piece that can move only diagonally along the black or the white squares counts as a bishop) or about who has the power to make further rules (it is a rule of etiquette that the host has the power to set the seating arrangement at a dinner party).

Hart's claim, then, is that law is a kind of normative social rule. He argues that the best way to understand the nature of a legal system is to see it as a complex web of social rules whose peculiarities are due to its status as a response to deficiencies in other kinds of social rules. To see why legal rules are as they are, you need to see why we might be dissatisfied living social life simply by means of other sorts of rules available to us.[19]

Imagine a society governed merely by rules of custom. Rules of custom are one sort of normative social rule. They can go quite a way in telling us how to behave, what to do and what not to do. But rules of custom come with certain drawbacks. For one thing, rules of custom can be *uncertain*. If there is disagreement between persons about what a rule of custom requires in a particular case, or about what the rule of custom is, or even about whether there is a rule of custom about a particular matter, there may be no way to resolve it. To call the problem one of uncertainty, as Hart does, may be a bit misleading: that makes it sound as if there may well be a fact of the matter whether there is a rule of custom and what it means, but people just are not able to come up with universally convincing arguments to show what the rules are. But the problem is likely to be even more severe than that: the problem is that it is *vague* in many cases whether there is a rule of custom. Remember that a normative social rule exists when members of a group use a standard for criticism of themselves and others; but how many members of the group must use it (half? three-quarters? all but a few? all?), and in what way (follow it all the time? only if they don't forget? occasionally?), for it to count as a customary rule?

A second difficulty for customary rules is that they are *static*. To say that they are static is not to say that they can never change – we know fully well that rules of custom do change over time. But it is to say that rules of custom are immune to *deliberate* change. The changing of a rule of custom requires lots of people to change their minds about using that rule – and one might have no interest in changing one's mind about using the rule unless one were confident that others would do so as well. So customary rules possess tremendous inertia. This would not be a problem if customary rules were always wise and well-suited to circumstances. But often they have their start in prejudice and ignorance; and even if they are at one time well-suited to their environments, environments can change, leaving customary rules without their original rationale. What's more, the same inertia that makes it hard to change or eliminate a customary rule that is in place

28

can make it very hard to get a customary rule established, even when some sort of alternative rule would make social life considerably smoother.

A third inconvenience of customary rules concerns the way that violations of them are to be detected, judged as such, and dealt with. Customary rules are *inefficient* with respect to the sanctioning of conduct that is contrary to the rules. When a violation occurs (or does not occur, but is believed or suspected of occurring), there is lacking an organized way to respond to the offense (or to make it clear that no such response is required). Thus there is no settled way to bring disputes with respect to the keeping of the rules to a close.

Customary rules can be uncertain, static, and inefficient. To some extent this vagueness, unchangeability, and wastefulness can be tolerated. But there is a way to ameliorate them. If we call these rules that dictate the basic duties and rights of social life *primary* rules, one way to deal with these difficulties is by the introduction of *secondary* rules – rules whose object is the identification of, addition to, modification of, or subtraction from, the primary rules.[20] To deal with the problem of *uncertainty*, a society's norms might come to include rules of *recognition*, secondary rules that specify what rules count as binding and how to identify them. To deal with the problem of *unchangeability*, a society's norms might come to include rules of *change*, secondary rules that specify how new rules can be introduced into the system. To deal with the problem of *inefficiency*, a society's norms might come to include rules of *adjudication*, secondary rules that deal with the settling of disputes about what the rules require.

Law, according to Hart's analysis, is a union of primary and secondary rules. He invites us to think of law in the following way. In paradigmatic legal systems, there is an accepted (usually very complex) rule of recognition that specifies what counts as binding legal norms within that society. This is the rule that is used – at least by officials, and perhaps by significant parts of the populace as well – for determining what counts as part of the law and what does not. It is in virtue of being recognized as such by the rule of recognition in a given community that other legal norms have their place within that legal system.

The rule of recognition has a very special place in Hart's account. It is the ultimate standard for determining legal validity and invalidity, and as such is itself neither valid nor invalid. Here is a useful analogy employed by Hart.[21] At one point the official standard for the length of a meter was a platinum bar in Paris. The length of that bar fixed the meter. To say that that bar was a meter long is true, but a bit misleading – it is not like saying that this desk is a meter long. While to say that the standard meter bar is a meter long is in some sense true, it is not true in virtue of its measuring up to some independent standard, in the way that "this desk is a meter long" might be true. It is, itself, the standard for meterhood. Such is the case with the rule of recognition – it sets the standard for legality within the community.

What makes something the rule of recognition? Again: what makes a meter the length of the standard platinum bar in Paris? It is simply because it is accepted as the standard that it counts as the standard. That the length of the meter is fixed by the bar in Paris is a matter of social fact – even if ordinary folks do not know that this is how the length of the meter is fixed, there are chains of influence (through scientists, meter-stick makers, schoolteachers, etc.) that establish that this is what a meter is. Similarly, the rule of recognition in a given society is what it is because it is accepted and used as the basis for determining legality. Its status as what constitutes legality within that society is simply in virtue of its acceptance. That such-and-such is the rule of recognition in a given society is a matter of social fact – even if ordinary folks are not able to say in detail what the rule of recognition is, there are chains of influence (through judges, legislators, lawyers, police officers, etc.) that establish that this is what the law is.

It is clear that Hart's version of legal positivism satisfies the sociality commonplace – whether law is in place is a matter of social fact, fixed by the attitudes, beliefs, intentions, and practices of people in their interactions with one another. How does it fare with respect to the other master commonplaces that we identified, those concerned with law's connection to authority and the common good? With respect to the authority commonplace, Hart's view certainly succeeds further than Austin's in respecting it. Recall that Austin's difficulty is that, on his view, the reason for compliance is the sanction attached to law; thus the reason for compliance that subjects have is not the legal norms themselves but the punishments that might follow upon non-compliance. But Hart's view does not share this feature. It is part of his analysis of what makes something a normative social rule that it is treated by the relevant persons as a reason to act in accordance with it. Law, however, is treated not just as a reason for compliance but a reason of a rather far-reaching and demanding sort. It seems, then, that Hartian positivism can account for the authority commonplace by ascribing de facto authority to the law: it is part of our concept of law that at least officials and perhaps large chunks of the citizenry as well treat it as a decisive reason for compliance.

What Hart does *not* claim is that it is part of the concept of law that law must be genuinely authoritative. There can be, on his view, law that is accepted as authoritative but is not really such, for it does not merit the sort of deference that genuine authority merits. Part of the reason for this is that, as Hart's rendering of the sociality commonplace makes clear, law can be very morally bad indeed – given the fact that law is a human institution, made by fallible and sometimes simply evil people, we have no basis for thinking that a system of law cannot turn out very rotten. One might think, then, that the only thing that Hart can say about the commonplace that law is oriented to the common good is what Austin says: we ought to make our law as morally good as possible. But in fact Hart says a little more than that.

What Hart says about the connection between law and the common good is that there is what he calls a "minimum content of natural law" in actual legal systems.[22] We will begin to discuss the idea of natural law more thoroughly later in the chapter, but for now understand it simply as morality – that there is a minimum content of morality in actual legal systems.

What on earth does he mean by this? What he wants to say is that, even though there are massive differences in moral belief among human societies, there is tremendous agreement on survival as a human aim, an aim that people have strong reason to pursue. The idea, then, is that it is an important truth about legal systems that unless those legal systems provide a basis for the survival of (a large proportion of) those living in that system, they will not take themselves to have adequate reason to comply with the norms of that system. Thus there is a kind of rational pressure in favor of legal systems providing at least a basic sort of protection from the evils that thwart human survival. There is at least, then, a minimal orientation of law to the common good, even if legal systems can deprive large chunks of their population of these protections or might cease to respect these constraints on their way to becoming defunct.

1.5   Interlude: Hard and Soft Positivisms

Hart's positivism remains a very widely affirmed account of the nature of law. But one line of criticism of Hart's view, that put forward by Ronald Dworkin, ultimately led to a division within the positivist camp, a division that is still a matter of serious intellectual debate among positivists.[23] Dworkin held that Hartian positivism does not adequately account for the way that *principles*, as contrasted with *rules*, play a role in law. Dworkin noted that it is common in cases at law for judges to appeal to principles in the justification of their decisions, principles for which there was no obvious account of how they found their way into the law. For example, in the case of *Riggs v. Palmer*,[24] a young man murdered his grandfather in order to receive an inheritance from the grandfather's will. Though convicted of the murder, the young man nevertheless made a legal claim on the estate, holding that there were no laws regarding inheritance that would prevent murderers from inheriting from the estates of their victims. While agreeing that plain readings of the statutes in place did not rule out the murderer's inheriting from his victim's estate, the court nevertheless found against him, appealing to the principle that no one should be permitted to profit by his or her own wrongdoing. Such appeals to principle, resulting in decisions that seem contrary to what plain readings of statutes or settled precedents would require, are rife in the cases, and so call for explanation. One available explanation, though, is deeply inimical to the positivist approach to law: that it is simply because those principles are morally attractive that they are part of the law and so can be used by judges to justify particular decisions. One who accepted *that* explanation would cease to be a positivist, for he or she would be denying that all legal norms ultimately have their status as such in virtue of social facts.

To remain a positivist, one must bypass the straightforward explanation and provide an alternative. The task of giving an alternative account of how moral principles end up as part of the law, so that judges can legitimately appeal to them in deciding cases, is the source of the division of legal positivism into two camps. The issue is whether legal positivism should be (to use the presently popular labels) "hard" or "soft," "exclusive" or "inclusive," "nonincorporationist" or "incorporationist." What is at issue between these two camps is how the constraint that law is a matter of social fact should be understood.

Both hard and soft positivisms allow that there is no necessary connection between law and morality. What they disagree on is whether it is *possible* for morality to be incorporated into law. The hard positivist says "No": law's sociality means that the existence of law in any community is entirely a matter of social fact, and not at all a matter of moral facts. The hard positivist responds to Dworkin, then, by denying that moral principles become part of the law to be used by judges; rather, when judges engage in moral reasoning, they are going beyond the law in rendering their decisions. The soft positivist says "Yes": whether the content of the law of some community includes moral norms is itself a matter of social fact within that community. The soft positivist responds to Dworkin, then, by saying that moral principles (such as *no one should profit by his or her own wrongdoing*) would be part of a society's law because, and only because, the rule of recognition within that society acknowledges morality, or some part of morality, as law.

Let us make what is at issue more concrete by considering an example. Suppose that we consider the provision of the United States Constitution that declares that cruel and unusual punishments shall not be imposed. One might think that "cruel" here is a moral notion – to call an action "cruel" is, in part, to make a moral assessment of it. Now, the question is: does the existence of this constitutional provision imply that morality has been *built into* the law, so that what the law is concerning punishment is not simply a matter of the rule of recognition holding sway in the United States and the status of the Constitution as law under that rule, but also a matter of what acts count as cruel in the morally relevant sense? The hard and soft positivists agree – because they are, after all, positivists – that whether *cruel and unusual punishments may not be imposed* is law in the United States depends on a social fact, the fact that there is a rule of recognition that fixes the text of the Constitution as law. They disagree about whether moral facts involving cruelty – *it is cruel to hang people from their fingernails over boiling oil; it is cruel to hit people in the kneecaps with sledgehammers* – are implicated in the law.

The soft positivist holds that there is no reason that law cannot incorporate these sorts of moral values. Though Hart was unclear about his views on this matter in *The Concept of Law*, he later wrote a Postscript to that work, published only after his death, in which (in response to Dworkin's criticisms) he affirmed soft positivism. While it is true, he allows, that permitting moral values to be incorporated into the law might make the content of law more uncertain – and remember uncertainty was one of the evils that the introduction of law aims to remedy – certainty is not the *only* value that law might aim to realize, and it might serve the community better to incorporate moral values in its legal norms.[25] It has also been noted that soft positivism seems to fit with the fact that when judges seek to apply norms that include this sort of morally loaded language, they see themselves as engaging in moral reasoning to discover what the law is – and it can hardly be the case that judges can engage in moral reasoning to discover what the law is unless moral values are themselves included in the law itself.

So there is some reason for thinking that soft positivism is a plausible version of positivism, and we might wonder why anyone would insist that moral values simply could not be incorporated into law. The hard positivist is committed, that is, to insisting that no matter how hard one tries, one cannot make a law that incorporates morality.

The most elaborate defense of hard positivism has come from Joseph Raz, who was himself a student of Hart's.[26] What is particularly interesting about this argument is the way that it employs the commonplace that law is authoritative in order to make the case that hard positivism must be right. Raz says that the commonplace that law is authoritative should be understood as, at least, the view that law *claims to be* genuinely authoritative – that whenever you have a system of law, it makes claims on its own behalf that it is genuinely authoritative. But if law claims to be genuinely authoritative, then it must be the sort of thing that can be genuinely authoritative – it would be very strange to think that law, everywhere and always, claims to be genuinely authoritative, but that even in principle it is not the sort of thing that can have genuine authority. From the law's claiming authority, we know that it has what we may call "authority-potential."

Here is Raz's second point. The role of authority, its function, is to give people dictates that help people act better – to do a better job acting on the reasons for action that they already have. (Raz calls this the "service" conception of authority.) In order for an authority's dictates to be capable of doing this job, those who are to follow those dictates must be able to understand and apply them even without being able to decide for themselves how they should act on the reasons that apply to them. If people are to act better on the reasons that apply to them by using legal norms, they must be able to grasp those legal norms apart from identifying the reasons that apply to them.

Raz combines these two points in an argument for hard positivism. For law must have authority-potential. But it has authority-potential only if folks can understand the law's requirements without going through moral deliberation on their own. So law must be understandable without going through moral deliberation on one's own. But if moral values are incorporated in law, one will be able to understand law's requirements only by going through moral deliberation on one's own. So moral values cannot be incorporated into law.

Raz of course recognizes that there is apparently morality-incorporating language in law. But what he denies is that this is any more than appearance. When the law says that cruel punishments are not to be imposed, this does not mean, on Raz's view, that law incorporates moral values. Until there is an authoritative ruling – for example, a judge's ruling from the bench – on what counts as "cruel," the law on punishment is *unsettled*. The law may authorize the judge to engage in moral reasoning to decide whether to strike down a certain statute (e.g., one that designated boiling in oil as a punishment), but we should not understand this as a case of the judge's *discovering* what the law is but in exercising a limited law*making* power.

The debate between hard and soft positivism is a debate about how sociality and authority fit together in our concept of law. The hard positivist claim is that the requirements of authority actually place a very high demand on the extent to which law is determined by social fact. Soft positivists deny this, holding that the extent to which the content of legal rules is determined by social fact is itself partially determined by social fact. These views are united by their positivism, but divided on the question on what sorts of constraints there are on what the rule of recognition in a society can acknowledge as law. On this question, interestingly and paradoxically enough, the hard positivists are united with the natural law theorists. We will return to this similarity below.

1.6   Natural Law Theory

The major opponent to legal positivism as a conception of the nature of law goes by the label "natural law theory." "Natural law theory" is probably not the best name for this view – it's a bit of a historical accident that this view in the philosophy of law came to have this name – but it is the traditional label, and I will not try to displace it here.[27]

Natural law theory is the view of the nature of law against which Austin set himself in propounding his command theory of law, and against which Hart set himself in offering his own revisionist positivism. Natural law theory, like legal positivism, comes in a variety of formulations, and we will have to spend some time thinking about how best to put the essentials of the view. But we can begin simply by treating the natural law view as a negation of the positivist thesis that it is not necessarily part of the criteria for legality that norms measure up to some moral standard. While the positivists treat social facts alone as the ground for the legality of all norms, natural law theorists want to say that there is a further test – some sort of morality test, or reasonableness test – that all genuine legal norms must satisfy.

You can think about it this way. The hard positivist says that social facts alone determine what the law is. The soft positivist says that morality might enter into the determination of what the law is, but only if a rule of recognition grounded in social fact alone says so, and it is by no means a necessary truth that morality enters into the determination of what the law is. The natural law theorist says that it is a necessary truth that morality enters into the determination of what the law is. Somehow morality constrains legality, not just as an ideal (law ought to be morally good) but as a matter of necessity (in order to be law, norms must be in some way morally acceptable).

The natural law thesis has seemed to many to be so counterintuitive as to be simply incredible. What kind of magic trick is it, one might ask, that a human-made institution like law should turn out to be necessarily morally acceptable? We will approach this by looking at the case that can be made for a contemporary version of the natural law view that is, from the standpoint of the mainline natural law tradition, a bit on the watered-down side, and see why one might be tempted to affirm it. Once we see why one might be tempted to affirm this watered-down view, we will be in a better position to understand and assess the more robust traditional natural law position.

1.6.1 Fuller's procedural natural law theory

One of Hart's more interesting critics was Lon Fuller, who was teaching law at Harvard at the same time that Hart was on the faculty at

Oxford. Fuller found fault with Hart's view insofar as it placed all of the emphasis on the *sources* of law in determining legality. On Fuller's view, the nature of legality is also to be found in the *content* of the norms themselves. We learn in Hart a great deal about what must be the case for people to treat certain norms as rules, but what we do not get from Hart is a close study of whether there are some norms that must fail to be law because they somehow intrinsically lack the potential to become laws.

Think back to Austin. For all of Austin's strict positivism, he placed one very interesting condition on the commands that count as laws. The condition was that the commands must be *general* in form. The commands must be of the form "All those in class C must do x" rather than "You – do that!" The idea is that our concept of law involves *generality* – that it is a guide to action not just on the particular occasion of its utterance, but in various kinds of situation that one might find oneself.

Fuller's view is that Austin is correct on this point, but that he failed to recognize the wide variety of constraints on the norms that qualify as law. He makes his view vivid by offering a thought-experiment about one King Rex, a woefully underqualified monarch who wipes the slate clean and sets about creating a new legal code.[28] At first, Rex decides not to announce any general rules, only to make particular decisions: the subjects are deeply dissatisfied, for there is no detectable pattern in Rex's decisions and they have no way to determine how Rex will decide from one case to the next. So Rex tries to make general rules, but is unsure of how sound they are, so he decides to keep the rules that he will apply a secret: again, the subjects are up in arms. Next Rex decides that it is easier to decide cases in retrospect, so every year he will make up the rules by which he will decide the cases of the previous year. Again, the subjects find this deeply wanting. Rex has further mishaps with his attempts to make law: his efforts generate rules that are incomprehensible, contradictory, impossible to follow, change from day to day, and bear no relation to his judicial decisions.

Fuller calls this thought-experiment "Eight Ways to Fail to Make Law."[29] His argument is that this parable counts as a sort of clear case against the positivist view. *For Rex's dictates need violate no positivist constraints.* All of the relevant social facts might be in place. What we need to appeal to in order to explain the failure of Rex's dictates to constitute law is not anything about the source of the norms, but about the norms themselves – they lack the proper *form* to count as law.

It is illuminating to think of Fuller's conditions not merely as a laundry list of constraints but as unified under the commonplace that law is authoritative – that it is meant to serve as a guide to the conduct of those living under it.[30] Each of Fuller's conditions must be met if folks are to use the norms of law as guides to their conduct. How, after all, is one to guide one's conduct by legal norms if those norms are impossible to follow – if they are contradictory, or incomprehensible, or ephemeral? Fuller calls this a "procedural" natural law theory, one that emphasizes that law be made a certain way, employing a certain form.[31] There is, then, a sort of constraint on the possible content of law, one arising from the requirements of law as an authoritative institution.

1.6.2 Aquinas's substantive natural law theory

As John Austin's legal theory is the paradigmatic formulation of legal positivism, Thomas Aquinas's legal theory is the paradigmatic formulation of natural law theory. It is very difficult to overstate Aquinas's influence on the philosophy of law, both on those who follow his view and on those that react against him.[32]

Aquinas's concern is not only with the sort of law that we are concerned with – that is, human law over some human community. His concern extends beyond that to the various sorts of law that God imposes on the universe and the rational creatures in it. Thus he begins his investigation by asking what law in general is. His conclusion is that "Law is an ordinance of reason for the common good, made by one who has care of the community, and promulgated."[33] How should we understand this definition, how does it apply in the case of human law, and how does Aquinas argue for it?

Begin with the part of the definition that law is an ordinance of reason. That it is an ordinance of reason means that law is a rational standard for conduct – a way that rational beings should guide their behavior. Why does Aquinas think this?

> Law is a sort of rule and measure of acts, according to which one is induced to act or restrained from acting, for *lex* (law) is said to be from *ligare* (to bind) because *obligat* (it binds) one to act. But the rule and

measure of human acts is reason, which is the first principle of human acts, ... for it belongs to reason to order things to the end, which is the first principle in practical matters, according to the Philosopher [that is, Aristotle]. However, that which is the principle of any given genus is the measure and rule of that genus. ... Hence it follows that law is something pertaining to reason.[34]

Though this argument is couched in unfamiliar terms, its gist is plain enough. Aquinas's idea is that, no matter what else we think about law, we agree that it consists in rules, mandatory standards by which our conduct is to be assessed. Furthermore, the sort of assessment involved is essentially practical: the standard that law sets is a standard by which one is "induced to act or restrained from acting." But the only standards that can induce *rational* beings as rational beings to act are *rational* standards. So law necessarily is a rational standard for conduct.

The other elements of Aquinas's full definition are subordinate to the element that law is a rational standard for conduct, in that Aquinas employs the claim that law is an ordinance of reason to show that law is for the common good, made by one who has care of the community, and promulgated. Why must law be for the common good? Because law is for the governance of *group* conduct, and what determines reasonable conduct for members of a group is the common good of that group.[35] Why must law be made only by one who has care of the community? Because while anyone can make *suggestions* about how it is reasonable to order group conduct, only one who is charged with making such decisions can render an *authoritative* ruling on what is to be done, thereby setting the standard that members of that group must follow.[36] Why must law be promulgated? Because a rational being cannot act on a rational standard as such unless he or she has the means to become aware of the existence of the standard, its status as authoritative, and its content, and the promulgation of the rule provides for this awareness.[37]

It might seem strange to say that law is a rational standard for conduct, when it seems clear that there are many laws that do not seem to be requirements of reason at all. Surely the details of the United States tax code, or the motor laws within the commonwealth of Virginia, are not the sort of thing that one *must* come up with if one sits down to reason clearly about what tax law ought to be for the United

States or what the motor laws ought to be in Virginia. (Taxes could be due on April 30 rather than April 15; the speed limit on Virginia highways could be 60 instead of 65.) Aquinas is aware of this potential criticism, and wants to distance his view from the idea that all law reflects already-existing requirements of reason. If we call the rules of reason that tell us how we ought to act within our political communities the "principles for common living," Aquinas wants to say that all human law is rooted in the principles for common living in one of two ways.[38] It might be rooted in those principles by way of *deduction*: part of human law simply reflects what we can independently know to be necessary for good common living. So we have human laws forbidding murder, and rape, and assault, and fraud: all of these are actions that are damaging to the common life of a political community, and we are rationally bound to refrain from these actions even apart from the law's forbidding them. On the other hand, some laws are rooted in the principles for common living as "determinations of certain generalities." In other words, in some cases human law functions not by copying the principles for common living, but by going beyond them to "fill in the gaps" where the principles and their implications are vague. It is clear that there need to be rules of the road: but which ones? It is clear that the operations of political authority need to be funded somehow: but how? There are numerous equally acceptable possibilities, but it is important that we fix on a common scheme. These determinations are not requirements of reason before they are laid down in law; on Aquinas's view, they *become* requirements of reason by being reasonable solutions to the problem of how to make the principles for common living more precise *and* by being laid down by the public authority who "has care of the community."

Regardless of whether the human law derives from the principles for common living by way of deduction or determination, Aquinas's view involves a firm denial that it is simply the pedigree of a norm, its sources, that fixes the status of the norm as law. And Aquinas does seem to draw these conclusions, much to the dismay of the positivists that followed. If we say that law is a rational standard, or that law is for the common good, then it would seem that even a norm that is passed by the accepted legislature, or issued by the sovereign, would fail to count as law, on account of its unreasonableness. And this seems to be Aquinas's conclusion: such rules are "acts of violence rather than laws."[39]

This is a bold claim. It is worth backtracking a bit to Fuller's view to see why one might be tempted toward this sort of position. Recall that Fuller's argument was that there are certain norms that fail so miserably to guide conduct that they cannot count as law, even if their social pedigree is impeccable. Now, one might respond to Fuller: "What do you mean, these formally defective norms can't guide action? Of course they can guide action. One might, in response to a contradictory norm, try to do both of the contradictory actions. One might, in response to an impossible norm, try to do what is impossible. One might, in response to an unclear norm, try to do precisely what it is unclear that one should do. So you are wrong to say that these norms cannot guide action." Why is this an inadequate response to Fuller? What is a more straightforward way to be guided by a rule that says one must x rather than try to x?

The most obvious way to respond here is to say that this is not the sort of action-guidedness we are looking for, because these are not *rational* responses; to say that one cannot be guided by a norm is to say that one cannot be *rationally* directed by it. But if one accepts this point, then Aquinas has an opening. For he can say that unless an alleged legal rule is *actually reasonable*, one cannot be *rationally* guided by it; one would be irrational to direct one's conduct by an entirely unreasonable norm. Once one allows that the *form* exhibited by some norm might render it nonlegal, it looks as though one might have to allow that a norm might be rendered nonlegal on account of its *substance*.

The natural law theorist might further try to enlist aid and comfort from a most unlikely source – the hard positivist. One might think that these views are fundamentally opposed: the hard positivist thinks that not only is legality not necessarily constrained by morality, legality is necessarily not constrained by morality; the natural law theorists think, of course, that morality necessarily constrains legality. But they have an interesting alliance against the soft positivist on one point: they agree that there are constraints on the kinds of norm that can be law, regardless of what the social facts about norm-acceptance seem to be. The hard positivist thinks that it is a prior constraint on law that it not incorporate morality. The natural law theorist thinks that it is a prior constraint on law that it operate within the constraints of the principles for common living. Both believe in prior constraints on the content of legal norms.

We will return in a moment to questions concerning the success of these points in favor of Aquinas's view and concerning the other objections that one might raise to the natural law position. But it is worth keeping in mind the case in favor of Aquinas's view. We can put this case in terms of the commonplaces about law. Aquinas's view satisfies the sociality constraint: Aquinas emphasizes that human law exists only when it has been *made* by one who has care of the community and *promulgated*: these are matters of social fact, so that there is no human law without some social facts that make it so. (Aquinas's theory seems to tend in the direction of Austin's sovereignty view, imagining a fundamental lawmaking authority; on this point a contemporary natural law theorist would probably look to Hart for guidance in revising Aquinas's position.) Where Aquinas departs from the positivists is in his insistence that there is more to law than social fact: there are normative standards that constrain whether pedigreed norms are law. Aquinas holds that law is essentially a rational standard for conduct, itself binding on those subject to it (thus satisfying the commonplace that law is authoritative), and he holds that the source of its authority is the way that it provides for the common good (thus satisfying the commonplace that law is for the common good).

The most serious difficulty for natural law views is that they seem to fly in the face of clear cases of law. It seems that there are countless examples of bad laws, laws that people did not have decisive reason to comply with, yet which were recognized and accepted as law by judges, legislators, and subjects alike. As Brian Bix writes,

> The basic point is that the concept of "legal validity" is closely tied to what is recognized as binding in a given society and what the state enforces, and it seems fairly clear that there are plenty of societies where immoral laws are recognized as binding and enforced. Someone might answer that these immoral laws are not *really* legally valid, and the officials are making a mistake when they treat the rules as if they were legally valid. However, this is just to play games with words, and confusing games at that. "Legal validity" is the term we use to refer to *whatever* is conventionally recognized as binding; to say that all the officials could be wrong about what is legally valid is close to nonsense.[40]

Andrei Marmor offers a similar basis for rejecting the natural law view:

> Take a certain legal system, say Roman law in the first century AD; let us presume that a certain norm, P, was recognized by the Roman

lawyers at the time as part and parcel of their legal system. Does it make sense to say that this community of lawyers has made a mistake, since according to the "real nature" of law, P did not lie within the extension of their legal system even then, despite their inability to recognize this?

I presume that a negative answer to this question is almost self-evident; such an extensive misidentification in law would be profoundly mysterious.[41]

Bix and Marmor seem to be right: it is hard to accept that we should simply treat a widespread consensus that a norm is law as a mere mistake. While there are some kinds of widespread error that are surely possible – errors about astronomy, or morality, or biology – errors about law are different: to say that all of the people in some society are mistaken about what the law in that society is seems almost as bizarre as to say that all of the English speakers are mistaken about what the English word "blue" means. The use of "blue" by these speakers fixes its meaning; similarly, the way that the people in some society treat some norm fixes its status as law. This burden of proof weighs heavily on the natural law theorist.

1.7 A Suggested Resolution

Positivism has its obvious attractions. Law's plain status as a social institution leads us to want to push as far as possible the explanation of legality in terms of social facts alone. But once we see the case to be made for appealing to certain formal constraints on the norms that can be legal, it is hard to resist the claim that there can be substantive constraints as well. Nevertheless, when we see that this would commit us to a rejection of the thesis that the Fugitive Slave Act was law, we rightly hesitate, wondering how we found ourselves at this paradoxical conclusion.

Let me close this discussion of the analytic fundamentals in the philosophy of law by suggesting a resolution. Perhaps it is a mistake to think that Fuller is right to recognize his "Eight Ways to Fail to Make Law" as constraints on legality. We accepted for the moment his view that the guidance of rational conduct requires that these constraints be satisfied. This may be true, but why do we want to say that the fact that a norm that cannot guide rational conduct is sufficient to preclude its legality? Even if it is the purpose of law to guide action rationally, the fact that a norm cannot do this does not show that it is not a law at all. It shows only that it is *defective*, screwed-up law.[42]

To see the distinctiveness of this position, we would need to say more about the idea of defect. To say that something is defective is not to say that there is something about it we don't like. I might like a defective alarm clock better than a nondefective one, because I don't like to be awakened in the morning. To say that something is defective is to say that it belongs to a certain kind, and there are certain standards of perfection that are internal to (that are intrinsic to, that necessarily belong to) members of that kind. To be an alarm clock just is, in part, to be the sort of thing that if it cannot sound an alarm when one wishes to be awakened, is defective. But something can be an alarm clock even if it cannot sound an alarm: it might be broken, or poorly constructed, or whatever.

The notion of defect is common both with respect to artifacts (alarm clocks, vacuum cleaners, chairs) and natural objects (ducks, begonias, humans). What I am suggesting is that perhaps the best way to understand the natural law alternative to legal positivism is not as an alternative account of legality, but as a more fully developed account of the idea of *nondefective* legality. Law, the natural law theorist can say, is a kind that has certain standards of perfection intrinsic to it. Fuller's views might go some way toward explaining the formal constraints that there are on nondefective legality. Aquinas's go further still, explaining how a substantive orientation toward the common good is required for law to be nondefective. These views need not be at odds with a positivist picture like Hart's: what Hart's view offers is in the main an account of the existence conditions of law rather than an account of its nondefectiveness conditions.

The most powerful case for this view is the strong way that it handles the commonplaces about law without requiring the counter-intuitive stands on clear cases that the more straightforward natural law position suggests. With respect to the sociality commonplace, we can say that law's existence is entirely a matter of social fact. With respect to the authority commonplace, we can say, first, that it is the nature of law to be de facto authoritative (at least over some relevant population, for example, officials) and that it is law's function to give genuinely authoritative guidance, so that nondefective law is genuinely authoritative. And, finally, with respect to the common good commonplace we can say that law is oriented to the common good in that the object of law's functioning is to serve the common good. Law that fails to serve the common good is defective as law, and that is why it would be weird and paradoxical for a legal system to deny that it means to serve that good. A system of law that announces that it is not for the common good is like an alarm clock that is labeled "not to be used to awaken people."

For Further Reading

The classic text for legal positivism is John Austin's *Province of Jurisprudence Determined* (Cambridge, UK: Cambridge University Press, 1995). Also very influential in the development of positivist thought was the work of Hans Kelsen: see, for example, his *Pure Theory of Law*, 2nd edn., trans. Max Knight (Berkeley, CA: University of California Press, 1967). H. L. A. Hart's *The Concept of Law*, 2nd edn. (Oxford: Clarendon Press, 1994) powerfully restates the positivist view in the form in which it is now most familiar. Joseph Raz defends his hard positivism in a number of essays in *The Authority of Law* (Oxford: Oxford University Press, 1979) and *Ethics in the Public Domain* (Oxford: Clarendon Press, 1994). A recent new defense of hard positivism is Scott Shapiro's "On Hart's Way Out," in Jules Coleman (ed.), *Hart's Postscript* (Oxford: Oxford University Press, 2001), pp. 151–91. Jules Coleman defends soft positivism in, among other places, *The Practice of Principle* (Oxford: Oxford University Press, 2001), pp. 67–148. An excellent discussion of the positivist thesis can be found in John Gardner, "Legal Positivism: $5\frac{1}{2}$ Myths," *American Journal of Jurisprudence* 46 (2001), pp. 199–227.

The classic text for natural law theory is the so-called "Treatise on Law" in Thomas Aquinas's *Summa Theologiae*: see Aquinas, *Treatise on Law*, ed. and trans. R. J. Henle (Notre Dame, IN: University of Notre Dame Press, 1993). Lon Fuller's *The Morality of Law* (New Haven, CT: Yale University Press, 1964) was an attempt to confront Hart's positivism. Another view sometimes described as a natural law position (but which, in my view, is more a theory of adjudication than of the nature of law) is that of Ronald Dworkin: see his *Law's Empire* (Cambridge, MA: Harvard University Press, 1986). The most important recent statement of the natural law position is John Finnis's *Natural Law and Natural Rights* (Oxford: Clarendon Press, 1980). See also Michael Moore, "Law as a Functional Kind," in Robert P. George (ed.), *Natural*

Law Theory (Oxford: Oxford University Press, 1992), pp. 188–242, and "Law as Justice," *Social Philosophy and Policy* 18 (2001), pp. 115–45, as well as Mark C. Murphy, *Natural Law in Jurisprudence and Politics* (New York: Cambridge University Press, 2006). Concise overviews of both the natural law and positivist views by Mark C. Murphy and Brian Bix (respectively) can be found in Martin P. Golding and William A. Edmundson (eds.), *Blackwell Guide to Philosophy of Law and Legal Theory* (Malden, MA: Blackwell, 2005), pp. 15–28, 29–49.

Notes

1 The case is a version of that offered by Bertrand Russell in *Human Knowledge: Its Scope and Limits* (New York: Allen and Unwin, 1948), p. 154.
2 John Austin, *The Province of Jurisprudence Determined*, ed. Wilfrid E. Rumble (Cambridge, UK: Cambridge University Press, 1995 [originally published 1832]).
3 Ibid., Lecture I, pp. 21, 25.
4 Ibid., Lecture I, pp. 21–2.
5 Ibid., Lecture VI, pp. 168–9.
6 Ibid., Lecture V, p. 158.
7 Ibid., Lecture V, p. 111.
8 Ibid., Lecture II, p. 41.
9 H. L. A. Hart, *The Concept of Law*, 2nd edn. (Oxford, UK: Clarendon Press, 1994 [first published 1961]), pp. 26–78.
10 Ibid., p. 28.
11 Ibid., pp. 29–33.
12 Ibid., pp. 51–4.
13 Austin, *Province of Jurisprudence Determined*, Lecture I, p. 23.
14 Hart, *Concept of Law*, pp. 82–3.
15 See Robert Alexy, *The Argument from Injustice*, trans. Bonnie Litschewski Paulson and Stanley L. Paulson (Oxford: Clarendon Press, 2002). He asks us what we would think of a constitution of a country, X, that begins with the declaration that "X is a sovereign, federal, and unjust republic" (p. 36). Alexy thinks that we would find this not just out of the ordinary but "defective" (p. 36) and "absurd" (p. 37).
16 Austin, *Province*, Lecture V, p. 157.
17 Hart, *Concept of Law*, p. 56.
18 Ibid., p. 55.
19 Ibid., pp. 91–4.
20 Ibid., pp. 93–9.
21 Ibid., p. 109.

22 Ibid., pp. 192–200.
23 Ronald Dworkin, "The Model of Rules – I," in *Taking Rights Seriously* (Cambridge, MA: Harvard University Press, 1977), pp. 14–45.
24 22 N.E. 188 (N.Y. 1889).
25 Hart, *Concept of Law*, pp. 250–4.
26 Joseph Raz, "Authority, Law, and Morality," *Monist* 68 (1985), pp. 295–324.
27 Aquinas says that the principles of practical rationality – that is, those principles that tell us how to act reasonably – both are God's law for our conduct and are knowable by nature, even apart from special divine revelation. So the principles of practical rationality are both *law* and *natural*, and hence are *natural law*. Because Aquinas says that law must be in accordance with reason, and he identifies the basic principles of rationality with natural law, he sometimes says that human law must be in accordance with reason and he sometimes says that human law must be in accordance with the natural law. But for Aquinas, these formulations are equivalent. So Aquinas's legal theory is called a natural law theory, because he holds that it is a constraint on the legality of human law that it accord with the natural law. The label is unfortunate because there are some writers who believe that the principles of rationality or morality place a constraint on legality, but who do not believe that these principles of rationality or morality are God-given law. These writers are called natural law theorists, even though they do not, strictly speaking, believe in natural law.
28 Lon Fuller, *The Morality of Law* (New Haven, CT: Yale University Press, 1964), pp. 33–8.
29 Ibid., p. 33.
30 Ibid., p. 53.
31 Ibid., pp. 96–7.
32 Aquinas's most important writings on law occur as a very small part of a very large 13th-century treatise on theology called the *Summa Theologiae*. This massive work is divided into three parts, with the second part divided into two parts; all citations to this work begin with the part number (Ia, IaIIae, IIaIIae, or IIIa). Each of these parts contains a number of "questions" (which are more like topics) and "articles" (which are more like particular issues). A complete citation to a specific discussion within the *Summa Theologiae* will give, then, the part number, question number, and article number. The "Treatise on Law" that contains the core of Aquinas's natural law doctrine occurs in the *Summa Theologiae* at IaIIae QQ. 90–7. Quotations in the text are from *Summa Theologiae*, trans. Fathers of the English Dominican Province (Westminster, MD: Christian Classics, 1981).
33 Aquinas, *Summa Theologiae*, IaIIae Q. 90, A. 4.
34 Ibid., IaIIae Q. 90, A. 1.

35 Ibid., IaIIae Q. 90, A. 2.

36 Ibid., IaIIae Q. 90, A. 3.

37 Ibid., IaIIae Q. 90, A. 4.

38 Ibid., IaIIae Q. 95, A. 2.

39 Ibid., IaIIae Q. 96, A. 4.

40 Brian Bix, "Natural Law Theory: The Modern Tradition," in Jules Coleman and Scott Shapiro (eds.), *Oxford Handbook of Jurisprudence and Philosophy of Law* (New York: Oxford University Press, 2002), pp. 61–103, quotation pp. 72–3.

41 Andrei Marmor, *Interpretation and Legal Theory* (New York: Oxford University Press, 1992), pp. 96–7.

42 For defenses of this view, see John Finnis, *Natural Law and Natural Rights* (Oxford: Clarendon Press, 1980), pp. 9–18 and Mark C. Murphy, *Natural Law in Jurisprudence and Politics* (New York: Cambridge University Press, 2006), pp. 29–59.

Chapter 2

Normative Fundamentals: The Basic Roles of Paradigmatic Legal Systems

2.1 What Are the Basic Roles in Paradigmatic Legal Systems?

Recall Hart's account of the nature of a legal system, discussed in Chapter 1. On Hart's view, we can make sense of legal systems by seeing them as a response to various problems that arise if communities' lives are organized only by primary rules. Living under primary rules alone generates difficulties concerning the uncertain status of the rules, the modification of the rules, and the application of the rules. A paradigmatic legal system is one that has introduced a rule of recognition, rules of change, and rules of adjudication that remedy these deficiencies.

With the introduction of new sorts of social *rules*, rules that are distinctively legal, come new sorts of social *roles*, roles that are distinctively legal. What is a social role? As I am using the term, a social role can be defined as a set of rules. A role is constituted by two kinds of rules: *occupancy* rules and *performance* rules. An occupancy rule specifies what must be the case for someone to be in that role. A performance rule specifies what is to be done by someone who occupies that role. So consider, for example, the role *teacher*. If we want to describe what sets that role apart from other roles, we would say two things about it: what characteristics a person has that make it the case that he or she is a teacher, and what one must do in order to count as a good teacher.

The Basic Roles of Paradigmatic Legal Systems

What, then, are the social roles that are fundamental to legal systems? Under a set of customary norms, people see themselves as bound by the rules, but with the introduction of a legal system, there is introduced a similar but nevertheless in important ways distinctive role: that of *subject*. Under a set of customary norms, the existence and content of the rules, and their application to particular cases, is often a loosely defined matter of how some segment of the population governs their own behavior, but with the introduction of a legal system, two distinctive roles are introduced: that of the lawmaker, the *legislator*, and of the law-applier, the *judge*. (These cannot in practice always be neatly separated: it is a commonly recognized phenomenon that judges often put forward new rules from the bench, making further law in the course of deciding disputes about which the law is presently unsettled. But, given our previous definition of roles as consisting in occupancy and performance rules, this does not count against the view that they are distinct roles: what it is to be a *good judge* is different from what it is to be a *good legislator*.)

The roles that are fixed by the nature of legal systems are that of *subject*, *legislator*, and *judge*. By contrast, and perhaps surprisingly so, the role *lawyer* is not. The reason is simple: there can be fully fledged legal systems without lawyers, so the role of lawyer cannot be basic to the legal system. (You cannot, however, have a fully fledged legal system without the roles of subject, judge, and legislator.) The role of lawyer is a secondary phenomenon in legal systems, on account of certain difficulties that exist in understanding and applying the law. If the point of rules of recognition and adjudication is to resolve difficulties about recognition and adjudication existing in schemes of customary rules, the existence of a lawyerly role within a legal system shows that this legal system has failed to resolve those difficulties. The fault may not belong to the system: it may be that due to the complexity of the rules that the society requires or the inequality between parties in disputes at law, a specialized class of lawyers is necessary for the recognition and adjudication functions to be carried out well. But the point remains that the role of lawyer is a functionally secondary one in legal systems.

Also functionally secondary are roles that we might collectively call "enforcement" roles, roles like that of police officer, prison warden, or executioner. Given that it is very hard to realistically imagine a developed legal system that does not require any such roles to be filled in order for the system to function effectively, one might wonder why we should think of these roles as functionally secondary. The reason is that all of these enforcement roles presuppose unwillingness to comply with the law; they are concerned with the employment of force to get the otherwise unwilling to fall in line with the law's requirements. But note that the difficulties concerning social life governed only by primary rules need not have anything to do with unwillingness to comply: a society of the most community-minded folk would experience the difficulties of uncertainty, unchangeability, and inefficiency to which Hart calls our attention. This is a very important point. Because we are not angels, our legal systems must include enforcement roles as well. But the roles of subject, legislator, and judge would have point and purpose even if we were all angels.

Subject, legislator, judge: with respect to these roles we can ask a number of questions, and it is important to keep the questions distinct from each other. With respect to each role, we can ask a *conceptual* question: what are the occupancy and performance rules that constitute this social role? This is a matter of unpacking what the role is, of defining its parameters more clearly. With respect to each, we can ask a *substantive* moral question: how ought persons occupying this role to act? (This question can be broken down into several others: what reasons do people have for acting in accordance with the requirements of this role? how strong are those reasons? in what circumstances do people have adequate reason to violate the requirements of the role? what relevant moral guidelines ought people in that role to follow when performing the duties of that role?)

Let's pause for a moment here to make sure that we see what these questions mean, and the distinctions between them. When we answer the *conceptual* question about the occupancy and performance rules associated with a certain role, we are not thereby advocating that anyone act in accordance with the requirements of that role. We are merely *describing* the role. If, for example, you were to ask "What are the requirements that constitute the role *member of the Hitler Youth?*," I would reply, "Well, that role requires one to cheer for Hitler, to advocate racial purity, etc." By giving this answer, I am not thereby advocating that anyone cheer for Hitler or advocate racial purity. I am not even saying that people who occupy the role *Hitler Youth* have good reason to cheer for Hitler or advocate racial purity. All I am saying is that one who fails to cheer Hitler or advocate racial purity falls short as a Hitler Youth, isn't the best Hitler Youth one can be. (But, to repeat: one should *not* be the best Hitler Youth one should be. If one is somehow stuck with being a Hitler Youth, one should be a *bad* one.) The conceptual task of making clear who occupies a certain role and what the role-requirements are is *morally neutral*: one is engaged in the descriptive task of filling in the blanks: one occupies Role R if and only if one is ___ (these are the occupancy rules) and one is acting as a good R only if one does ___ (these are the performance rules).

The substantive question is a different matter. In answering the substantive moral question, we are no longer able to be morally neutral. Once we answer the conceptual question "What are the performance rules for Hitler Youth?," we can ask whether one has good moral reasons to act in accordance with that role; and we can answer "No," holding that the support of a monster like Hitler is morally indefensible and that racial purity is no sort of worthwhile moral ideal. With other roles, we might offer more nuanced answers. Consider the role *student*. There are various requirements associated with it – attending class, writing papers, and so forth – and we might think that there are good reasons for students to follow these requirements. But we might also think that there are exceptions: when a friend seems down and needs someone to talk to, one might flout the requirements of class attendance in order to be with the friend. One might then be a worse *student* but a better *friend*. Whether this is a good idea in the circumstances would depend on a careful evaluation of those circumstances and the alternatives to skipping class.

So we have identified two questions concerning social roles: a conceptual question about the rules that make up that role, and a substantive question concerning how persons who occupy that role should act. Both of these questions can be raised about the fundamental legal roles of subject, legislator, and judge. Who are subjects, legislators, judges? What is it to be a "good subject," a "good legislator," or a "good judge"? What reasons are there to adhere to the requirements of these roles, and how should one go about adhering to them? And in what cases might one reasonably flout those requirements?

2.2 The Role of Subject

To be a subject is not necessarily a voluntary undertaking. Indeed, it is very difficult to live anywhere in the world without being a subject under some legal system. While there may be some choice concerning the legal system to which one is subject, being subject to some legal system is not a matter of choice. So we should not think of the occupancy rules of the role subject as including a voluntariness condition: to be a subject does not require one to adopt that role voluntarily. Neither does being a subject involve any self-definition constraints: one might refuse to define oneself in those terms, might deny the very existence of the legal system that one is under, while still being a subject. This should not be surprising. *Subject* is a social role, constituted by social rules, and for there to be social rules involves how members in some society use those rules as standards for criticism and action-guidance. To say that the role of subject does not include voluntariness or self-definition among its occupancy rules is just to say that one is expected to adhere to the demands of that role regardless of whether one can agreed to it or not and regardless of whether one wishes to think of oneself in those terms or not.

To be a subject of some legal system is defined by the rules of that legal system. Legal systems claim to govern the behavior of certain people and not others; those that they claim to govern are typically those who are citizens of the political community to which that legal system belongs, or those who are living in the territory over which that legal system holds sway, or both. At the moment I am a subject of the legal system of the United States, whether I like it or not. There are steps that I could take to no longer be subject at all to that legal system: I could renounce my citizenship and emigrate to Australia. But until I take such steps I am a subject of the United States legal system. The occupancy rule for subjects is, then, something like: S is a subject of legal system L if and only if L's jurisdiction is so defined as to include S. (Note that this definition makes possible one's being a subject to more than one legal system: I am subject to the laws of the United States, the commonwealth of Virginia, and the town of Herndon; while traveling in Ireland I am subject to the laws of the United States – US law claims to govern some actions of US citizens while abroad – and the laws of Ireland.)

The Basic Roles of Paradigmatic Legal Systems

So much for the occupancy rules for the role *subject*. What are the performance rules? What is it to be a good subject? To be a good subject, I think, is a matter of *obedience*: the good subject obeys the law, and in particular, the law as it is officially interpreted. It is this addendum about official interpretation that makes the role *subject* differ from the role *custom-follower*. In a society ruled by merely customary norms – remember that this is the backdrop that Hart uses to help us understand the distinctive character of legal rules – one is basically left to one's own lights to determine what the rules are, how far they extend, what they mean, and how violations are to be dealt with. The good custom-follower is thus one who obeys the customary rules – but it is a vague and uncertain matter indeed who this person is, given that it is a vague and uncertain matter what precisely the customary rules are. The introduction of rules of recognition and adjudication cuts down on this uncertainty considerably (though not, of course, entirely): rules of recognition give guidance as to how to determine what the legal norms are, and rules of adjudication give guidance as to where subjects can look for clearer understandings of those norms. Deference is required both to the legal norms and to the legal officials charged with interpreting and applying those norms.

Why should we characterize the role of subject in this way? There are at least two reasons, one of them conceptual, built on our earlier observations on the nature of law, and the other empirical, built on observation of legal systems. The conceptual point is that this is how we would expect the role of subject to be defined, given the authority commonplace. Law is authoritative, giving (or being taken to give) decisive reasons for action; the parties to whom it gives those decisive reasons are subjects, those under the law's jurisdiction. The empirical point is that this is how official pronouncements from legal systems treat the demands of the role of subject. Courts tend to treat rather dismissively the claim that subjects are not bound to adhere to its norms.

So the role of subjects is obedience, obedience to legal norms and to the official interpretation of those norms. It may not seem to be a very attractive picture of the role of subject that it is a matter of simple obedience. But let us keep in mind the qualification noted above: to say that the good subject is the obedient subject is not to say that, morally speaking, we should at all times be good subjects. The circumstances in which we are bound by that role may be limited, mildly or severely:

this is a question we have not yet discussed. And we should also keep in mind that obedience is usually not the passive matter that it is sometimes made out to be. Following legal rules is often not simply a mechanical process: subjects need to be able to interpret the rules where there is no settled interpretation of them, and this requires a sort of sensitivity to the point of those norms, the sensitivity exhibited by good judges.

Let us then turn from the preliminary questions about the role of the subject and to the more pressing substantive questions about the extent to which one is bound to adhere to the demands of this role. It is of course obvious that even one who entirely rejects the role of subject might have good reason to do a lot of the things that good subjects do. Many of the demands of law involve prohibiting behavior that decent folks would not engage in anyway – murder, assault, rape, robbery, extortion, theft, fraud, and so forth. But the question that we need to face is the extent to which being a subject ought to make a difference to the way that one acts. Is one morally bound to comply with the demands of law? If so, under what circumstances, and what are the limits of this required obedience?

One explanation, an extremely popular one, for why persons are bound to adhere to the role of subject by exhibiting obedience to law is a consent explanation: generally speaking, people consent to the requirements of being a subject, and thus are morally bound to comply with legal norms. The first, most obvious point to note here is that very few of us explicitly consent to the requirements of being a subject. As we already noted, the role of subject is imposed on one willy-nilly, regardless of whether one consents to it. There are thus not all that many folks who ever explicitly consent to adhere to the demands of that role: immigrants, some political officials, some members of the military. Explicit consent of this global sort is a comparatively rare phenomenon in legal systems.

In the absence of explicit consent the characteristic response of defenders of consent is that while people do not usually *explicitly* consent to carry out the role of subject, they somehow *implicitly*, or *tacitly*, consent.[1] Tacit consent is consent that occurs in ways other than the standard written or spoken words. The task that faces a defender of tacit consent views is to explain what subjects generally do in order to tacitly consent to their roles and to explain why this tacit consent is binding in the way that standard explicit consent is binding.

If the problem with explicit consent is that it is too rare to serve as a general basis for subjects' moral requirements to honor the demands of their role, then defenders of tacit consent will want to identify some very common action as the action that counts as tacitly consenting to honor the demands of that role. Different writers have offered different suggestions, but the most prominent, for obvious reasons, is that of remaining in residence. If remaining in residence counts as consent to adhere to the role subject, then generality is guaranteed – for, after all, one way to occupy the role of subject is just to be living within the jurisdiction of that legal system.

But there are deep difficulties involved in holding that remaining in residence counts as consent to be governed. The problem is that remaining in residence is an act that is so very different from saying or writing "I consent to be ruled by law" in suitably serious circumstances that it is hard to see why we would take the former also to bind one to compliance. Here are three important facts about explicit consent. The first is that uttering "I consent to be ruled by law" and refraining from making that utterance are both, of themselves, low-cost options. The second is that by uttering "I consent to ___," one can bind oneself to a clear set of terms: what one is bound to do is whatever set of terms with which one fills in the blank. The third is that consenting by using the "I consent" phrasing is widely understood and accepted: it is clear to most everyone how to consent and what normative consequences follow if one consents.

The difficulty with the tacit consent theory is that remaining in residence is different on all these counts. Remaining in residence is not a matter of relative indifference, and so we cannot tell whether folks remain in residence because they aim to undertake the obligations of a subject or because they do not want to leave their homes, loved ones, jobs, and so forth behind. As David Hume writes in his demolition of consent theory, "Of the Original Contract":

> Can we seriously say, that a poor peasant or artisan has a free choice to leave his country, when he knows no foreign language or manners, and lives from day to day, by the small wages which he acquires? We may as well assert, that a man, by remaining in a vessel, freely consents to the dominion of the master; though he was carried on board while asleep, and must leap into the ocean, and perish, the moment he leaves her.[2]

56

Second, it is not at all clear what terms one is agreeing to by remaining in residence. There is a clear and simple rule for determining the action to which one is binding oneself when one says "I consent to x": it is (minor complications aside.) x-ing. But there is no such public rule for determining what action one would be agreeing to perform by remaining in residence. Since the attractiveness of the principle that people are bound by their own consent is, in part, that they can see what they are agreeing to and can refuse their consent if they wish, this is a serious difficulty.

Third, it's pretty obvious that residing within the jurisdiction of some legal system is not conventionally understood as an attempt to place oneself under an obligation. It is not typically understood as a linguistic act at all — one lives somewhere because it is convenient, or comfortable, or inexpensive, but not in order to perform a speech-act. But that makes it hard to believe that we should take residence to constitute tacit consent to honor the duties of a subject.

It seems that residence is not to be construed as tacit consent to the authority of law. One might suggest an alternative indication of tacit consent, perhaps, say, voting. But this is also an implausible suggestion. Aside from the fact that it would have the implication that those that fail to vote are under no requirement to adhere to the demands of the role of subject, it is hard to see why we would construe voting as consent to the authority of the legal system in place. When one votes, all that one really registers is one's preference for one candidate, or policy choice, over another; there is no basis for thinking that one submits oneself to the authority of the legal system *as a whole* by stepping into the voting booth to cast a ballot. And, furthermore, voting fails as an alleged sign of consent for the same reasons that residence does: it is not otherwise a matter of mere indifference whether one votes or not; it is unclear what scope of authority one would be placing oneself under by voting; and it is not at all obvious that voting is conventionally regarded as a sign of consent at all.

Consent is now roundly rejected as a basis for explaining why persons occupying the role subject ought to honor the requirements of that role. As an alternative it is tempting to appeal to the *consequences* of flouting that role: one might say that it is in virtue of the bad results of falling short in the demands of the role of the subject that people are bound to comply with those demands, irrespective of one's consent. There is an ambiguity here that needs to be resolved, though.

On one version of the argument, it is the bad results of all (or most) subjects under a legal system failing to comply with the demands of their role that makes each person morally obligated to comply. On another version of the argument, it is the bad results of each person's failing to comply with the demands of his or her role that makes him or her morally obligated to comply.

Consider the latter, individualistic version first. What we lack is any reason to think that overall results will really be worse if each person fails to comply with his or her role as subject. After all, the withdrawal of, say, my tax payments from the United States revenue system is likely to make no practical difference whatever. I could take that money and put it to use in ways that would surely produce better overall results than if I paid them into the system as the law requires. So it seems hard to believe that, from each person's decision-making perspective, the overall good is better served by acting as a good subject than by being willing to disobey on a variety of occasions.

Suppose that we go with the former interpretation, then: it is because it would be disastrous if none of us honored our roles as subjects that each of us is bound to compliance. But there are a number of serious worries here as well. First, we have to be very careful in making the move from the claim "it would be disastrous if no one honored the demands of the role *subject*" to "each person is bound to honor the demands of the role *subject*." For one thing, we would need some explanation as to why the fact that everyone's doing something would be disastrous places each person under a requirement not to do it. (It would be disastrous if everyone spent today working on a philosophy of law textbook. Yet here I am, doing that; surely I am not morally remiss as a result?) Second, we should keep in mind that it is probably false that it would be disastrous if no one honored the demands of the role *subject* – at least if we interpret that to mean that no one fully honors those demands. After all, it probably is true that no one fully honors the demands of subject. (Have you ever broken the law? Think you ever will again?) Further, there is an awful lot of lawbreaking that simply has no tendency to bring about bad consequences. The standard example is the person who runs a red light in the middle of a desert, with excellent views from all sides. Surely this does not contribute, even in the least, to a bad outcome. So, given the existence of harmless lawbreaking, how can an appeal to consequences show that subjects are under a duty of obedience?

A line of argument more promising than a postulation of tacit consent or a direct appeal to the bad consequences of lawbreaking is that which takes *fairness* as its normative basis. One of the defenders of this view was Hart, and it also was at one time advocated by John Rawls. They defended a moral principle, called either the "principle of fairness" or the "principle of fair play," which according to their view showed that certain occupants of the role of subject – those who occupy that role in a reasonably just society – are bound to obey the law.[3]

It is easiest to see the force of the principle by beginning with an example. Suppose that there is a loosely organized group of cyclists whose members take turns leading their weekly rides. When one's turn to lead comes around, one's responsibilities include scouting a route, writing up and copying a sheet of cues so that if members of the group become separated they will know what course to follow, and riding in front in order to call out road hazards along the way. Suppose I fall in with this group, knowing how it is organized, and begin to enjoy their weekly rides. I get the benefits of a well-scouted route, a nice cue sheet, and protection from tire damage along the way. After months of participating, my turn to lead comes around, and I balk. "No thanks," I say, "too much trouble. Yes, I know the rules you all have been following. But I never *agreed* to adhere to them. And it's not like my participation cost you anything: the leaders would have done their jobs regardless of whether I tagged along or not, and there were always extra cue sheets thrown away anyway, so it is not like I was taking a cue sheet that someone else would have used. So why am I bound to serve as ride leader?"

I have, it seems, defused the arguments that I am bound because of my consent or because of the harm that I imposed: I did not consent, and am doing no harm. Yet it does seem plausible that I really ought to take my turn. Why? Because it is *unfair* that I should reap the benefits of others' efforts, which were produced by their adhering to a rule that divides up the burdens of a regular ride. By taking the benefits and refusing the burdens, there is an unjustified inequality among us – by being a free-rider, I take advantage of their efforts, making me better off than they without any adequate rationale.

Here is Rawls's formulation of the relevant moral principle:

> Suppose there is a mutually beneficial and just scheme of social cooperation, and that the advantages it yields can only be obtained if everyone,

59

or nearly everyone, cooperates. Suppose further that cooperation requires a certain sacrifice from each person, or at least involves a certain
restriction of his liberty. Suppose finally that benefits produced by cooperation are, up to a certain point, free: that is, the scheme of cooperation is unstable in the sense that if any one person knows that all (or
nearly all) of the others will continue to do their part, he will still be able
to share a gain from the scheme even if he does not do his part. Under
these conditions a person who has accepted the benefits of the scheme is
bound by a duty of fair play to do his part and not to take advantage of
the free benefit by not cooperating.[4]

This principle applies to the facts of the cycling group situation: the
cycling group scheme is beneficial to all, and just, and the benefits are
produced only by there being widespread cooperation. (Frequent flouting of the rule would make the benefits unreliable, and seriously
devalue them.) But the benefits are gotten only through the cooperation of the group members, through their adhering to a common rule.
In these circumstances, those that take advantage of the benefits of the
scheme are required in fairness to shoulder their share of the burdens –
that is, the share of the burdens determined by the rules.

How does this principle of fairness apply in the case of subjects'
duties to obey the law? Suppose we live in a not-too-defective legal
system – one whose rules are for the common good and divide the
benefits and burdens in a reasonably just way. It is not as if the mere
existence of the rules themselves churns out the benefits: it is only
because of the compliance of large numbers of people, people who often
accept sizable burdens as a cost of compliance, that we receive the
benefits of life under the rule of law. These benefits range from safety
and security (provided by criminal law) to means for redress against
those that harm one (provided by tort law) to techniques for implementing one's wishes (provided by contract law and the law of estates).
And we should not underestimate the benefit of simple predictability –
knowing that there is a set of rules that one's fellows by and large
comply with. Given the fact that these benefits are generated through
broad compliance with the demands of law, it seems that if one accepts
the benefits of the legal system one would be a parasitical free-rider if
one did not adhere to the law as well.

It seems to me that the notion of fair benefits and burdens must be
central to an account of why subjects ought to obey the law, but the

principle of fair play as formulated by Rawls does not seem to do the work Rawls needs it to do. The problem is that the principle as formulated requires one to *accept* the benefits of the system in order to be bound, and it is hard to make sense out of the notion of acceptance of benefits when one is going to receive them regardless of whether or not one chooses to take them.[5] There is a marked contrast between the cycling group case and the case of the subject in a legal system. In the cycling case, I went out of my way to get the benefits of the club; in the case of a legal system, as the passage from Hume above notes, we simply find ourselves under a legal system, with all of its benefits and burdens thrust upon us. Just like the argument from consent, the argument from the principle of fair play requires an appeal to a voluntary act in order for the principle to apply; but, like the argument from consent, the argument from fair play requires a voluntary act that is not widely present in actual legal systems. (Rawls himself later rejected the principle of fairness as the basis for political authority for that reason.[6])

One could take as the result here the idea that fairness is not the basis for a subject's duty to obey the law. But that might be too hasty. Perhaps what needs to be done is not to jettison the idea of fairness as a ground for the obligation of obedience to law but rather to revise the principle so that voluntary acceptance of benefits is not required. Instead of suggesting that we assimilate disobedience to law to free-riding in a voluntary and optional cooperative enterprise, perhaps we should assimilate disobedience to law to failing to shoulder one's share of a collective responsibility.

Here is what I mean. As a matter of common sense we have responsibilities toward the good of groups in which we find ourselves, even if not wholly as a matter of voluntary choice. We take ourselves to be bound to promote the good of our families, for example. It seems plausible that we would be under a similar obligation with respect to the common good of our political communities. But, of course, the promotion of the common good is a chore that belongs not just to one person but to all of the members of the community; each is bound by the duty, not to realize the common good on his or her own (that would of course be beyond our powers), but rather to do his or her *share* for the common good.

Suppose that each of us in a political community has a moral duty to do his or her share for the common good. The problem is that there are an infinite number of ways to divide up the collective task of acting for the common good. Some of them are fair ways, and some are unfair ways, and we should not be bound to adhere to a division of duties that makes excessive, extremely unfair demands on us. But even among the fair ways there are a number of possibilities, and we need to settle on one of these ways in order to coordinate our action for the common good in a reasonably efficient and just way. If one has a decent legal system in place, though, it will provide for just this sort of division: law, when working well, provides a salient and just way to divide up the job of promoting the common good of the political community.[7]

The suggestion, then, is that subjects ought to obey the law because subjects are bound to do their fair share for the common good and the law provides a reasonable way to determine what counts as one's fair share. There are, of course, other reasons to worry about this account (e.g., why is it that the law gets to decide what counts as each person's fair share? what gives it the privileged position of rendering these decisions about how the burdens of promoting the common good are to be distributed?) but I will leave the positive account of obedience to law behind at this point, asking instead what the limits of such obedience are.[8]

It is always worth asking, of any account of obedience to law, in what cases one is morally free to disobey the law and in what cases one is even bound to disobey. The idea behind the fairness/common good account I just sketched is that one is bound because by obeying the law one is doing one's fair share for the common good. This rationale would of course be absent if law did not fairly divide up the task of promoting the common good: if it, for example, placed unjustly high demands on some parties, allowing others to get away with very few burdens. In such a case we should say that one is not bound to obedience, though there might be reasons to be selective about when and how one disobeyed. (After all, legal systems tend to wield sanctions, and sanctions are often a good reason for compliance even with unduly burdensome laws.) We should also keep in mind that even in systems that are reasonably just there may be cases in which laws are passed that are simply not fit to be obeyed. A law that required one to do harm to a vulnerable person, for example, might fail to be morally binding, just because one cannot become obligated to perform that kind of action. (Think of the Fugitive Slave Act: we can hold that even if we can see politically why it was passed, no one can be morally bound to assist in the return of a runaway slave to bondage.)

The important point here is that an account of obedience to law need not be an account of *absolute* obedience: even if the good subject is an obedient subject, the best theory of why folks are morally obligated to obey the law will include both a positive account of why such obedience is morally required and an account of the limits of such obedience. There is no major political theorist who has held that people should everywhere and always put the demands of being an obedient subject superior to all other demands, so that those under legal systems are morally required to obey the law *no matter what.*[9] Sometimes legal norms are so unfair, or so unwise, that disobedience is the only appropriate response.

2.3   The Role of Legislator

One might think that to be a legislator is a role whose occupancy rules are, at least in part, a matter of one's choice. For, after all, even if we are born into subjecthood rather than choosing it for ourselves, we are not born to the task of legislation but choose to enter into the arena where laws are drafted, adopted, rescinded. But a moment's reflection shows that this would be a mistake. First, it is a mistake simply as a matter of empirical fact: at some times and places in the world, people did not choose but were rather born to the role of legislator.[10] One might also have the role of legislator thrust upon one at some time by popular acclaim or by the demands of some other authority, for example, religious authority. Second, it is a mistake when one reflects on the fact that there is nothing about the idea of the rules of recognition and change – recall that these are the social rules that establish how law is constituted and identified and how law can be transformed – that even suggests that the parties who are empowered to make law must occupy that role by their own voluntary choice. The qualifications to occupy the legislative role – that is, to hold the legal power to make rules deemed valid by the rule of recognition – are fixed by social practice, and social practice might authorize as legislators persons who have never wished to and in fact may strenuously want not to occupy that role.

The job of the legislator is, of course, to make law. But it would be silly to describe the role-requirements of the legislator in quantitative terms: the more law made, the better. (Indeed, some libertarians or anarchists would hold that the best legislators make *less* law.) Rather, we can use our commonplaces about law in order to say something about good lawmaking: to make good law, the law made must be *authoritative* and it must be for the *common good*. Otherwise, that law is *defective*. Whether a good legislator should make more law or less, and precisely which laws should be adopted or rescinded, is to be regulated by the constraints that law is to be authoritative and that it is to serve the common good.

In the next chapter we will enter into some discussion of the ways that the demand that law serve the common good and that law be authoritative shapes the appropriate aims of law. But we can, in advance of that discussion, remind ourselves of some of the points about authority and the orientation of law toward the common good, and note how they enter into an account of the role-requirements on legislators.

One constraint on the role of legislator is that the norms that are made into law must be authoritative. What this means, recall, is that the norms that are made must be able to provide genuinely decisive reasons for action for subjects. This places the legislator under two sorts of constraints with respect to the making of law.

The first is that the legislator's proposed norms must exhibit authority-potential – they must possess the formal features that make it possible for agents to treat them as guides to action. Recall from Chapter 1 Fuller's discussion of the eight ways to fail to make law. Fuller argues that there are a number of features that rules must possess in order to serve as guides to subjects' action, and that rules that fail to display these features fail to attain to the status of law. Rules must be general, public, prospective, comprehensible, consistent, within the subjects' powers of compliance, enduring, and sincere. At the end of that chapter we considered the possibility that rules that lack these features, even in extreme cases, might still be law, though gravely deficient. But that is sufficient to support the point that it is part of the legislator's role to formulate rules that display these positive features.

The second is that the legislator's proposed norms must exhibit not just formal authority-potential but must genuinely count as decisive reasons for subjects. What this entails is that the substance of the rules that are laid down must be sufficiently reasonable that subjects can rightly take those rules to be binding. If, for example, I am correct in the suggestions above that subjects are morally bound to obey the law insofar as it provides for a fair distribution of the burdens that must be shouldered in pursuit of the common good, then legislators will have to ensure that the norms that they offer distribute those burdens in a fair way. They will also need to ensure that all of the norms that they posit as law can be reasonably complied with in respect to other values – that laws do not require what is unacceptably cruel, or intemperate, or cowardly. For subjects can rightly see law as lacking authority on account not only of unfairness but on account of its being vicious in some other way.

So the fact that law is defective if it is not authoritative places important requirements on the exercise of the role of legislator. The fact that law is defective if it does not serve the common good places important constraints as well. For law is not supposed to be directed merely to the good of the legislator himself or herself (or itself, or the legislators themselves); it is supposed to be directed to the common good. Thus any exercise of legislative authority that serves not the good of all but only the good of some partial group is contrary to the very role of legislator.

The notion that the legislator is bound to exercise his or her authority for the common good raises an interesting question about how the legislator should carry out that task. One way to put this question is to ask whether the role of legislator is essentially *representative* – that one who carries out the role of legislator must do so in a way that represents the community of subjects (including, presumably, himself or herself) who will be bound by the law.

What I mean is that when one says that law should be for the common good, one way to understand this claim is as the claim that law should *benefit* subjects (that is the *good* part) in an impartial (that is the *common* part) way. In making law, one should take every subject's well-being into consideration, and decide on rules that advance subjects' well-being in an evenhanded way, a way that treats no subject's well-being as intrinsically more important than another subject's well-being. If this is the picture of appropriate lawmaking for the common good that we endorse, though, there does not seem to be anything particularly representative about the role of the legislator – no important sense in which he or she stands in place of, legislates on behalf of, the people who are subject to the law. The perspective taken by such a legislator is instead one of *objective benevolence*: one's job is to examine potential acts of lawmaking by asking the master question: "What would the results be on the people in terms of their well-being?"

A rival picture of lawmaking is representative: it holds that the legislator's role is not merely to make law for the people, but to ensure that law is in some important sense *by the people*. The legislator's job is not, then, to deliberate about lawmaking from the perspective of the objectively benevolent person. The legislator's job, by contrast, is to legislate from the perspective of the people, taking on their opinions, attitudes, preferences, and so forth, so that the lawmaking activity that flows from the legislative office is one that reflects the people's own views of what ought to be done. This picture of the legislator as representative is not, I should add, one that is entirely tied to democracy. One could have a monarch, like Fuller's Rex, who is the sole lawmaking authority but who views that role as requiring him or her to take on the commitments and judgments of the various classes of people who are subjects of the law, and deliberate from those judgments until he or she reaches a coherent legislative policy. But it does seem to be true that this representative ideal seems easier to realize, and more fully realized, in a structure of legislative authority that allows a representative to be one among many, and thus to advocate and vote on behalf of one of a variety of well-worked-out views.

We have contrasted here legislation from the objectively benevolent point of view and legislation from the representative point of view. Let me offer an example of the ways in which deliberation about legislation can differ depending on which perspective one takes. Suppose Rex is considering the legislative possibilities with respect to punishment in some community. (We will consider the problems of punishment in some detail in Chapter 4.) One way that Rex could carry out this deliberation is by examining patterns of crime and their effects on the prosperity of the citizens of that political community, by looking to the conclusions of experts in the social sciences about the effects of various sorts of penal law on the rates of crime, along with their associated costs; and on that basis making a judgment about what would best further the common good of the political community. On this view, the aims, desires, attitudes, and beliefs of the subjects is relevant to deliberation only insofar as it will make a difference to the effectiveness of implementing particular proposals. If, for example, it is Rex's reasoned view that extremely harsh punishments generally tend to lower crime drastically, but the subjects of that political community are likely to balk at such a policy, undercutting support for it and ultimately making it ineffective within that political community, then Rex will take that fact into account in deciding whether to implement harsh penalties.

This way of proceeding differs from the more representative way, in which Rex adopts the point of view of the people: Rex takes on the considered views of the populace, starting not with a fresh slate but asking what the citizenry takes the proper goals of punishment to be and what information would be necessary to implement those goals as the people understand them. Note the difference in the way that the people's beliefs, aims, commitments, and so forth are taken into consideration under the representative way of proceeding. Under the objective benevolence approach, the people's beliefs and attitudes are just one more set of facts that the legislator should take into account in crafting effective, benevolent policy. Under the representative approach, the people's beliefs and attitudes serve as the premises that determine what the legislator should view as the proper aims of his or her legislative activity.

Here is an illustration of the difference between objectively benevolent and representative rulemaking. Consider the different ways that parents make rules for their young children and that babysitters make rules for their charges. The parent typically makes rules for his or her children from the perspective of objective benevolence. The parent wants the children's lives to go well, and aims to craft rules for the household that will foster the children's good. Of course, the parent will have to take the children's beliefs and aims into account in crafting policy – even the most promising rules might be undercut if made without taking into account the particular psychological features of the children governed by those rules. (However great it would be for a parent to have his or her "Eat all of your Brussels sprouts" rule followed, a parent that does not take into account whether his or her children can possibly stomach Brussels sprouts is not taking all relevant factors into consideration.) But parents do not see themselves as *representing* their children in the sense I have described. By contrast, babysitters typically do not make rules for the children in their care from the perspective of objective benevolence. The way that they make such rules is by representing the children's parents. If I am an atheist babysitting for the children of devout religious believers, I may think that from the perspective of objective benevolence it would be a good idea for them to skip prayers before bed, perhaps reading some accessible antitheistic writers instead, but I would hardly take it to be my place to make this rule for them, even a rule that is to remain in force only while I am in charge of them.

That there is a distinction in principle between the two ways of proceeding is clear enough. In practice the gap between them might close a bit. For, after all, it could be that from the objectively benevolent point of view, it is very detrimental to subjects' good to have their views on legitimate lawmaking flouted, and it is likely that subjects' consensus on some question of lawmaking will be excellent evidence for the wisdom of accepting public opinion on the matter. And, after all, it could be that from the representative point of view, the legislator will have to deal with so many conflicts of attitude and belief once the legislator takes on the people's beliefs, commitments, and so forth, that the task of winnowing and refining the public point of view will require deliberation that is not much different from that which would be carried out by an objectively benevolent lawmaker.

Whether good lawmaking must be representative is a difficult question. It has been argued that representative lawmaking is a requirement of impartiality: it is an affront to impartiality to fail to treat each subject's view of the proper aims of legislation as a contribution to legislative deliberation.[11] It has been argued that representative lawmaking has important good consequences: people more vigorously develop their powers of thought and judgment and inform themselves about public matters much more thoroughly when their decisions substantially contribute to the ultimate official outcome.[12] On the other hand, one might claim that these points can be adopted into a more inclusive objectively benevolent perspective, which treats contribution to legislative outcomes and development of powers as relevant to, but not determinative of, the common good. One might even claim that the question of the preferability of the objective benevolence or the representative approach is itself a matter to be decided by social rule: there might be different social contexts in which objectively benevolent or representative perspectives are required, so that different legal systems' legislators are subject to different role-requirements about how they are to deliberate with respect to the common good.

We still have not asked why those who find themselves in the role of legislator would be bound to act in accordance with the role's requirements, making only rules that can be authoritative and which serve the common good. We might appeal to consent: legislators often take an oath to carry out faithfully the demands of their role, and we would take this oath to be a reason for them to comply with their role-requirements. We might appeal to Rawls's principle of fair play: legislators often go out of their way to accept the benefits of their position, and thus in fairness take on the burdens of acting under the constraints required of legislators. Though these are good reasons, and legislators who fall down on the job may scold themselves (and be scolded by the rest of us) for violating their oaths or taking unfair advantage of the system, we noted above that there is nothing about the legislative role that is essentially voluntary. Imagine a society in which, for example, the role of legislator is determined by lot, or assigned on a rotating basis. Voluntariness would then have little to do with it; becoming a legislator would be like being drafted to serve in the military. What would the basis be for adhering to the demands of the role if one comes to occupy it in this nonvoluntary way?

I take it that the answer here would be very little different from the answer offered above for why folks would be bound to the role of subject. The role of legislator is, as Hart argues, one that is introduced into societies for good reasons: it enables the introduction of new, useful norms, the abolition of old, useless norms, and the modification of subpar norms. The effective functioning of this role, like the effective functioning of the role of subject, is helpful in the promotion of the common good. And, furthermore, there must be some fair way of dividing up the labor of legislating. Thus, so long as there is a fair way to assign persons to the role of legislator, one is bound to carry out the role of legislator as one's fair share of one's responsibilities to the common good.

2.4 The Role of Judge

We turn, finally, to the role of the judge. It may now come as no surprise that the occupancy rules for this role include no voluntariness conditions: the persons who are designated as judges within some legal system depend on the rules in place in that legal system, and the extent to which one's own choice is necessary in being a judge is a contingent matter. To be a judge is to be designated by the rules as someone whose applications of the rules of that system, or some of the rules of that system, count as authoritative. You might be extraordinarily well informed about the law in your society, about the cases that are now under dispute, and the relevant facts that would need to be applied; and you might then have extremely intelligent things to say about how these cases should be understood. But you lack the power to decide the cases; you have not been authorized by the rules of adjudication in the legal systems in which you live to decide them.

The performance rule for the role of judge is that judges are to apply the law in their resolution of disputes. That is to say: in occupying the role of judge, one who resolves a dispute should resolve it in a way that is determined by the law that bears on the dispute. Occasionally cases are *easy*: there is relevant law that bears on the case, both the law and the facts of the case are perfectly clear, and the proper legal outcome follows as a matter of straightforward deductive logic from the clear law and the clear facts.[13] If the speed limit on a highway, declared by statute and promulgated by multiple signs, is 55 miles per hour, and one drives 70 miles per hour on that highway, fully aware of what one is doing and without further excuse or justification, then the legal consequence is that one is guilty of speeding: there is simply no room for the judge to maneuver, and no difficulty at all in reaching the decision. It would be flouting the judge's role, to decide cases in accordance with law, to fail to find the speeder guilty -- regardless of whether the judge thinks that the speeding rule is silly, or a bit on the severe side. It is not the judge's job to deliberate on the merits of the law's existence, only to apply it.

Easier said than done. When the law is as crisp and clear as the speed limit statute, and the facts entirely plain, the case is easy. But cases are often *hard*. (Easier cases tend to be handled apart from disputes in front of judges: if it is clear that a tort has occurred and compensation is owed, there will typically be a settlement out of court; if it is clear that a crime has been committed, a plea arrangement will be made.) Putting to the side difficulties that arise from lack of factual clarity -- about just what happened -- the distinctive difficulties concern the discovery of relevant law, something that is legally sufficient to decide the case, and the interpretation of the relevant law.

The questions of interpretation are too varied and complex for us to do more than to get a sampling of the difficulties that arise, and I will focus here on one relatively straightforward set of interpretive questions arising from the interpretation of statutes. But it is important to keep in mind that statutes are by no means the sole source of the law that judges are called upon to interpret. Aside from statutes, judges must deal with constitutional matters (whether the constitutions in question are written or unwritten), precedents (whether general rules or particular decisions reached by previous judicial decisions), and custom, to take three sources of law that might be acknowledged within some society's rule of recognition. Statutes should be, one would think, one of the easier types of legal source to deal with as a matter of interpretation: they can be deliberately drafted to ease problems of understanding, and they are typically easier to pass or repeal than constitutional provisions, so there is less inertia to combat if the legislators wish to keep the law in good condition. So the fact that statutes generate interesting puzzles of interpretation should give a sense of how vexing problems of legal interpretation can be.

Here is a statute passed in 1885:

> Be it enacted by the Senate and the House of Representatives of the United States of America in Congress assembled, That from and after the passage of this act it shall be unlawful for any person, company, partnership, or corporation, in any manner whatsoever, to prepay the transportation, or in any way assist or encourage the importation or migration of any alien or aliens, any foreigner or foreigners, into the United States, its Territories, or the District of Columbia, under contract or agreement, parol or special, express or implied, made previous to the importation or migration of such alien or aliens, foreigner or foreigners, to perform labor or service of any kind in the United States, its Territories, or the District of Columbia.

This statute was passed at a time in which companies were paying for the passage of large numbers of unskilled laborers, with the aim of securing cheap workers to undercut the prices current on the labor market.

Consider now the situation of the Church of the Holy Trinity in New York, which aimed to employ as their pastor the colorfully named E. Walpole Warren. In 1887 they hired Warren, a citizen of England, to come to the United States to serve as their pastor, and they paid his passage for the trip. The United States government initiated legal proceedings against the church, holding that their actions were made unlawful by the statute. Was the United States's contention correct? Does the statute, properly interpreted, render illegal E. Walpole Warren's subsidized travel to New York?[14]

All judges agree that it is crucial to attend to the *text* of the statute: the words that were used, and actually voted into law by the relevant legislature. No one is advocating simply ignoring the text of the statute. And all judges agree that the text has its meaning only by way of a *context*. Most boringly, the context of these statutes include the fact that English is the language used by the drafters and ratifiers of the statute, and that its meaning is in part determined by the fact. But part of the question is what counts as the *relevant* context of interpretation.

Here are two lines of thought, somewhat idealized, concerning how the relevant context ought to be understood and thus how the text should be construed. "Look," it might be argued, "it is often false that when one says to you 'Do not x' one means for you never to x. When I say to my child 'Do not cross the street without looking' I do not mean for her not to cross the street without looking, ever, at any time. If she is being chased by rabid dogs, then obedience to my rule does not require her to stop and look. The import of my command is to be found in my *purpose* in giving her the command: in ordinary circumstances, it is a bad idea to cross without stopping and looking; and what I mean for her to do is, in ordinary circumstances, to stop and look. Now, when the legislators who passed this statute said 'no labor or service of any kind,' they meant to prohibit manual labor – that's what they had in mind, and in the context of its deliberation and passage that is what gives point to their passing the law. So that's what the statute means, and the church did nothing unlawful by prepaying the transportation of E. Walpole Warren."

Here, though, is a rival, "textualist" view. "We should distinguish between what the legislators *might have wanted to say*, or *could have said if they were more careful about their words*, and what they *in fact said*. What the statute *in fact says* is that it is unlawful to prepay the passage of a foreigner to the United States to enable that foreigner to perform any sort of labor or service. E. Walpole Warren was a foreigner, and his passage was paid for by the church, and he was coming to serve the church as its pastor. The users of the law cannot, after all, go poking about to find out the legislative context of each statute; they should be able to take a statute and, from their own situation, use that statute to make their decisions. From that perspective the statute is clear: the Church of the Holy Trinity should have been able to look at it and see that what they were planning to do was unlawful."

Both of these are intelligible views. Let me say three things about them. The first is that each of them takes a certain context of understanding the text to enjoy primacy. The former view takes legislator's context to be primary. It takes the task of understanding the statute to be that of figuring out what the legislature meant to say by producing the legal text that it produced: given the context of the legislators' proceedings, this is what they meant to say in forwarding this legal text. The latter view takes the subject's context to be primary. It takes the task of understanding the statute to be that of figuring out what the subjects bound by the statute would take the statute to require of them: this is what subjects would reasonably construe the legal text to require, given the circumstances in which subjects confront these legal texts.

The second is that while these contexts can be labeled the legislator's and the subject's contexts, it is obvious that they enter into each other to some extent. Part of the legislator's context, the circumstances in light of which the legislators choose how to draft the statute, consists in the way that subjects are likely to approach and understand various formulations of the text. Part of the subject's context, the circumstances in light of which the subjects assess what the implications of the statute are, are whatever aspects of the legislator's context that are common knowledge to them.

The third is that while these contexts enter into each other, they remain distinct, insofar as legislators may misunderstand how subjects will approach various formulations of the text, may be sloppy in choosing a formulation, and so forth; and subjects will of course often be unaware of, or have false beliefs about, the various circumstances that shape the aims of the legislators in passing a particular formulation of a statute.

So one level of tension in interpreting statutes is generated by the conflicts possible between legislator's and subject's perspectives. One way to make this tension vivid is to connect it back to our commonplaces about law – that law must be authoritative and it must be for the common good. The commonplace that law is for the common good suggests a canon of interpretation that favors the legislator's perspective: it is legislators who are in charge of articulating and promoting a vision of the community's common good, and so their context of interpretation should be accorded deference in the interpretation. What the legislator means to realize for the sake of the common good by passing a statute is what is ultimately relevant in interpreting that statute. On the other hand, the commonplace that law is authoritative pulls in favor of the subject's context: law is meant to guide the conduct of subjects, and so we should interpret the law in accordance with those resources that subjects have when they aim to use the law as a guide to action. Given the centrality of both of these common-places in our understanding of law, it is no surprise that judges would experience tension between these perspectives in offering interpretations of statutes.

There are also important questions that arise *within* each of these contexts. Suppose that one is considering the question how the statute ought to be construed given the legislator's context – what the legislator meant to say by means of the statute's language. There are still questions about what judges should focus on in determining what the legislators meant to say. Consider, for example, a statute that forbids employers from "discriminat[ing] against any individual with respect to his compensation, terms, conditions, or privileges of employment, because of such individual's race, color, religion, sex, or national origin."[15] Legislators, we can assume for the moment, have an idea of the *concept* of discrimination and have an idea of what sorts of acts are *instances* of discrimination. The question is: when the law forbids "discrimination on the basis of race," does it forbid what falls under the legislator's concept of discrimination, or does it forbid whatever the legislator counts as an instance of discrimination?[16]

The questions are practically important ones because cases will be decided differently depending on how they are answered. Suppose, for example, that the legislator's concept of "discrimination" is "treating persons or groups differently with respect to benefits granted to them and burdens placed upon them without adequate justification" and that the legislator believes that affirmative action in offering government contracts does not count as an instance of discrimination, because there are adequate reasons to count race as a factor in the granting of contracts. Is the judge bound by the legislator's concept of discrimination alone, or also by the legislator's beliefs about what count as instances of discrimination? Suppose that a judge is hearing a case in which a plaintiff is claiming that she was discriminated against because of the government's race-based affirmative action policies in awarding contracts, and she offers evidence that the judge finds persuasive that there is no adequate rationale for the race-based program: should the judge decide that this policy violates Title VII, because it really falls under the legislator's concept of "discrimination," or should the judge

74

decide that this policy does not violate Title VII, because the legislator did not believe that such affirmative action policies count as discrimination? If the judge is not entirely bound by the legislator's beliefs about instances of discrimination – after all, legislators can make mistakes about what cases their concepts apply to – what standard should the judge use to make these decisions? Should the judge ask what the community treats as an adequate reason for race-based classification? (If the community is prejudiced, the answer might be absurdly under-cutting of the point of the law.) Should the judge undertake to make moral decisions on his or her own about what are adequate reasons for such classification, of course trying to be as objective as possible? (This is a version of the objective versus representative question that we considered above in the case of the legislative role.)

So much for these problems of interpretation. A distinct set of problems arises when law "runs out" – when judges are called upon to decide a case in which it is simply vague what the law says on that issue. There may be nothing from the legislator's or speaker's context that settles the question of whether a set of facts falls under a given law. Take the famous example discussed by Hart: suppose that there is a statute that declares "No vehicles in the park."[17] The judge might be able to determine, from the legislator's context or from the subject's commonsense assessment of the purposes of the statute, that the statute does not preclude an inoperable tank from being included in a war memorial within the park, or ambulances from entering to take away accident victims; and the judge might be able to determine that automobiles, motorcycles, and buses are precluded from entering the park as a matter of course. But it may simply be a vague matter whether the law precludes bicycles. There might be a temptation here to try to posit an interpretive rule to cover these cases and restore clarity: for example, if it is vague whether a case falls under a statute, then it is to be considered as not falling under the statute. But this does not work: it can be a vague matter whether it is vague whether a case falls under a statute. Sometimes it is clear that a case is a vague one; sometimes that is itself something that is unclear. (Thus two people can reasonably disagree about whether it is unclear whether some case falls under a statute.)

What is a judge to do in these cases? The law is vague, but the decision cannot be: either bicycles will be allowed into the park or they will not; the person who rode a bicycle into the park will be found in violation of the law or not. The judge's role is to decide cases within his or her jurisdiction, and so to allow the resolution of the case at hand to be a vague and uncertain one is to fail to fulfill one's role as a judge. What we can say here is that in these cases the judge exercises *discretion*: the judge is not compelled by the authoritative legal sources to reach one decision rather than another.

Almost everyone agrees that judges sometimes have discretion in the making of their decisions, and that it is not entirely objectionable for those who occupy the role of judge also to be charged to engage in limited discretionary decision making. What there is much more disagreement about is the extent of the discretion that exists in typical legal systems. Hart's view, for example, is that discretion is a pervasive phenomenon: legal rules characteristically have a "core" and a "penumbra," where the core consists in a set of cases in which the rule's application is determinate and the penumbra a gray zone in which it is simply an indeterminate matter whether the rule applies.[18] We can think of Hart's as a moderate position: there is a solid core of legally determinate cases and a penumbra of legally indeterminate ones. One can be less moderate than Hart in more than one direction: going in one direction, one claims that the phenomenon of legal indeterminacy is more limited than Hart suggests; going in the other direction, one claims that the phenomenon of legal indeterminacy is much broader than Hart supposed.

On the side of less extensive legal indeterminacy are the views of Ronald Dworkin, one of Hart's most persistent early critics. Dworkin argues that judicial discretion is actually a very limited phenomenon – in some texts he seems to deny that there are any cases in which judges are free simply to exercise discretion in resolving disputes – for the law contains a wide variety of general principles that help to determine correct legal answers when the law's plain meaning is exhausted. The notion that judges simply exercise discretion when the law in a case becomes hard to discern does not sit at all well with the way that judges present their decisions: they present them not as simply free choices within the space left undetermined by law but rather as rulings constrained by all of the legal materials at hand. What justifies this common mode of presenting judicial rulings is that judging involves a thoroughgoing interpretation of the law as a whole: when a judge decides a case, he or she should rely upon those principles that best justify the entire body of legal materials.

The best-justified method of judging, by Dworkin's lights, is this. When a judge issues a ruling, he or she should aim for that ruling that fits best with the entire body of legal materials. When cases are easy, as in the speeding case described above, it is obvious that it would not best fit with the whole body of legal materials to hold that someone who is driving 70 in a 55 zone without justification or excuse is not guilty of speeding. But when cases are hard, it is harder to see what ruling best fits that whole body of materials. To determine what decision best fits the materials, one will have to develop an account of what are those principles that underlie the various rules and decisions that make up the law. In thinking through the question of what constitutes "discrimination" in the Civil Rights Act, a judge will have to ask what sort of understanding of individual rights can best account for the various rules forbidding or allowing differential treatment of members of distinct races, religions, sexes, and so forth. The correct decision in a case is that which proceeds from the most defensible account of the principles that underlie the law as a whole.[19] Dworkin has no illusions that judges will be able to show, by way of some sort of transparent procedure, that their decisions thus defended really do rest on the most adequate account of the principles underlying the legal materials at hand. But he does take it to be the most plausible account of how judges actually try to decide cases and of how decisions could be determinately correct or incorrect in hard cases.

On the other extreme is the view of a group of philosophers of law called the "American legal realists" who claim that all or nearly all judicial decisions are discretionary, that the role of judge as a discoverer of what the pre-existing legal rules require is, for the most part, a charade or illusion. Because of the seriousness of the charge that the legal realists level against the practice of judging, I treat legal realism as a challenge to our commonplaces about law, and will consider the realists' views in some detail in the concluding chapter (6.4).

The issues brought up here barely scratch the surface of the problems that arise when judges set themselves to render decisions, especially in complex legal systems whose rule of recognition acknowledges a variety of sources of law. What we have not considered is why one ought to adhere to the duties that constitute the role of judge. The judge does not enjoy the relative freedom of the legislator: where there is law, the judge is bound to act in accordance with it. Why ought those that occupy the role of judge to defer to these standards in rendering decisions?

77

The Basic Roles of Paradigmatic Legal Systems

Our usual answer, offered for both the subject and the legislator, is that judging is doing one's fair share for the common good, at least when the burdens of judging are equitably distributed. We should not find it surprising at all that the same answer is offered for "Why act in accordance with the role of subject?," "Why act in accordance with the role of legislator?," and "Why act in accordance with the role of judge?" For if the point of the introduction of these roles is to serve the common good, then each role is justified in terms of its doing a part in serving that good, and so one is bound to carry out that role insofar as one has a duty to do one's share for the common good. If the common good requires the existence of authoritative legal rules, then (as, we have seen, Fuller argues – see 1.6.1), there should be congruence between the standards as enunciated and how they are applied to subjects; and there will be such congruence only when judges act in accordance with their roles.

We can see the rationale for the law's being applied faithfully by judges. But we should note that the ideal of judicial fidelity to law can generate enormous tensions when the law to be applied is substantively deeply unjust. Consider, for example, the Fugitive Slave Act, which required the return of runaway slaves from free states and which required the cooperation of local law enforcement officials and even private citizens. While appreciating the responsibilities of a subject to defer to the law's apportioning of benefits and burdens, it is not too hard to see that one might reasonably reject the authority of this law and disobey. We are tempted, then, to say the same thing with respect to judges who were called upon to apply that law: they might use their office to subvert the Fugitive Slave Act. But if we accept this resolution as reasonable, it should only be in full awareness of the reasons that militate against it. What alternatives should judges adopt rather than simply to apply the Fugitive Slave Act? If the judge wants his or her actions to have legal effect, he or she must profess to be acting within the law; and thus some sort of duplicity will be required – duplicity that will be as public as can be, and may well lead folks to wonder, especially when judges are flouting clear and settled law, to what extent judges are fulfilling their roles. Perhaps the judge should simply reject decision making in these cases, publicly declaring that he or she cannot in good conscience apply the law and thus will not do so. This refusal to cooperate may not change the consequences one bit, as there are always those who are willing to step in and carry out that role. But there are reasons to refuse to cooperate with evil that go beyond the consequences of that refusal.[20]

For Further Reading

There has been a great deal of interesting work recently on the subject's duty to obey the law, inspired by (among other important works) A. John Simmons, *Moral Principles and Political Obligations* (Princeton, NJ: Princeton University Press, 1979). A number of articles on the topic appear in William A. Edmundson (ed.), *The Duty to Obey the Law* (Lanham, MD: Rowman and Littlefield, 1999); an article by Edmundson on the current "state of the art" in the theory of political obligation, which also contains a valuable bibliography, appears in *Legal Theory* 10 (2004), pp. 215–59. Jeremy Waldron has done some important work in the (sadly neglected) theory of legislation: see his *The Dignity of Legislation* (New York: Cambridge University Press, 1999). For a spirited defense of textualism, along with replies by critics, see Antonin Scalia, *A Matter of Interpretation* (Princeton, NJ: Princeton University Press, 1997). For Dworkin's theory of interpretation, see both "Hard Cases," in his *Taking Rights Seriously* (Cambridge, MA: Harvard University Press, 1977), pp. 81–130, as well as his *Law's Empire* (Cambridge, MA: Harvard University Press, 1986) and *Freedom's Law* (Cambridge, MA: Harvard University Press, 1996).

Notes

1 See Thomas Hobbes, *Leviathan*, ed. Edwin Curley (Indianapolis, IN: Hackett, 1992), ch. 18, p. 90; see also John Locke, *Second Treatise on Government*, ed. Peter Laslett (Cambridge, UK: Cambridge University Press, 1988), §119, and Jean-Jacques Rousseau, *Social Contract*, trans. Maurice Cranston (New York: Penguin, 1968), IV, 2.

2 David Hume, "Of the Original Contract," in Henry Aiken (ed.), *Hume's Moral and Political Philosophy* (New York: Hafner, 1948), pp. 356–72.

3 See H. L. A. Hart, "Are There Any Natural Rights?," *Philosophical Review* 64 (1955), pp. 175–91, and John Rawls, "Legal Obligation and the Duty of Fair Play," in Sidney Hook (ed.), *Law and Philosophy* (New York: New York University Press, 1964), pp. 3–18.

4 Rawls, "Legal Obligation," pp. 9–10.

5 This line of criticism is prominent in A. John Simmons, *Moral Principles and Political Obligations* (Princeton, NJ: Princeton University Press, 1979), pp. 129–40.

6 John Rawls, *A Theory of Justice*, 2nd edn. (Cambridge, MA: Harvard University Press, 1999), p. 296.

7 See, for one formulation of this argument, John Finnis, "The Authority of Law in the Predicament of Contemporary Social Theory," *Notre Dame Journal of Law, Ethics, and Public Policy* 1 (1984), pp. 114–37.

8 We return to these questions briefly in 6.2.

9 Thomas Hobbes is sometimes said to be a defender of absolute obedience to law. This is just a mistake: much of Chapter 21 of *Leviathan* is devoted to the question of when subjects can without injustice disobey their sovereigns.

10 One can be born into the role of king or queen; and until recently one could be born to membership in Britain's House of Lords, which is (among other things) a legislative body.

11 See Thomas Christiano, *The Rule of the Many: Fundamental Issues in Democratic Theory* (Boulder, CO: Westview, 1996), pp. 59–93; see also Henry S. Richardson, *Democratic Autonomy: Public Reasoning about the Ends of Policy* (New York: Oxford University Press, 2002), p. 28.

12 See John Stuart Mill, *Considerations on Representative Government* (Amherst, NY: Prometheus Books, 1991), Chapter III.

13 I draw this nice description of easy cases from Neil MacCormick, *Legal Reasoning and Legal Theory* (Oxford: Clarendon Press, 1978), p. 32.

14 The case is *Church of the Holy Trinity v. United States*, 143 U.S. 457 (1892).

15 Title VII, Civil Rights Act of 1964.

16 See, for example, Ronald Dworkin, "Constitutional Cases," in *Taking Rights Seriously* (Cambridge, MA: Harvard University Press, 1977), pp. 131–49.

17 H. L. A. Hart, *The Concept of Law*, 2nd edn. (Oxford, UK: Clarendon Press, 1994 [first published 1961]), pp. 126–7.

18 Ibid., p. 123.

19 Ronald Dworkin, *Law's Empire* (Cambridge, MA: Harvard University Press, 1986), p. 255.

20 For a powerful treatment of the problems of judging in the Fugitive Slave Act era, see Robert M. Cover, *Justice Accused* (New Haven, CT: Yale University Press, 1984).

Chapter 3

The Aims of Law

3.1 The Aims of Law and the Common Good

What are the appropriate aims of law? What should we aim to accomplish, to realize, through law?

Instead of launching immediately into a discussion of the variety of answers that have been offered to these questions, it will be helpful to pause for a moment to consider how our commonplaces about law – in particular, the commonplaces that law is authoritative and law is for the common good – should shape our answer to the questions we wish to pose about the aims of law. As I will use the terms, there is a difference between the notion of *the appropriate aims of law* and the notion of *the common good*. In coming up with an account of the common good of a political community, one is coming up with an account of what positive, desirable features we think a political community should exhibit. But the appropriate aims of law, while oriented by the common good, may be limited by the fact that the use of law involves the exercise of authority. Perhaps we should not use the law as far as it can be used in order to promote the common good, for there may be limits as to how authority should be wielded, even for the sake of admittedly valuable goals. Or perhaps certain ways that we might want to use the law to achieve valuable goals are self-defeating, so that we will achieve these goals less fully if we attempt to achieve them through the law.

Here is an analogy. Suppose that you are an employer, and enjoy some authority over the lives of your employees. You may come to believe that it is for the good of your employees that they, say, read more books. You might be interested in using your authority to make them read more books, because you might believe (even rightly) that reading more books would make your employees more informed and more well-rounded people. But it seems pretty clear that in many such cases you would not count as a prudent user of authority but rather as a petty tyrant if you chose to wield your authority to make your employees do more reading. Furthermore, there is always the possibility that your goal would be achieved less well if you tried to use your authority to realize it: in some cases, the employees might resent your heavy-handedness so much that they would be less inclined to do more reading; or you might be so out of touch with your employees' tastes that your book recommendations would bore them to the point that they would be turned off the idea of reading as a pastime. To use your authority as an employer to mandate that your employees spend more time reading seems out of place, and objectionable, and in some cases might be simply imprudent. It is objectionable in part because it strips the employees of an important good in their lives, that is, discretion with respect to their choice of leisure activities; and it is objectionable in part because the power relationship is such that brings with it the realistic fear that sanctions of some sort will be associated with non-compliance. If use of your authority as an employer to get them to read more causes them to read less, then it is pretty obviously imprudent as well.

This might very well be the situation with respect to use of law to realize the common good of the political community. Even if the common good is a wonderful thing, it might be that there are certain ways of acting for it that the law should not require of people, or certain aspects of the common good that law should not take as its task to promote. Law's authoritative character strips folks of discretion, placing them under a standard that binds them; given the importance in human life of choosing for oneself, this is itself a burden that should be avoided if possible. Law's authoritative standards are often backed by sanctions, placing folks under a threat of burdens being imposed upon them if they fail to comply; given the importance in human life of being free from coercion, this is itself a burden that should be avoided if possible. Law is not a good tool for all purposes, and so there may be some aspects of the common good that, while worth promoting, cannot be effectively realized through authoritative legal rules.

So what I will mean by "the appropriate aims of law" is "those aspects of the common good that the law should support by means of authoritative rules." In answering the question of what counts as the appropriate aims of law, we will of course have to take some view about the nature of the common good and some view of the moral and practical limits of authoritative imposition, and consider how these views come together to determine the appropriate aims of law.

3.2 The Harm-to-others Principle

In *On Liberty*, John Stuart Mill formulated a conception of the appropriate use of legal authority that has been massively influential.[1] This principle, which went unlabeled by Mill, is sometimes called the "harm principle," or (more accurately, if less briefly) the "harm-to-others principle":

> The object of this essay is to assert one very simple principle, as entitled to govern absolutely the dealings of society with the individual in the way of compulsion and control, whether the means used be physical force in the form of legal penalties or the moral coercion of public opinion. That principle is that the sole end for which mankind are warranted, individually or collectively, in interfering with the liberty of action of any of their number is self-protection. That the only purpose for which power can be rightfully exercised over any member of a civilized community, against his will, is to prevent harm to others.[2]

Mill meant for his principle to apply not just with respect to limitations on legal constraint but also to limitations on social pressure toward conformity. But we will restrict our questions concerning the meaning, application, rationale, and plausibility of the principle as a limitation on law.

Of course, the plausibility of Mill's principle rests on how the notion of "harm to others" is to be understood. Mill allows for three distinctive sorts of action to count as harming others. The first sort of action that counts as harm to others is action that directly diminishes another's well-being, that sets another's interests back in some way. (We will consider below what sorts of interests count for the purposes of the harm-to-others principle.) The second that counts as harm is failure to perform some obligations that one has to identifiable persons. So, even if my failing to provide food for someone usually does not count as my harming him or her, my failing to provide food for my children does count as my harming them, as I have positive obligations to provide for their needs. The third that counts as harm is failure to perform one's share of what is required for a decent common life in society. This obligation to do one's share for society is not owed to identifiable persons (unless one simply says that one owes it to *everyone*, that is, *all* of society), and includes requirements on one "to give evidence in a court of justice, to bear his fair share in the common defense . . . and to perform such acts of individual beneficence, such as saving a fellow creature's life or interposing to protect the defenseless against ill-usage."[3] The Millian principle is thus not a principle that holds that so long as one is not positively doing damage to others, one is in the clear. The emphasis should be placed, rather, on the "others" part: legal restrictions on conduct should be in place only in order to compel the subject to respect what is due *to others*, whether by way of avoiding damaging their interests or by way of fulfilling the subject's clear obligations to them. What does *not* justify any restrictions, by contrast, is the fact that some conduct would harm the subject himself or herself, or that it is unpopular, vulgar, or immoral. Unless it can be shown that the action under consideration clearly generates harm to others, there is no legitimate basis for legal restrictions.

Mill applies this principle with respect to questions of legal restrictions on both speech and conduct. He rails against the claim that restrictions on speech – the example he has in mind are laws against denying belief in God or in life after death – are somehow necessary for the preservation of the good of society. For any given opinion is either true, or false, or a mixture of the true and the false. Suppose that the opinion is true: if so, then legal restrictions against discussing or affirming it make it much harder for people to come to correct beliefs on the subject, and that is surely harmful to society. Or suppose that the opinion is false. In that case, restrictions on its discussion or affirmation make it much harder for the falsity of the view to be made publicly clear, and it makes belief in the contrary true opinion untested and stale. Or suppose that the opinion is a mix of the true and the false: legal restrictions against its affirmation or discussion make it much harder for people to separate the wheat from the chaff, to distinguish the important truth from the unimportant or even pernicious falsehood.[4]

Mill allows restrictions on conduct, of course: it is conduct that harms others that is ruled out. In that sphere of an individual's life that can be shaped different ways without doing harm to others, each individual is sovereign over his or her own affairs. Mill takes pains to note that this does not mean that our attitudes toward others and their self-regarding choices should be one of indifference. The harm-to-others principle declares only that we must not restrict and punish self-regarding conduct, not that we must not care about others and the way that they treat themselves.[5] Mill is of course fully aware that teasing apart self-regarding and other-regarding behavior can be difficult: any self-regarding choices can be shown to affect, in some way, the extent to which one is able to carry out one's duties toward others. But Mill thinks it a poor idea to use this sort of slippery slope argument as a basis for rejecting the existence of a sphere of choice outside of the control of law. When a person's actions affect himself or herself in ways that cause him or her to violate a "distinct and assignable" obligation to others – think of a person who gambles away his or her paycheck, leaving no money to feed the hungry children at home, or a person who gets drunk at a bar, but plans to drive home in that condition – we can then rightly fix blame on the wrongdoer, and legally restrict that person's actions.[6] But the link between the self-regarding and other-regarding conduct must be direct and definite, and it must be clear that the basis for restriction of the conduct is the effect it has on others, not the effect it has on the subject himself or herself.

What, then, is the rationale for the harm-to-others principle? Why should we think that this is a correct account of the aims of law? It is illuminating to think of the harm-to-others principle as shaped by Mill's conception of the common good of the political community and by his views about the intrinsic limits of authoritarian intervention to achieve this common good. With respect to the nature of the common good: Mill, like Austin (see 1.2), was a utilitarian, and he held that the sole justifying end of any action, whether that of an individual or a state, was the promotion of the overall happiness. Mill is insistent that the harm-to-others principle is a derivation from nothing "independent of utility," for utility is "the ultimate appeal on all ethical questions."[7] But this raises a pressing question for Mill: if the overall happiness is ultimate good to be sought by individuals and states, then why shouldn't the constraint on lawmaking simply be "legally constrain individual conduct only when it promotes the overall good to do so" rather than the seemingly more restrictive "legally constrain conduct only if that conduct harms others"? The overall good can be diminished by actions that cause harm to self, so why shouldn't the law prohibit such conduct?

Mill has a number of arguments here. One of the arguments concerns a point about the limitations of knowledge of those who exercise lawmaking authority.[8] If the subject willingly and knowingly chooses to perform some action, then presumably he or she thinks that the harm to self that might accompany the action is worth it, in light of his or her goals, aims, and preferences. The lawmaking authorities are not nearly as likely to be able to make a fine-grained assessment of subjects' situations in passing laws that prevent subjects from performing actions that are harmful to themselves. To put it another way: if the aim is the overall good, that aim is better served by allowing subjects to judge for themselves what will promote their own happiness rather than by having lawmaking authorities judge for others what will promote those others' happiness.

One might think that this view could rest only on a general skepticism about knowledge of what makes for happiness that actually undercuts the rationale for the harm-to-others principle. After all, the lawmaking authorities have to have a view on what counts as people's interests if they are going to make laws that forbid people from harming others' interests; but if they are supposed to know so little about people's interests that they are not competent to make laws forbidding subjects from harming themselves, why wouldn't that give us reason to suspect that lawmaking authorities are not competent to make laws forbidding subjects from harming others, either? But the puzzle is only apparent. All Mill needs to make his case against the law's forbidding A from doing something that harms A is that A is probably more motivated by the prospect of A's happiness than the lawmakers are and is probably more knowledgeable about what will make for A's happiness than the lawmakers are. All Mill needs to make his case in favor of the law's forbidding A from doing something that harms B is that the lawmakers are at least as motivated by the prospect of B's happiness as A is and that the lawmakers are at least as knowledgeable about what makes for B's happiness as A is. With respect to what makes for one's own happiness, one is in a good position to claim a right to decide for oneself on the basis of one's superior knowledge and superior concern, but one is not in a good position to make this claim with respect to what makes for anyone else's happiness.

Mill has a second line of argument. The first line of argument appeals just to the fact that the subject himself or herself is more likely to know what actions are for his or her happiness than the lawmakers are. The second line of argument appeals to the more remote effects of allowing lawmakers to prohibit conduct simply on the basis of protection of the subject from himself or herself. The idea is that our common views of good and bad ways of life are constantly changing, in part as a result of various "experiments in living": the only way to find out whether a certain way of living one's life is to be commended or rejected, adopted or refused, is to see it tried out, and assess what happens.[9] To put law into place that forbids folks from undertaking these experiments in living, even though these experiments neither threaten anyone else's interests nor violate any clear obligations, is to deprive both the experimenters and the wider community of the possibility of learning more about what makes for human happiness.

There is a third line of argument. This line of argument suggests that there is an important value to the fact of choice itself, a value that is independent of the wisdom or correctness of the choices that one makes. Call this condition of choosing for oneself *autonomy*. Mill suggests that part of the point of rejecting laws that are not in keeping with the harm-to-others principle is that it fails to respect the value of autonomy. Part of what makes our lives go well is just the possession and use of autonomy: and so one has reason not to interfere with a subject's choices about how to live his or her life.[10]

It is impossible to dismiss the appeal of Mill's principle. Part of its appeal rests in its conception of the common good as the happiness of the members of the political community. Mill's view is *welfarist*: it holds that what is ultimately of importance is the well-being of the people whose lives are affected by legal and social policy. Part of its appeal rests in its expansive picture of human happiness: it includes not just pleasure and the absence of pain, but also the exercise of autonomous choice and the development of knowledge and creativity. Part of its appeal rests in its lack of dogmatism about, combined with optimism concerning, our knowledge of well-being: Mill does not take it that we have reached anything like the height of our knowledge about what makes life go well, though there are better and worse answers out there to be discovered through argument and experiment. And part of its appeal rests in its healthy skepticism concerning the motivations and knowledge of those who exercise lawmaking authority: Mill seems just right to think that lawmakers can be closed-minded and ignorant, whether in particular instances or more generally, with detrimental effects on the good of those living under norms they create. Mill combines a very ambitious vision of the common good with a more cautious account of what legal authority can and should do to realize that vision.

3.3 Challenges to the Harm-to-others Principle

3.3.1 Types of harm

In order to challenge the harm-to-others principle, one must know precisely what its scope is. We saw above that Mill includes within the notion of "harm to others" action contrary to another's interests, actions that are in violation of an obligation to some particular person, and actions that constitute failures to carry one's share of the social burden. We might wonder about the first of these categories: precisely what sorts of effects on another count as harm to him or her? What counts as one's interests, such that whenever these interests are set back by another's actions, one is harmed?

There is an easy answer that cannot be right. The easy answer is that a subject harms another whenever the subject does something that the other does not want the subject to do, or whenever the subject causes some effect that the other does not want to occur. The mere fact that one has performed an action that is out of step with someone's preferences cannot count as harm, for if it did, then the harm-to-others principle would lose almost all of its bite. The harm-to-others principle is an important curb on the use of legislative authority only when lawmakers otherwise would want certain subjects not to act in certain ways. If merely acting contrary to someone's preferences counts as doing harm, then the harm-to-others condition would be satisfied every time someone was interested in passing a law to restrict conduct, and so it would lose its power to limit lawmaking activity. (Surely Mill does not want to allow, say, forbidding private consensual homosexual conduct on the basis that some people would rather that such conduct not take place, and so those people are harmed if that conduct does take place.)

There are a couple of ways that one can try to deal with the harm question. One way is to stick with the idea that harm consists in acting contrary to someone's desires but to say that it is only *certain desires* that count. One might say, for example, that only *self-regarding* desires count: while you might harm me by frustrating my desires about how my own life goes, you do not harm me by frustrating my desires about how your life goes. We would, of course, need some way to determine what makes a desire about one's own life. Is a desire not to be in the presence of others who are acting in a certain way a desire about one's own life? Is a desire not to live in a community with others who have a certain lifestyle a desire about one's own life? If so, then the harm-to-others principle will again lose much of its bite.

Another way that one could try to spell out the notion of harm is by appealing to certain natural interests that people have, and to define harm in terms of what immediately sets back, or has a very strong tendency to set back, those natural interests. So one might say that one has a natural interest in being alive, and free from injury; and one has a natural interest in avoidance of physical pain and suffering; and one has a natural interest in freedom of thought and conduct; and so forth. One might also say that there are certain goods that are not part of one's natural interests, but at least in certain types of society are very closely connected with realizing one's natural interests: in a market society, for example, the safe possession of one's property is needed for securing one's natural interests, and so deprivations of one's property count as harms.

This might be seen as a merely academic dispute if it were not for the fact that how we understand the harm-to-others principle, what it allows and what it forbids, will depend so heavily on how we understand harm. Consider, for example, Mill's brief and cryptic discussion of "offenses against decency" in the "Applications" section of *On Liberty*:

> There are many acts which, being directly injurious only to the agents themselves, ought not to be legally interdicted, but which, if done publicly, are a violation of good manners and, coming thus within the category of offenses against others, may rightly be prohibited. Of this kind are offenses against decency; on which it is unnecessary to dwell, the rather as they are only connected indirectly to our subject, the objection to publicity being equally strong in the case of many actions not in themselves condemnable, nor supposed to be so.[11]

This passage is circumspect to the point of mysteriousness. But what is clear about the passage is that Mill thinks that there are some actions that can be legally proscribed in the public square insofar as they are *offensive* or *indecent*. Not only actions that we think of as harmful to the subject would be in this class, though; we might think there are some things that are distinctly not harmful to the subject, but which should not be carried out in public for the very same reasons.

The real question, though, is what the rationale is supposed to be for forbidding actions in public that are contrary to good manners. In order to get us to see the variety of ways in which such actions can be hard to tolerate, Joel Feinberg takes us on an imaginary "Ride on the Bus."[12] He has us imagine that we are on a crowded bus, with a variety of unsavory passengers coming aboard. Some of these passengers produce affronts to the senses ("A passenger sits down next to you, pulls a slate tablet from his briefcase, and proceeds to scratch his fingernails across the slate"); others are disgusting ("Itinerant picnickers practice gluttony in the ancient Roman manner, gorging until satiation and then vomiting onto their tablecloth"); others shock our sensibilities ("A group of mourners carrying a coffin enter the bus and share a seating compartment with you.... they refer to the corpse as 'the old bastard' and 'the bloody corpse.' ... At one point they rip open the coffin with hammers and proceed to smash the corpse's face with a series of hard hammer blows"); others produce intense embarrassment (individuals and couples and individuals with dogs performing a variety of sexual acts); others are simply annoying ("The passenger at your side is a friendly bloke.... You quickly tire of his conversation and beg leave to read your newspaper, but he persists in his chatter despite requests to desist"); and others cause fear, humiliation, and anger ("A passenger seated next to you reaches into a military kit and pulls out a 'hand grenade' (actually only a realistic toy) and fondles and juggles it throughout the trip to the accompaniment of menacing leers and snorts. Then he pulls out a (rubber) knife.... He turns out to be harmless enough. His whole intent was to put others in apprehension of harm").

No matter how amusing all of this might be in print in a philosophy book, it would likely be distinctly nonamusing to find oneself confronted with all of these exhibits on a bus, on a train, in the town square, or on the sidewalk in front of one's home. It might be tempting to say that the rationale for forbidding such actions is just that they generate a sort of harm – the shock and upset and irritation that one encounters when faced with the reality or appearance of such

90

behavior. One might say that this shock and upset triggers the harm-to-others principle, because it is unwanted, and about one's own life (one thing one wants for oneself is not to be shocked and upset); or one might say that avoidance of shock and upset are part of one's natural interests, and indeed can be more important to one than some of one's property and liberty interests.

However plausible these answers seem, they seem to have further implications that are out of step with the harm-to-others principle. For shock and upset are sensitive to one's moral evaluations of conduct: folks can be shocked and upset to see someone eating pork or someone eating a hamburger, and folks can be shocked and upset to see a man and a woman kissing in public, or two men kissing in public, or a man and a woman of different races kissing in public. It is hard to know why someone who is insistent on the value of experiments in living and the point of autonomy in the living of one's own life would come down on the side of rules that could allow the proscription of any public behavior that offends the sensibilities of the majority. But it is equally hard to see how the parade of horrors laid out by Feinberg can be legally prohibited under the harm-to-others principle without also providing a basis for legally prohibiting other, less horrible but nevertheless (in some times and places) shocking sorts of behavior.

Consider further how Mill's arguments concerning free speech would have to be revised and reformulated if one includes emotional distress or shock and alarm as a sort of harm that legal means can be used to suppress. While relying on a distinction between speech and conduct in the articulation of his position, Mill notes:

> Even opinions lose their immunity, when the circumstances in which they are expressed are such as to constitute their expression a positive instigation to some mischievous act. An opinion that corn-dealers are starvers of the poor, or that private property is robbery, ought to be unmolested when simply circulated through the press, but may justly incur punishment when delivered orally to an excited mob assembled before the house of a corn-dealer, or when handed about among the same mob in the form of a placard.[13]

Mill's suggestion, then, is that speech, when it has a direct and immediate tendency to cause harm – a harm that cannot be practically prevented by means other than legal – might fail to have the blanket immunity that his earlier argument might seem to suggest. This is, after all, what common sense dictates, and is the basis for a variety of legal doctrines circumscribing that freedom ("fighting words," incitement to riot, and so forth).

But imagine what happens if we start counting emotional distress as harm. For there is much speech the very public articulation of which immediately generates emotional distress. Sincerely religious people can be very distressed by public criticism of religion; sincere atheists can be very distressed by public criticism of godlessness. Members of racial and religious minorities who have suffered in the past and continue to deal with ongoing discriminatory conduct may be very distressed to encounter public articulations of racism and religious bigotry. If emotional distress is harm, then a *lot* of speech causes harm, and a lot of speech will thus fail to come under the protection of the harm-to-others principle. The massive difficulties that various communities have had with respect to the formulation of "hate speech" codes is merely a reflection of the tremendous conceptual and philosophical problems that exist in trying to come to terms with the notion of harm and the ways that speech can be, and cannot be, itself harmful.

3.3.2 The party harmed

So one set of worries that arise with respect to the harm-to-others principle concerns the scope of the action that counts as harm: there are difficult questions both concerning how that scope is to be understood and whether one can interpret it in a way that does not turn out to be counterintuitive or arbitrary. A distinct set of worries concerns the plausibility of the view that legal restrictions are to be employed only to prevent harm to others, as opposed to preventing harm to self as well.

Let us return to Mill's argument – not because Mill enjoys exclusive control over how we should understand the harm-to-others principle, but because Mill's concessions concerning the scope of that principle are illuminating and independently plausible. Almost immediately after Mill enunciates the harm-to-others principle he cautions his readers not to overestimate the range of the persons to whom it applies:

It is, perhaps, hardly necessary to say that this doctrine is meant to apply only to human beings in the maturity of their faculties. We are not speaking of children or of young persons below the age which the law may fix as that of manhood or womanhood.... For the same reason we may leave out of consideration those backward states of society in which the race itself may be considered as in its nonage.[14]

Mill also notes a couple of kinds of cases involving adults in developed societies which may nevertheless call for treatment other than that suggested by the harm-to-others principle.

> If either a public officer or anyone else saw a person attempting to cross a bridge which he had ascertained to be unsafe, and there were no time to warn him of his danger, they might seize him and turn him back, without any real infringement of his liberty; for liberty consists in doing what one desires, and he does not desire to fall into the river.[15]

Mill also claims that the harm-to-others principle does not justify allowing persons to sell themselves into slavery: while in ordinary contracts,

> The reason for not interfering, unless for the sake of others [not party to the agreement] with a person's voluntary acts is consideration for his liberty. His voluntary choice is evidence that what he so chooses is desirable, or at least endurable, to him, and his good is on the whole best provided by allowing him to take his own means of pursuing it. But by selling himself for a slave, he abdicates his liberty; he foregoes any use of it beyond that single act.... The principle of freedom cannot require that he should be free not to be free.[16]

So Mill allows that there are a variety of cases in which one can interfere with others' choices, even for the sake of looking after the good of those very people. In some cases, the justification is that some people – less controversially, children, the severely mentally retarded, and the insane; more controversially, whole societies that have not yet attained a certain level of stability, maturity, and civility – are not able to look after their own good, and thus "despotism,"[17] at least despotism of a caring and enlightened sort, is the proper way of dealing with these folks and their actions. In other cases, cases where we are dealing with people who are in the maturity of their faculties, there are occasionally emergencies in which people's choices may be interfered with in order to prevent them from doing what they, at a deeper level, really do not want to do. One may want to cross this bridge; but one wants to cross this bridge only because one wants to cross the river and believes this is a safe way across; if potential interveners are unable to get the message across that the bridge is really not a safe way across, then it would be for the sake of rather than contrary to one's liberty to have one's choice to cross the river impeded. In still other cases, there may be certain actions that are so undermining of the possibility of liberty itself that we could not reasonably say that the value of liberty precludes interference with that action.

The tenor of Mill's argument is that these are isolated cases and do not generate deeper questions for one who is considering endorsing the harm-to-others principle. It is hard to fault the idea that children, at least very young children, require for their rearing a host of limitations on their liberty. While Mill allows that whole societies might be unfit for the harm-to-others principle, he assures us that all nations with which "we need here concern ourselves"[18] (he probably means all nations in which *On Liberty* is likely to be read and considered) have reached that level of maturity. And while Mill allows that in emergencies interference with subjects' choices is justifiable to prevent them from undermining their deeper desires, he is explicit that it is better for one to deliver warnings of dangers that another may heed or refuse to heed upon his or her own judgment than to interfere forcibly with another's choices.

One important matter of discussion, though, has concerned whether Mill's allowance of exceptions to the harm-to-others principle expands even further than to the limited cases that Mill had in mind. Mill's strong case for the harm-to-others principle is that authoritative legislation justified by the prevention of harm to the subject himself or herself is likely to be based on inadequate knowledge and is likely to undermine the goods of experimentation in lifestyle and autonomous choice. But once we allow that there are several cases in which harm-to-self interference is justified, we are committed to thinking that there are some cases in which the presumption in favor of noninterference can be overcome. And if it can be overcome in these particular cases, why not others?

This line of thought is influentially explored by Gerald Dworkin.[19] Dworkin's concern is to defend a limited paternalism – "paternalism" is a label for the view that legal restriction on a subject's conduct is justifiable for the sake of protecting or promoting that subject's good – in a Millian spirit. Dworkin suggests that what underlies our willingness to accept the exceptions to the harm-to-others principle that Mill allows is a principle that autonomy is only to be limited for the sake of autonomy itself: it is justifiable to interfere with another's freedom of choice only if by this interference that other's freedom of choice is ultimately supported rather than undercut. The physically immature, mentally ill, or developmentally disabled need paternalistic guidance just so that they will not act in ways that destroy whatever limited capacities for autonomous action they possess and or may someday possess. The person who is, unawares, about to cross a bridge that is unsafe will not get to make many more choices after this one. If one sells oneself into slavery one is depriving oneself of a future of autonomous choice.

That is the rough idea: limitations on autonomy must be for the sake of autonomy.[20] Dworkin introduces a test that we can use to decide what sorts of paternalistic limitations on autonomy are justifiable. We are all familiar with cases in which one realizes that one will later not be in a good position to make choices that are rational and in line with one's overall set of commitments and values, and takes steps to protect oneself against one's foreseen poor choices. Ulysses wanted to hear the song of the Sirens but knew that if he could control the ship while listening to their siren-song he would wreck the ship and doom the entire crew; so he had himself tied to the mast so that when he later wanted to direct the ship into the rocks, his choice would be thwarted. Often someone who plans to have a few drinks hands over his or her car keys to a friend, with the instruction that the friend is not to return the car keys if he or she is in no condition to drive. In both cases one is protecting oneself against one's future poor choices.

Paternalistic intervention cannot always be justified with the actual prior consent of the person whose liberty is to be limited. In some cases, this is impossible or pointless (for example, with respect to children) and in even more cases would be massively impractical. Dworkin suggests reliance on a test of *hypothetical* consent: paternalistic interference is justified only if it *would be* rational for one to agree in advance to that sort of interference. He suggests that this sort of test suggests that several broad types of paternalistic restriction on conduct could turn out to be justifiable.

The first is that, when thinking clearly, people should realize that there are certain goods that are needed in order to make decisions at all – for example, health, or a certain level of education. If there are certain goods that are needed to live an autonomous life at all, and certain actions that by any reasonable measure promise far too little of value to the subject to justify the risks to these goods that they generate, then paternalistic restrictions on these types of conduct might be justified under Dworkin's test. One might object, along Millian lines: if these goods are so crucial to an autonomous life, why must the state take steps to prohibit these actions? Why wouldn't subjects simply refrain from them on their own? The answers are various: some folks do not understand the plain facts about the risks; some folks appreciate the risks properly, but out of sheer dull habit or laziness fail to take the steps that they in some sense know they should take; some folks might have risk-aversion profiles that are simply irrational.[21]

The second type of paternalistic interference that Dworkin thinks might be justified through his hypothetical-rational-choice test is constituted by restrictions instituted in order to prevent irrevocable or very costly choices from being made under duress. Some choices that are life-altering – the choice to commit suicide is pretty obviously life-altering – often arise under conditions of psychological distress and panic, and with inadequate opportunities for deliberation. Thus even if legal proscription is not justified, perhaps some legal requirement to wait before acting might be justifiable.

So one might rationally want to be protected against oneself, one's failures of knowledge or will, or one might rationally want to be protected against one's circumstances, the situations that interfere with the normal operations of one's deliberative faculties; as Dworkin writes, "Since we are all aware of our irrational propensities, deficiencies in cognitive and emotional capacities and avoidable and unavoidable ignorance, it is rational and prudent for us to in effect take out 'social insurance policies'."[22] The general justification for paternalistic interference is that *if you were to think about it clearly, rationally, and knowledgeably, this is what you want to be done to and for you.* Of course, use of this test is subject to abuse: legislators may overestimate the extent to which they can accurately employ this test. But there is a strong case for thinking that even taking for granted the broadly Millian framework there are broader grounds for paternalistic interference than the harm-to-others principle, even as qualified by Mill, allows.

There are questions, though, about the extent to which Dworkin's friendly amendment to Mill's view is a sufficiently stable alternative to a more straightforward harm-to-others view. Suppose we say that autonomy in choice is only to be limited for the sake of autonomy. There are a couple of reasons why we would defend this view. The first is that we might think that protecting autonomy is in general the best way for people to satisfy their desires, whatever those desires happen to be; in those cases where satisfaction of one's desires is thwarted by allowing autonomy (as in the cases when people are ill-informed, weak-willed, etc.), then paternalistic intervention is justified. The second is that we might think that autonomy – the capacity and opportunity and exercise of one's free capacities of choice – is a great human good, regardless of one's desires, and so is not to be sacrificed for the sake of other goods. I do not see a third way to defend the view that autonomy is to be restricted only for the sake of autonomy.

But both of these answers are subject to criticism. With respect to the first: if what ultimately matters is the satisfaction of the subject's desires, then we should ask Mill why the law should be so much concerned with guaranteeing (as far as is feasible) subjects the ability to act for the sake of realizing their desires, rather than with guaranteeing (as far as is feasible) subjects the satisfaction of their desires. Given the broad similarities in basic desires among agents, and the broad similarities in the infirmities of will and knowledge among agents, why shouldn't the law more directly restrict liberty for the sake of overall desire-satisfaction?

With respect to the second: if what ultimately matters is the objective good of autonomy, then we may well want to know why it is that, for all of our uncertainty about the nature of the good, we are so certain that autonomy is the most fundamental, irreplaceable of human goods. If we make a list of plausible objective goods in a human life, we are likely to include autonomy, but we are also likely to include life and health, knowledge, friendship, enjoyment, and achievement. Why is autonomy so much more important than these, so that paternalism is justified for the sake of autonomy, but not for the sake of any of these other human goods? (I will return to this question of human goods other than autonomy below.)

3.4   Morals Legislation

"You can't legislate morality." The claim is often made, but is itself none too clear, and it is worth disentangling the senses in which it is clearly true, the senses in which it is clearly false, and the senses in which it is neither clearly true nor clearly false, and thus in need of further investigation.

If we take "morality" to consist of the accepted norms that are used within a community to guide one's own conduct and criticize others', and noncompliance with which will generate social pressure toward conformity on account of the nature of the forbidden action itself, then it is absolutely, obviously true that morality cannot be legislated. One cannot magically bring it about by passing a law that suddenly a new norm is introduced into everyday morality, so that folks will take the action legislated against to be bad or base or repugnant or unworthy. This is, after all, the whole point of Hart's distinction between a society ruled by customary norms alone and a society ruled by law. Under law new norms can be introduced that are binding, even if those norms have not worked their way into the everyday standards of conduct employed by the bulk of the populace.

Corresponding to this obviously true sense of "You can't legislate morality" is an obviously false sense of it. The obviously false sense would be that lawmaking cannot influence the course of a society's moral consciousness. That is just false. One boring reason that it is false is that almost any public institution's activities can influence the course of a society's moral consciousness. One more interesting reason is that law has the authority to make rules, and, typically, to back them up with motives for compliance, that can get the unwilling to fall in line with respect to the behavior required. In many cases, what begins as mere law can become habitual and eventually enters into the public morality as required on its own account. It is hard to deny that antidiscrimination laws, for example, had a positive influence on the extent to which discrimination is seen as morally blameworthy. It is hard to deny that laws cracking down on driving under the influence of alcohol were themselves part of what changed public perception of drunk driving. So while it is true that morality cannot be legislated in one fell swoop, legislation can make a difference, whether for good or for ill, in the content of social morality.

There is another thought that people are sometimes trying to express when they say "You can't legislate morality." What they mean is that there is something self-defeating about legally requiring morally upright conduct. To force someone to act morally is like forcing someone to volunteer: the sense in which one is "volunteering" if required to do so is only a false, shadowy sense, and moral action that is done under compulsion is "moral action" in a similarly false and shadowy sense. In this way "You can't legislate morality" is supposed to be analogous to "You can't make someone volunteer."

Again, there is a true sense to this claim and a false sense to this claim. The true sense is that in the central cases of morally upright conduct the action is undertaken for the sake of doing the right thing – that is, one intends to do x, knowing that x is a worthwhile thing to do and choosing x because of its worthwhile features. If one chooses to do x not knowing that x is worthwhile or not choosing it because of its worthwhile features – if one instead chooses it because one has been told to, or because one has been threatened – then that is not a central case of morally upright conduct. All that seems correct. But there is a false sense as well. For while it is true that one who performs a morally upright act under legal compulsion does not epitomize morally good conduct, he or she does not epitomize morally bad conduct either. For if the legal compulsion prevents one from choosing what is morally bad, knowing it to be such, then while law has not made one act in the morally best way, law has at least made one refrain from acting in the morally worst way. And there is more. For it may be that by preventing one from acting in the morally worst way – the compulsion wielded by law might neutralize one's weakness for the morally bad – the result is that one is freed up to pursue other, morally worthy aims, which one will choose in full awareness of their value.

So while it is true that legislation cannot bring about instantaneous changes in social morality and it is true that the force of law cannot make people act in highly morally praiseworthy ways, it is also true that legislation can bring about some gradual changes in social morality and can prevent people from acting in highly morally blameworthy ways. Sometimes, though, by "You can't legislate morality" what is meant is not that it is impossible to use law in the service of morals but that, regardless of its possibility, it ought not to be done. Law should not be used to promote morality or prevent immorality.

Almost everyone agrees that just because an act is immoral, it does not mean that it should be legally prohibited and that just because an act is not immoral, that does not mean that it should not be legally prohibited. To take the second point of agreement: there are a lot of actions that are prohibited, but not on account of their prior immorality. Think of all of the laws that Aquinas calls "determinations" of general norms needed for good common living (see 1.6.2) – laws that require you to drive on the right (or left), to pay your taxes by a certain date, and so forth. These actions are not requirements of morality, but it seems perfectly permissible to require them by law for the sake of realizing worthwhile social ends. To take the first point of agreement: even Aquinas agrees with Mill that we should not try to legally prohibit all actions that we take to be immoral. Sometimes it would do more harm than good to try to prohibit certain immoral actions: people might be simply unwilling to comply, and their disrespect for that law might transform into disrespect for law as such; or it might be too invasive or costly to enforce; or it might be the sort of immorality that is so difficult to judge that it is better left to God or the individual conscience rather than to the legal system.

Not all actions that are rightly made illegal are in themselves immoral, and not all actions that are in themselves immoral are rightly made illegal. We need some criterion for deciding what to legislate against (or for), and *because it is morally wrong* (or *because it is morally required*) would be a bad criterion. But even if we reject the criterion that conduct ought to be forbidden if and only if it is immoral, we are left with a live question about legislation and morality: is the fact that an action is immoral a good reason – not necessarily a decisive one, but *a* good reason – to outlaw it? Mill says that harm to others counts in favor of outlawing a form of behavior; others would claim that harm to self or offense to others should count as well. The real question about morals legislation is whether immorality should be included in the list of reasons that a legislator can rightfully rely upon to justify legally prohibiting conduct.

The terms in which the current discussion of morals legislation is carried out were framed in the aftermath of the Wolfenden Report, a statement issued by an appointed British commission that was charged to consider whether homosexual conduct and solicitation of prostitution should be criminal offenses.[23] The Report concluded that these forms of conduct should not be criminal, and in so doing articulated an account of the appropriate reaches of legislation:

> The function of criminal law . . . is to preserve public order and decency, to protect the citizen from what is offensive or injurious, and to provide sufficient safeguards against exploitation and corruption of others, particularly those who are specially vulnerable because they are young, weak in body and mind, inexperienced, or in a state of special physical, official, or economic dependence.[24]

The Report explicitly rejected the view that morality as such could be a reasonable basis on which to justify legislation: there is a range of actions that belong only to private morality, and such actions are "not the law's business."[25]

The standard offered by the Wolfenden Report reads not too differently from Mill's harm-to-others principle, supplemented with Mill's remarks about offenses against decency and the qualifications for those who are by birthdate or infirmity in their "non-age" with respect to their autonomy. This is how it was read by Patrick Devlin, a British judge who argued at length that the restriction of the aims of law to preventing harm or offense is a gravely wrongheaded mistake.[26]

Suppose that we distinguish between *critical* and *positive* morality.[27] Critical morality consists in those moral norms that correctly prescribe what is to be done from a moral point of view, and thus can be used to accurately criticize actual choices and prevailing moral beliefs and attitudes; positive morality consists in those social norms that are in fact accepted within some society. Devlin's argument is framed in terms of the desirability of legislating positive morality: he rejects the view that critical morality should be legislated, on the basis that critical morality is on the whole religious rather than secular in origin and thus any society that has sworn off enforcing particular religious beliefs as true should, in consistency, swear off enforcing particular religiously grounded moral norms as correct.[28] His argument is framed instead in terms of the importance of positive morality – that morality that often remains implicit, but is generally accepted within a community, and the contours of which can be discovered by getting the reactions from 12 jury members or from the randomly chosen "man in the Clapham omnibus."[29] This positive morality manifests itself in judgments about right and wrong, but it also manifests itself in what pleases or attracts or disgusts or repels us; it elicits not only belief but also emotion.

Devlin's view was that we have a strong interest in enforcing positive morality through law, and that while there might be countervailing reasons against doing so on many occasions, we cannot fence off a zone in which morals legislation is not allowed to intrude. His reasoning is this. We all have an interest in the preservation of society. But society consists not just in a group of individuals: one cannot collect a bunch of individuals together and thereby have a society. What makes a collection of individuals a society is that these individuals are unified in some way – in particular, through common habits of judging, assessing, deciding, and feeling. If that is the case, then society is threatened by whatever tends to break these unifying bonds of common moral assessment, and is preserved by whatever tends to hold these bonds firm. But morals legislation is one way of keeping these bonds in place: such legislation expresses the common sentiment against certain actions; it discourages those whose are tempted, either through failing to share the common opinion or through weakness of will, from carrying out these acts; and it helps to prevent an atmosphere in which the as-yet-immature will be tempted to form habits inconsistent with this positive morality.[30] Because society (in Devlin's sense of a group of individuals united by common judgment and sentiment) is itself threatened by private immorality, the refusal to countenance legislation against immorality is, in Devlin's view, like the refusal to countenance legislation against treason. Both immorality and treason are threats to society; both immorality and treason are proper objects of legal proscription.[31]

Hart immediately called Devlin's views into question, suggesting that there was no consistent way to understand "society" such that private immorality always constituted a threat to society and that society is something worth preserving.[32] Think about it this way. On one hand, we might understand "society" to mean "individuals sufficiently organized and at peace with one another to make possible a decent life for those individuals." Under this definition of "society" it is clear that society is worth preserving, and that legislation toward this end could be justified. But it is not clear that morals legislation would be needed to preserve this end. Why must private morality be regulated by law in order to make possible a peaceful, orderly life for those living under it? Why wouldn't a regulation of more obvious and direct threats to peace and order – harm and serious offense – be sufficient to preserve society?

On the other hand, we might understand a society as defined in part by the moral outlook of its members: we might think that it is constitutive of a given society that it has the positive morality that it has.

Even a society that has all the same members would be a different society if the positive morality were different; changes in a society's positive morality are thus better described as one society's supplanting another instead of a society's positive morality undergoing a transformation. If it is essential to a society that it have the positive morality it has, then the survival of that society will depend on the preservation of positive morality. But it is unclear why society, in this sense of "society," is worth preserving. Even if we put to the side the point that a society's positive morality might be repugnant and thus not worth keeping, it is unclear why we would ascribe value to the existence of a social unit defined by its common moral stance.

It is widely agreed that in the Hart–Devlin debate, Hart emerged as the victor. But, as in all debates, one should be cautious about equating one side's winning a debate with one's side's having the weight of reason on its side. It is worth asking whether there are other ways to defend morals legislation that do not succumb to the weaknesses of Devlin's argument.

Here are some possibilities. One way to defend morals legislation is as a species of paternalism. The idea is that when we sit down to reflect on the things that make a life a good one, we are likely to include far more of substance within it than autonomy; we are likely to include a number of items that are worth having in a life, items without which a life goes worse. It is good to be alive and healthy, rather than dead or sick; it is good to have some knowledge rather than to be ignorant; it is better to have friends rather than to be friendless; and so forth. These are rather boring truths, and when called into question the usual point is not to deny them ("Are you crazy? It's better, or no worse, to be ignorant than knowledgeable" is not often heard) but to deny what one might take to be implications of these truths (e.g., "Does that mean that we should always be trying to improve our knowledge?" "Does that mean that there can be no conflict between goods?"). Now, one might reasonably enough think that *acting rightly rather than wrongly* is on this list as well – that among the things that make a life go well is not only *being alive*, and *knowing things*, and *having friends*, but also *acting morally*.

If this is right, then there is a basis for an argument from paternalism to the justification of morals legislation. Suppose that we adopt Dworkin's standard: if one would be rational to accept in advance a paternalistic constraint on one's action, then that paternalistic constraint can be justifiably imposed on one. Now suppose that I am trying to decide what constraints on me I should accept. If I think that accepting a constraint on me would improve the extent to which my life goes well, then I rationally would accept it. But my life would, all things being equal, go better if I did not engage in immoral conduct. So I rationally would, all things being equal, accept the imposition of morals legislation upon me.

Here is a thought experiment to make this point more vivid. Suppose that you are reliably informed that when you wake up in the morning tomorrow, you are going to have a very strong desire to do something that you now believe to be deeply, deeply morally repugnant. What is more, you will no longer have the view that the action is deeply, deeply morally repugnant. This should be very alarming to you. You are going to want to do something that you now believe to be evil, and your beliefs are going to change so that you do not recognize the badness of what you do. Now, here is the question. In this circumstance, would you want there to be a legal restriction on your conduct, so that you could not act on your newfound desire? You can foresee that you might well resent this restriction on your conduct, given that you will not at that time believe that the action that you are being prevented from performing is morally bad, and you will want very much to do it. But, on the other hand, you might well go to bed happier with the restriction in place, knowing that even though you will come to have a desire for something morally repugnant, at least you will be prevented from performing the repugnant action. You might well genuinely want there to be this restriction on your conduct, given the importance of not acting in vicious ways and the fact that the restriction on your conduct will enable you not to act in vicious ways. In this way morals legislation can be justified using a version of the hypothetical consent test that Dworkin offers.

One might raise objections to this proposal in a variety of ways. One might object that acting morally rather than immorally is not really a human good. This is a hard dispute to settle – questions about fundamental values are notoriously hard to settle – but we should keep in mind that if one is inclined to reject the status of this as a human good, one has to decide whether that is because one rejects such claims about *all* fundamental human goods (if so, what's wrong with thwarting autonomy?) or because one rejects only the claim that, specifically, acting morally is a human good (if so, what evidence do we have that autonomy is more defensibly a fundamental human good than acting morally is?).

By contrast, one might, in Millian style, say that this is not an agreement that one should be willing to make, for it would involve the assumption that the legislators have more knowledge than one does about one's own particular situation, and thus that they are competent to interfere to get you on the right path or perhaps the assumption that legislators are in general more knowledgeable about morals than individual subjects are. To this objection there are a couple of responses available, though none can be developed here in nearly adequate detail. The first is that this Millian counterargument underestimates the extent to which the problem to be combated by morals legislation is not one of knowledge but of will: it is not that the legislator's knowledge is superior, it is that the legislator is able to render an authoritative rule that can combat weakness of will with respect to vices that both the legislator and the subject can equally acknowledge as such. The second is that in those cases where there is disagreement between someone subject to a morals law and the legislator who passes it, we need not cast the contrast as that between the moral knowledge of the subject and the legislator, as least when the legislator is acting as a representative rather than merely in an objectively benevolent way (see 2.3): if the legislator is acting on behalf of the people, then the relevant competing judgments are those of the subject whose conduct is restricted and the collective wisdom of the people on whose behalf the legislator makes law. And while this collective wisdom cannot reach to the details of particular cases, we should say that (1) we do not in general think that people are privileged in knowing what it is right for them to do, as opposed to what will make them happy or satisfied, and (2) if the legislator thinks it best, the legislator can restrict morals legislation to cases in which the particulars of the case are in the vast majority of cases irrelevant. (I will illustrate this below.)

A second defense of morals legislation is due to Robert George, who has offered a friendly reinterpretation of Devlin's views.[33] Call this the neo-Devlinian account. George suggests that we can move away from the weak argument that is the plainest reading of Devlin toward a more nuanced and defensible view. The first revision George suggests is that Devlin's argument cannot be used to defend whatever positive morality happens to be in place; it is critical morality that should be the basis of morals legislation. Devlin's error, George argues, is to suppose that critical morality is necessarily religious in its justification: this claim of Devlin's is not only implausible as a general thesis about moral justification, given the variety of nonreligious justifications for moral norms that have been offered, but is not even plausible as a thesis about a number of religious traditions that defend their conception of moral norms by reference to natural reason as well as divine revelation. The second revision is to provide an alternative understanding of the importance of society: the idea is that society is an element of human well-being, so that social relationships are part and parcel of what make human life go well.

George puts these two revisions to work in an argument for morals legislation. The idea is that being related to others in friendship and community is part of human well-being, and thus an aspect of the common good worth promoting. But the value of this common life is undercut to the extent to which virtue (whether public or private) languishes and to the extent to which vice (whether public or private) flourishes. Think, for example, of the good of friendship, and how it is more fully realized between those who are good through and through than between those who are bad through and through or even between those whose lives are generally good but nevertheless marked with serious vice. George invites us to think of the good of social life as distinct from, but analogous to, the good of friendship. And if the virtue of citizens can be fostered by the existence of laws that discourage even private vice, then such laws may well be justified by reference to the common good.

Both the paternalist and the neo-Devlinian defenses of morals legislation can agree with Mill's broad views about the nature of the common good: the common good should be understood in a welfarist way, consisting in nothing other than the well-being of the subjects. The paternalist view argues that morals legislation can help to support the human good of acting morally, while the neo-Devlinian view affirms that there is a good of community that is more fully realized when folks act on a common and correct moral view. There is a third possibility that merits mention here, in part because it is not based on the welfarist picture of the common good.

The starting point is the idea that the common good that law should take as its objective might include more than well-being as its target. Consider, for example, the claims that some environmentalists make on behalf of the intrinsic goodness of certain flourishing ecosystems, or on behalf of the survival of certain species. One way to justify taking the preservation of ecosystems or the survival of species as aims of law is by way of their effect on the well-being of people. Some ecosystems are inhabited by humans whose well-being depends on the ecosystem's stability, some are just fun to visit, and, as one might note, the cure for cancer might be hidden in there somewhere. The interconnection of species is such that the elimination of one has unpredictable results, and thus it might be bad for human well-being to allow their destruction.

Such arguments, while perhaps plausible in some specific cases, are singularly unpromising as a way to explain why in general ecosystems should be freed from destruction or species protected from elimination. And so some have argued that we should simply take the survival of ecosystems or species to be intrinsically valuable, even apart from the way that their existence and flourishing affects or fails to affect human well-being. Once we include these objectives in our notion of the common good, then we can place persons under authoritative requirements to do their share to realize them: to refrain from dumping trash in a wilderness preserve, to refrain from hunting members of endangered species, and so forth.

Call objectives that are valuable, but not entirely in virtue of their contribution to human well-being, *ideals*. If I complain that my liberty is restricted because I am not allowed to dump my trash in a wilderness preserve or to hunt and eat bald eagles, the response would have to be framed in terms of the claim that these ideals are valuable and that it is not an overly burdensome imposition on one to do one's share in these ways to promote these valuable ideals. But if one accepts the existence of ideals and of this general strategy justifying restrictions of liberty in light of them, then one has opened up at least the possibility of an alternative defense of morals legislation. For one might take *the preservation of a moral community in which virtue flourishes (or vice languishes)* to be an ideal: it is simply a marvelous thing, much like the thriving of an ecosystem or the ongoing life of a species, for a community to be morally good in that sense. And one way to realize that ideal – or to approximate it more closely – would be to restrict certain sorts of immoralities. The justification would be, just as in the case of the ecosystems and the species, that the restrictions on liberty are not overly burdensome: for while liberty is indeed being restricted, it is only options that one should not want to choose anyway that are being taken off the table.

A general worry about morals legislation is that legislators are not to be trusted to enact such legislation well: either they will fail to represent the people's considered, reflective views on the matter, or they will accurately represent the people's unconsidered, unreflective, prejudiced views on the matter. This is of course a proper worry to have, but no different from worries that we should have about all legislation. Some might, echoing Mill, worry about the blocking of the possibility of moral progress that can result only if people are free to engage in experiments in living that run contrary to dominant views of private morality, even those that are considered and reflective. This is indeed a worry, but it is not clear that the proper way to respond to it is to eliminate morals legislation in its entirety: perhaps the proper way to respond to it is to make *damaging to experiments in living* one of the considerations, along with *costly to enforce, possibly self-defeating*, and so forth, that can give reasons not to legislate against private immorality. But even with these concessions in place, it seems that there are some types of action that remain candidates for morals legislation.

Take a concrete example: the actions of distributing and purchasing child pornography. Suppose that one wishes to argue that this should be legally forbidden. One might say that the justification of prohibition of this behavior is the harm done to the child in the making and distributing of this material. To succeed, one would have to show that the harm alleged to the child is indeed generally present, and that this harm is of a properly uncontroversial variety. It is not clear that the evidence of that sort for harm is available and sufficiently noncontroversial. But if we wish we can put this to the side by noting that the pornography targeted might be computer-generated, though extremely realistic, depictions. No children need be involved in its making.

It is hard to see how a consistent defender of the harm-to-others principle could support legal proscription of the distribution and purchase of child pornography of this form. Some have claimed that use of such materials makes users more likely to harm children, but the actual evidence is slight and it is unclear whether it shows nothing more than that those inclined to harm children are more likely to purchase child pornography. And if there is anything that defenders of the harm-to-others principle have wanted to rule out, it is the appeal to vague, indirect, and uncertain future harms to others for the sake of proscribing an action that is primarily self-regarding.

A defender of morals legislation might claim here that the point of distributing and purchasing child pornography is, in the main, that the end users can obtain sexual satisfaction through it. And the defender of morals legislation might claim that there is not much to be said against the view that seeking gratification through use of explicit sexual depictions of children is debasing, corrupt, and vile. It is hard to believe that there will be any results forthcoming from some experiment in living that will show us that it is anything but that, or that whether it is debasing, corrupt, and vile is something that varies among persons based on their circumstances, circumstances that legislators are not in much of a position to know about. If it is plausible that legally proscribing the distribution and purchase of child pornography will discourage the seeking of gratification through the use of sexually explicit depictions of children (while not encouraging other forms of equally bad or worse conduct), then there may well be justification for use of morals legislation in cases of this type.

For Further Reading

The classic source for discussions of the appropriate aims of law is John Stuart Mill's *On Liberty*, ed. Elizabeth Rapaport (Indianapolis, IN: Hackett, 1978). Contemporary defenders of versions of Mill's view – though not always for Mill's reasons – include Joel Feinberg's magisterial multi-volume *The Moral Limits of the Criminal Law* (New York: Oxford University Press, 1985) and Joseph Raz, *The Morality of Freedom* (Oxford: Clarendon Press, 1986), Chapter 15, pp. 400–29. The debate between Patrick Devlin and H. L. A. Hart sets the agenda for contemporary discussions of morals legislation; see Devlin's *The Enforcement of Morals* (London: Oxford University Press, 1965) and Hart's *Law, Liberty, and Morality* (Palo Alto, CA: Stanford University Press, 1963). The volume *Morality and the Law*, ed. Richard A. Wasserstrom (Belmont, CA: Wadsworth, 1971), is a useful collection containing pieces by Devlin, Hart, Gerald Dworkin, and others. Recent defenses of morals legislation can be found in Robert P. George, *Making Men Moral* (Oxford: Clarendon Press,

1993) and John Kekes, "The Enforcement of Morality," *American Philosophical Quarterly* 37 (2000), pp. 23–35.

Notes

1 John Stuart Mill, *On Liberty*, ed. Elizabeth Rapaport (Indianapolis, IN: Hackett, 1978 [first published 1859]).
2 Ibid., Ch. 1, p. 9.
3 Ibid., Ch. 1, pp. 9–10.
4 Ibid., Ch. 2.
5 Ibid., Ch. 1, p. 9; Ch. 4, pp. 75–6.
6 Ibid., Ch. 4, p. 79.
7 Ibid., Ch. 1, p. 10.
8 Ibid., Ch. 4, p. 81.
9 Ibid., Ch. 3, p. 54.
10 Ibid., Ch. 3, pp. 54–5.
11 Ibid., Ch. 5, p. 97.
12 Joel Feinberg, *The Moral Limits of the Criminal Law: Volume II, Offense to Others* (New York: Oxford University Press, 1985), pp. 10–13.
13 Mill, *On Liberty*, Ch. 3, p. 53.
14 Ibid., Ch. 1, pp. 9–10.
15 Ibid., Ch. 5, p. 95.
16 Ibid., Ch. 5, p. 101.
17 Ibid., Ch. 1, p. 10.
18 Ibid., Ch. 1, p. 10.
19 Gerald Dworkin, "Paternalism," *Monist* 56 (1972), pp. 64–84.
20 Ibid., p. 76.
21 Dworkin treats the knowledge and will infirmities as different categories, but I treat them as one: they are both infirmities of choice that are internal to subject and thus conveniently discussed together.
22 Dworkin, "Paternalism," p. 78.
23 *Report of the Committee on Homosexual Offenses and Prostitution* ("the Wolfenden Report") (New York: Stein and Day, 1963 [first published in 1957]).
24 Wolfenden Report, paragraph 13, p. 23.
25 Ibid., paragraph 61, p. 48.
26 Patrick Devlin, *The Enforcement of Morals* (London: Oxford University Press, 1965). The first part of this book, "Morals and the Criminal Law," was delivered as a public lecture in 1959, shortly after the appearance of, and in response to, the Wolfenden Report. Devlin's appeal to the "man in the Clapham omnibus" is an appeal common in English law – the expression

is a shorthand reference to the ordinary, decent member of the public; it was coined by Lord Justice Bowen in the case of *McQuire v. Western Morning News*, 2 K.B. 100 (1903) at 109.

27 Hart makes this distinction in one of his discussions of Devlin's views: see H. L. A. Hart, *Law, Liberty, and Morality* (Palo Alto, CA: Stanford University Press, 1963), p. 20.

28 Devlin, *The Enforcement of Morals*, pp. 4–5.

29 Ibid., p. 15.

30 Ibid., p. 22.

31 Ibid., pp. 24–5.

32 H. L. A. Hart, "Immorality and Treason," *Listener* (July 30, 1959), pp. 162–3; reprinted in Richard A. Wasserstrom (ed.), *Morality and the Law* (Belmont, CA: Wadsworth, 1971), pp. 49–54.

33 Robert P. George, *Making Men Moral* (Oxford: Clarendon Press, 1993), pp. 65–82.

Chapter 4

The Nature and Aims of the Criminal Law

4.1 Types of Legal Norms

As Hart emphasized in his criticisms of Austin's view (see 1.2), legal norms come in a variety of types. Some confer powers; some grant rights or privileges; some impose duties. Contract law, for example, deals with individuals' mutual imposition of duties and the way that such duties will be recognized and enforced by the legal system. Constitutional law, for example, deals with the conferring on and limiting of powers of various governmental actors. There is no field of law that is not rich with philosophical presupposition and thus no field of law that is not ripe for philosophical discussion; there is not enough room in this book for a discussion of all of them, and none can be excluded for lack of interest. We will have to be selective, and so we will focus on two fields of legal norms, both primarily concerned with the ways in which persons are bound by legal duties with respect to one another and with the appropriate responses that are due when subjects fail adequately to honor these duties. One of these fields is *criminal law*. What distinguishes criminal law is that those that violate its norms are subject to punishment. Another of these fields is *tort law*. What distinguishes tort law is that those who injure others through violations of its norms – norms without a contractual basis – are liable for compensation to their victims. In this and the next chapter we will deal with criminal and tort law, respectively.

4.2   Crime and Punishment

A crime is a violation of a legal norm for which a punishment is authorized. Crimes are (almost) universally constituted by two elements: a mental element and a performance element.[1] To commit a crime, one must have both a guilty mind, or *mens rea*, and one must have engaged in a forbidden behavior, or *actus reus*.

The necessary conditions of *mens rea* differ for different crimes: sometimes intention is required; sometimes knowledge; sometimes recklessness; sometimes negligence, whether gross or garden-variety. But in all of these cases having a guilty mind means that the criminal knows (or should have known) certain things and that the criminal chose (or failed to choose) certain things. *Mens rea* is a state of mind, but "mind" understood as including both the cognitive, knowing aspects of one's mind and the volitional, choosing/willing aspects of one's mind.

The guilty act is a voluntary performance. It includes some behavior on the agent's part, where a behavior can involve doing something or failing to do something. (It can be criminal to run someone over with your car, and it can be criminal to be idle after you run someone over with your car.) In either case, the *actus reus* includes not only the behavior but also that behavior's being voluntary. "Voluntary" is to be understood here in a very thin sense – for a behavior to be voluntary in this sense is just for it to be something that the agent *did*, something that was an exercise of the agent's agency, rather than something that simply *happened to* the agent. Failures of this sort of voluntariness are of a particularly extreme variety. If one engaged in a criminal behavior while sleepwalking, or under hypnosis, or while in a coma (crimes of omission!), then the *actus reus* voluntariness condition would not be met.

What, then, is punishment? There are number of features of punishment that seem to be essential to it, but which together do not seem to separate punishment adequately from other legal phenomena.[2] First, it is essential to punishment that, in itself, it is an evil of some sort. Punishment involves the deprivation of goods or the imposition of bads: to be punished may be to lose one's wealth, one's liberty, one's status, one's citizenship, perhaps one's very life; to be punished may be to have pain or injury inflicted on one. Second, a punishment is imposed for the failure to measure up to some binding standard.

When one is punished, it is because one has not lived up to a guideline that one can be expected to live up to. (This is not to say that innocent people are never punished; obviously, tragically, sometimes they are. The point is that when an innocent person is punished, it is necessary that he or she is *believed to have* violated a standard or at least is *claimed to have* violated some standard.) Third, a punishment is imposed by a personal agency who is authoritative. The imposition of a punishment is the work of beings who can think and judge; it is not, that is, simply a natural process. (It is true that we sometimes speak of punishment without reference to such an agency – one might say, groaning, ''This is my punishment for drinking too much last night'' – but this is metaphor; punishment requires a personal touch.) And punishment is an activity by an authority, whether that authority is genuine or de facto only (see the Introduction for this distinction): a private person can carry out vigilante justice, but he or she cannot punish.

So punishment is a deprivation imposed on one by an authority because of one's failure to adhere to some standard of conduct. The interesting question is whether these conditions are sufficient to distinguish punishment from other sorts of intentionally and authoritatively imposed deprivations. Here are two cases that suggest that these conditions are not jointly sufficient.

Consider the case of *Flemming v. Nestor.*[3] In this case United States law allowed past membership in the Communist Party to count as grounds for noncitizens to be deported and have their social security benefits revoked. This law was passed after Ephram Nestor, a Bulgarian immigrant, had joined and then left the Communist Party. Nestor was deported and his benefits revoked, and he appealed the decision to revoke his benefits, holding that this was a punishment imposed ex post facto, in violation of the United States Constitution. The central question of the case, which reached the Supreme Court, was whether Nestor's deprivation of social security benefits counted as punishment. The Court's decision was that it did not: while there was indeed a deprivation authoritatively imposed on Nestor because of Nestor's past Communist Party affiliation, this was not a case of punishment; it was merely a rule that was being used to regulate United States immigration. To make sense of this decision – if one accepts its correctness – one must say that the three conditions on punishment we have seen are not together sufficient to distinguish punishment from nonpunishment, and that Nestor's case did not meet this as-yet-unnamed fourth condition. But even if one holds that the court's decision was incorrect, one must think that there is something more to punishment even to make sense out of the question it posed. For it is obvious that Nestor's case meets our first three conditions.

Here is another case. Games have rules, and often impose setbacks on those who violate those rules, and often these setbacks are imposed by officials who are authorized to identify the violations and impose the setbacks. If a basketball player takes more than one step while holding the ball, this constitutes traveling and is a rule violation; the referee who identifies traveling stops play and turns the ball over to the opposing team. This is a deprivation authoritatively imposed on a player for violating a binding standard. But it seems an awful stretch to say that every time a sports official imposes a penalty for violating a rule, there is a punishment taking place. If this is indeed a stretch, then we will want to know how exactly we should distinguish punishments from penalties.

Punishments are to be distinguished from penalties; punishments are to be distinguished from those regulations that set back some people's interests. How are they to be distinguished? The most obvious place to look is at the *point* or *purpose* or *function* of the deprivation. In the *Flemming v. Nestor* case, the Court's argument hinges on the claim that the aim of the rule in question was merely to promote desirable immigration patterns. In the basketball case, the point of the penalty is simply to define acceptable ball movement within the game and to ensure that teams do not unfairly violate the rules. Why do these cases fall short of instances of punishment? Joel Feinberg suggests that punishment has an essentially *expressive* function: whenever punishment is found, it expresses judgments of disapproval and attitudes of indignation and resentment.[4] The punishment itself expresses the condemnation in a particularly vivid way. This expression of condemnation might very well be absent in the immigration and basketball cases: regardless of whether one thinks Nestor is to be condemned for being a Communist, one might think that sound immigration policy requires the deportation of ex-Communists, with no continuation of benefits; and it is indeed rare to harbor indignation and resentment toward those who travel in basketball games.

The idea of punishment as essentially expressive requires a bit more comment. Who or what is being condemned in punishment? It would be misleading simply to say that it is just the *person* who violates the norm in question: punishment need not be a total condemnation of the person's character. Nor can it be just the *act*, the *failing*: even penalties are imposed because officials see the failings *as failings*, which is in a way to condemn them, and thus we would lose our basis for distinguishing punishments and penalties. The object of condemnation must be the person in a particular respect, that is, *the person as performer of this act*.

If this conception of punishment is right – and I will take its correctness for granted in what follows – then it is easy to see why crimes must be understood in terms of guilty minds and guilty acts. The criminal law is concerned to impose standards for conduct. But a person as performer of an act cannot be *condemned* unless he or she chose that action that is contrary to binding standards with the requisite state of mind. It may not matter on a basketball court whether traveling is chosen with a guilty mind or not, and it may not matter whether Communist Party membership was something that folks should have avoided; what is relevant is (respectively) that allowing traveling would confer an unfair advantage in the game, regardless of whether it was chosen with a guilty mind, and that Communist Party membership was (allegedly) correlated with a threat to the United States's stability.

4.3 Two Normative Theories of Punishment

Legal punishment is an exercise of legal authority: it occurs when one who is authorized to do so imposes hard treatment that condemns the criminal for violating an authoritative legal standard. Authority enters into the practice of punishment in a number of places: it is occasioned by the breaking of an authoritative rule; judges are often required to impose a punishment within some range of severity for those found guilty of violations; and parties are authoritatively charged with carrying out these punishments. Now, it is by reference to the common good that laws are justified. But the fact that laws are justified by reference to the common good produces the basic problem of punishment. The basic problem of punishment is that punishment aims to make people worse off. When one punishes, one imposes hard treatment on another, setting back his or her interests. But how is it for the common good to make people *worse off*?

The basic problem of punishment is that of explaining how we can justify the law's aiming at making persons worse off. This is the question of the *point* of punishment. But there are a couple of other problems that a theory of punishment should be expected to handle as well. One of these is the question of *target*: what sorts of acts should be made subject to punishment? This is not the same question that we treated above (Chapter 3) in asking about what sorts of laws should be limited by authoritative legal rules: we are asking here which sorts of authoritative legal rules should be enforced by punishment (as opposed to: not at all, or by public opinion, or by requirements for compensation). Another of these is the question about *amount*: for a given crime, how is the appropriate size of a punishment to be determined?

Two general types of view have dominated debate over the point, target, and amount of punishment: utilitarianism and retributivism. The basic idea of the utilitarian view is that punishment has a point because (and insofar as) it promotes good consequences for society to punish. The appropriate targets for punishment are those acts whose criminalization is optimal in terms of the benefits and costs, and the amount of punishment that should be set is fixed by the level of punishment that generates the best overall consequences.

4.3.1 Utilitarian theories

The classic statement of the utilitarian view is that offered by Jeremy Bentham.[5] Bentham is a utilitarian about all matters of decision, whether individual or social: all decisions are to be made by reference to the promotion of the overall good of society. Rules concerning legal requirements and legal punishments are no exception: we should ask what criminal laws should be laid down, and what punishments should be assigned to the violation of them, by asking what scheme of crime and punishment would best promote the overall good. (Utilitarians as a class do not say that judges should simply have discretion to assign guilt and punishment on the basis of their own calculations about the overall good: rather, they claim that the general rules that guide the choices of criminal laws that subjects and judges should follow should be made in a way that is for the overall good of society.) Bentham understands the goods of individuals within a political community as pleasures and the bads as pains. We have employed a broader conception, allowing the possibility of a wider variety of elements of human well-being (3.3.1), but even under this broader view one can still affirm the utilitarian thesis that criminal law is to be guided by the promotion of the overall well-being of the members of the political community.

Bentham takes the problem of punishment to be that punishment is essentially "mischief"[6] – as we said above, punishment is in itself about making people, the criminals, worse off. The point of punishment, though, is that it can be for the overall well-being of society to have rules that dictate that subjects will suffer if they act in certain ways.

Why is this so? Suppose that the actions that are criminalized are those the performance of which tends to produce lower overall happiness in one's political community. Perhaps the performance of these actions harms others, or harms the agent himself or herself, or causes offense to others. Now, we would like to see to it that these actions are not performed, and one way that we can do so is by attaching punishments to these actions as their consequences. The point of making it a rule that one will suffer punishment if one performs certain unhappiness-causing actions is that there will be greater happiness overall.

The mechanisms that might explain such a connection between punishment and the general happiness are many, and may differ from case to case. For one thing, a rule against performing some action may provide *general deterrence*: if the rule is well-known, and people think both that there is a significant chance that they will be caught if they perform the action and that the punishment is significantly damaging, then they will have further reason to avoid that conduct. The implementation of a rule may have additional effects of *special deterrence* as well: one who commits an offense and is caught and punished will have vivid, firsthand knowledge of what it is like to be punished, and may have reasons for avoiding criminal conduct above and beyond what the general population has. There may be other happiness-promoting effects as well. If the form of punishment employed helps convicts to see the error of their ways, then the security of society may be improved by the *reformation* or *rehabilitation* of criminals. (This was the idea behind penitentiaries – they were places in which one could repent for one's crimes.) If the form of punishment sufficiently isolates criminals from the means or opportunity for further wrongdoing, then *incapacitation* may be a benefit of punishment as well.

What we have focused on so far is the way in which rules prescribing punishments for crimes may prevent future criminal conduct and thus secure additional measures of social well-being. We should also note that there are other effects on the overall happiness that may result from choosing one scheme of punishment over another. Suppose that it is true that people in general take a certain satisfaction in criminals being punished for certain crimes. If people take satisfaction in severe criminals being punished, then this fact might be taken into account in making out a case for punishing certain crimes.

On the other hand, the utilitarian view serves as a basis for classifying certain sorts of action as being, as Bentham puts it, "unmeet for punishment."[7] In some cases, punishment is *groundless*: there is no action that is in need of deterrence. In some cases, punishment is *inefficacious*: while we might want to deter the action, punishment might be an ineffective way to do so. In some cases, a punishment rule would be *unprofitable*: the costs to human happiness of implementing the rule would not be worth the good that can be gotten from it. Punishment is not just bad for the punished, after all: it costs resources in terms of capturing criminals, bringing them to trial, convicting them, and imposing the punishment. In some cases, even where punishment would be useful in deterring undesirable actions, the punishment would be an inefficient means of preventing it. (Bentham includes a fourth category, in which the punishment is *needless*, because the good effects could be brought about by other means: I prefer to think of this as another case of inefficiency, for, after all, the means alternative to punishment might be much costlier than the punishment, and thus unjustifiable from a utilitarian point of view.)[8]

The attractions of utilitarianism as an account of the justification of punishment are many. When we imagine away the institution of punishment and ask what would be lost thereby, the immediate thought is *security* – that punishment's justification is grounded in the fact that a world without effective punishment would be a very insecure and unhappy world indeed. The utilitarian view extends this thought into a full account of punishment, holding that the range of actions fit for criminalization and the scheme of punishments due for various offenses should be carried out in a way that takes fully into account both the costs and the benefits of punishment for societal happiness. Not only is the normative rationale a plausible one, but utilitarianism tells us what information we need in order to decide which specific actions to criminalize and which punishments to impose, and how in principle we could resolve disputes on these questions. For such questions will be turned into questions of social science, asking what sorts of correlations there are between criminalization and societal happiness and between certain levels of punishment and the social benefits and costs that result.

One criticism that is often leveled against the utilitarian view of punishment is that it would sanction the punishment of the innocent: if in some case it turned out that framing an innocent person would produce the best overall results, then the utilitarian view entails that this punishment ought to be imposed. But this is a bad criticism, if we keep in mind that what the utilitarian view of punishment aims to justify is a system of *rules* for punishing: no rule for punishment that included the provision "but officials may frame innocents in order to promote the overall good" is likely to be a rule that promotes the best overall consequences. The anxiety that would accompany such a rule, and the uncertainty and distrust that would accompany judgments of guilt in hard cases, surely would undercut the potential utility that the rule might have.[9]

Other criticisms are harder to escape. It is a straightforward implication of the utilitarian view, embraced by Bentham, that those crimes that are not well deterred by punishment are not to be punished. But it is contrary to some of our deep convictions about punishment that in some types of cases punishment is merited even if punishment is not a profitable response to it. Consider the crime of unpremeditated spousal murder. It may be that this is a crime that is characteristically committed in the heat of passion and with little regard to the personal consequences. Suppose it is true that spousal murder is very little sensitive to general or special deterrence, and that those who commit it tend not to commit murder again, or indeed tend not to have future criminal records that look much different from those who do not commit that crime. It would look as though we would have to say that unpremeditated spousal murder is not the sort of thing that we should bother with punishing. But most of us would be very alarmed by the view that someone who murders his or her spouse should be immune from punishment.

The worry about spouse murder is that the utilitarian view suggests that in this case we should punish too little. The opposite worry arises with other cases. Consider a crime that is committed deliberately, for the sake of great personal gain, and that it is relatively difficult to detect and punish. In such cases, the deterrence effect of punishment will not be sufficient unless the punishment of those few who are caught is very high. So, for example, in the case of *Harmelin v. Michigan*,[10] a man who was arrested with 672 grams of cocaine was treated as a potential dealer and sentenced (as the statute required) to life in prison without possibility of parole. It may well be that massive punishments would be very effective at reducing that sort of crime. (In part the massive statutory punishment was used by prosecutors to get defendants to give evidence against other criminals in return for a reduction of the charges against them.) The result here suggests that in some cases the utilitarian view will imply that we should punish too much.

Indeed, things may be more severe for the utilitarian than it appears here. One could object that utilitarianism does not even provide a clear rationale why the person who is made to suffer must be the *same* person who is guilty of violations of authoritative standards. Utilitarianism might sanction *vicarious* punishment. One might think that this is impossible, given the analysis of punishment as expressing condemnation for wrongdoing: how can a punishment express condemnation for A's wrongdoing by imposing hard treatment on B? But this is not obviously crazy, for one might say that it is made clear to A how bad A's action was by imposing a punishment on someone close to A – A's nearest relative, perhaps, or closest friend. Whether this is justifiable would depend on the extent to which, as a general rule, vicarious punishment can bring about good consequences. On the one hand, one might be apprehensive that those close to one will commit crimes and thus subject one to vicarious punishment; on the other hand, one might take more action than one otherwise would to prevent those close to one from turning to crime. On the one hand, some people might be more inclined to commit crimes knowing that the punishment for the misdeeds will fall on others; on the other hand, some people are more willing to place themselves at risk than their loved ones. On the utilitarian view, this will be simply an *empirical question*: we cannot pronounce on the justification of vicarious punishment in advance of what the relevant social sciences tell us about its likely effects.

Another line of argument concerns the availability of the social science research that will enable us to carry out the utilitarian program of determining which actions to criminalize and the extent of punishment to assign to them by reference to the likely consequences. A straightforward criticism is that these sort of calculations are notoriously controversial and the evidence for them far from conclusive.

Consider, for example, the extremely closely studied question of whether the death penalty has a general deterrent effect over and above that of common alternative, less severe punishments. There is in fact nothing like a consensus among experts for or against the claim that it has such an effect.[11] (Of course, it has a *special* deterrent effect![12]) What we have are mostly vague impressions, anecdotal evidence, and a priori speculations about the effect that certain punishments have on the incidence of criminal violations. But matters are of course harder than merely determining whether certain punishments have certain deterrent effects; we would need to decide whether the benefits of generating those deterrent effects are sufficient to overcome the inevitable costs of criminalization.[13]

The objection just discussed is an "in practice" objection: there are overwhelming amounts of information that would be needed to do the sort of calculation that utilitarian punishment theorists require, and as a matter of fact we lack at present much that is really reliable with respect to such calculations. There is a harder line that one can take against the utilitarian, and that is that these sorts of calculation are in principle impossible. The utilitarian view requires a cost–benefit analysis with respect to punishment. But given the tremendous variety of human goods involved – money, pain, loss of freedom, loss of life, security, emotional stability, and so forth – it is hard to see what common standard can be used to assess the various costs and benefits of different proposals for punishment schemes.

The difficulties for utilitarianism arise out of its virtues. Its appeal to the importance of punishment in achieving goods for social life generates the result that punishments can be surprisingly mild or surprisingly severe because of the fact that different crimes are differently susceptible to deterrence through punishment. Its appeal to a source for deciding controversies on the questions of criminalization and the amount of punishment to be imposed – the findings of social science – places such decision making at the mercy of the existence of expertise in this field, which in practice or in principle may simply be absent.

4.3.2 Retributivist theories

An alternative model to the promising but troubled utilitarianism is retributivism. Utilitarian theories of punishment are frequently described as "forward-looking": the rationale for criminalizing and for setting certain punishments is that future happiness can be attained by having effective rules in place. Retributivist theories, by contrast, are described as "backward-looking": on the retributivist view, the aim of punishment is to *respond to the wrongful act itself* – there is something intrinsically appropriate about imposing a punishment for crimes. When one violates a legal norm, one performs a morally blameworthy act to which an appropriate legal response is punishment, and the extent of the punishment should be proportionate to the gravity of the offense.

We will postpone for a moment retributivism's response to the "What is the point?" question in order to examine its way of dealing with issues of which acts to criminalize and how levels of punishment are to be determined. The question of criminalization does not admit of an obvious answer in retributivist terms, and it seems to me that the retributivist's best response is simply to follow the course charted in the previous chapter. Recall that in the previous chapter it was argued that the appropriate aims of law are determined jointly by the most defensible conception of the common good and by the limits of legal authority (3.1). *Any* law that is formulated in light of these conditions and which is imposed on a subject as a matter of duty should be fit for criminalization, given the retributivist outlook. For to violate one of these laws is to fail to do one's share for the common good, which is morally blameworthy and thus (given the retributivist's viewpoint) a wrong to which punishment is an appropriate response.

Two clarifications should be noted here. First, the retributivist is not committed to the view that there is some reason to punish by law *every* moral wrong. The retributivist is, rather, committed to the view that every moral wrong *the forbidding of which falls within the aims of law* is a fit object of punishment. It could be that there are some morally blameworthy acts that are not treated as offenses with respect to the common good, and thus not fit to be punished. For example: if one agrees that the aims of law should not comprehend prevention of harm to self, the retributivist can hold that it is no part of the law's concerns to punish such actions.

Second, the retributivist need not claim that punishment is a *mandatory* response to every such morally blameworthy act. There have been some retributivists who have made this very strong claim. On Immanuel Kant's retributivism, a society that decided to dissolve itself would be duty-bound before it did so to execute all convicted murderers:

the imposition of retribution was a matter of moral requirement that overruled competing social concerns.[14] But a sensible retributivism could reject this view, holding that punishment is an important objective of the law, though one that might have to be sacrificed in the face of competing political concerns. So while it might be the case that certain sorts of acts merit punishment, the difficulty or expense of prosecuting and punishing offenders might make it reasonable even for a retributivist to endorse a refusal to criminalize them. This does not turn the retributivist into a utilitarian: the *point* of punishment remains the backward-looking aim of responding to wrongful deeds. Its effect is to recognize that responding to wrongful deeds is an objective that can come into competition with other important objectives the law might pursue. (Here is an analogy. One might think that a citizen who performs a particularly heroic deed merits a public ceremony in his or her honor. But one might also think that whether giving a public ceremony in the citizen's honor is justified, overall, will depend on whether there are sufficient public funds to carry it out and what public projects must be put to the side if this ceremony is to take place. That does not make it any less the case that the point of the ceremony is to honor the citizen for the heroic deed.)

With respect to the question of the amount of punishment due for any given criminal offense, retributivists affirm a principle of proportionality in punishment. The claim is that the severity of the punishment should be proportioned to the gravity of the offense. There is, however, a great deal of disagreement and uncertainty as to how strongly this notion of proportion should be understood. On any view, the retributivist is committed to putting forward a rank ordering of punishments from less severe to more severe and to putting forward a rank ordering of crimes from less grave to more grave. The disagreements concern how much one can say about the proportion between crime and punishment that retributivism requires.

On a very strong view – the *lex talionis*, or "eye for an eye" standard – the severity of the punishment can be measured by the level of harm that it does to the punished, and the gravity of the criminal offense can be measured by the level of harm that the offense does to its victim. By measuring both the gravity of the offense and the severity of the punishment by a common standard – level of harm – one can interpret the proportionality requirement in an especially strong way: one can say that punishment should *match*, or be *equal to*, the crime.

But a little reflection shows that the "eye for an eye" standard is untenable. One difficulty is that the standard obviously fails if one allows that there can be crimes that do no harm: either because they are concerned with morals as such (see 3.4), or because, while they involve an unwillingness to do one's share for the common good, the failure to perform them does not generate any harm. (Does a failure to pay some share of my taxes actually *harm someone*, as opposed to simply taking unfair advantage of others?) Another difficulty is that there are crimes that generate equal levels of harm but which seem to involve differences in levels of blameworthiness that we recognize by assigning different punishments: intentional homicide is more blame-worthy than involuntary manslaughter, but the victims of these crimes end up just as dead, just as harmed. Another difficulty concerns attempts: often attempted crimes do no harm at all – the bullet flies by, unnoticed by the intended victim – but surely attempts call for *some* punishment. (Attempts are discussed in more detail below.) There is very little sense to be made of the idea that punishment should equal crime in this sense: blameworthiness of deed and severity of punish-ment have two different standards of measure, and as such cannot be considered equal or unequal to each other; that is simply a category mistake.

By contrast: on a very weak view, all that the retributive propor-tionality requirement mandates is that less grave crimes receive less severe punishments and more grave crimes more severe punishments. Imagine two columns labeled "possible crimes" and "possible punish-ments," and under each column one lists possible crimes from least to most grave and possible punishments from least to most severe. Now suppose that one draws a line from each crime to the punishment that one proposes. Under this weaker reading of the proportionality require-ment, all that is required is that *no lines cross or touch*. If crime C2 is more grave than crime C1, then the punishment assigned to C2 must be more severe than the punishment assigned to C1 (see figure 4.1).

This version of the proportionality requirement does seem too weak, though. This proportionality requirement would be satisfied if all of the punishments were no more severe than, say, a $1000 fine and 30 days in jail – so long as the worst crimes were assigned the $1000 fine and 30 days in jail and lesser crimes assigned punishments less severe than this. It is possible, that is, to have actually assigned punishments that cluster in a relatively small space in one's array of possible punishments,

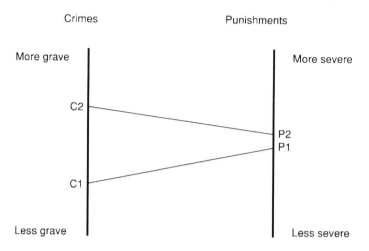

Figure 4.1

and for these clusters to permit very mild punishments to be imposed for very extreme crimes (see figure 4.2). Correspondingly, it is possible to have a cluster that occurs relatively high in the scale of possible punishments, with the result that these clusters permit very extreme punishments for fairly trivial offenses. So one can, consistent with the requirement of weak proportionality, assign 10 years in prison for the most minor offense, so long as every other offense received more than 10 years in prison as its assigned punishment. It is possible, that is, to

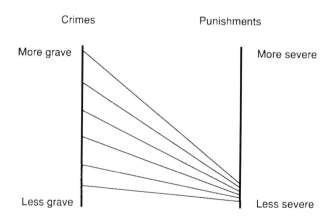

Figure 4.2

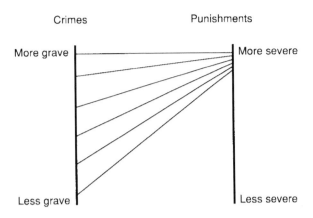

Figure 4.3

have actually assigned punishments that cluster in a relatively small space in one's array of possible punishments, and for these clusters to permit very severe punishments to be imposed for very minor crimes (see figure 4.3).

The very weak interpretation is correct as a constraint on retributivist proportionality, but it cannot serve all by itself as what proportionality requires. It seems inescapable that the retributivist has to say that we can somehow *see*, within a certain range of precision, that certain levels of punishment are *fitting* for certain crimes. While an adequate grasp of the nature of the criminal act in question will be necessary for one to come to such a judgment about a fitting punishment for it – one will want to know the details of the *mens rea* and *actus reus* conditions as well as whether there are any excuses or mitigating factors – determining the fitting level of punishment will not be an exercise of social scientific expertise but an exercise of moral insight and judgment. Compare, for example, the task of determining what punishment fits a crime with the task of determining what sort of grateful response one should show if a stranger does one a good turn at a sacrifice to himself or herself. We make such judgments in part by considering the nature of the good deed done and the intentions behind it; our judgments are tempered by facts about what we can afford to do in return; but there is also a more basic assessment as to what would be too much or too little to do. If one is saved from having to walk home on a rainy night by an acquaintance who goes out of her way to drive one home, it would be too little to just say "Thanks!" while later driving on past the next time one sees her in a bind ("I don't owe her anything; after all, I said thanks") while it would be too much to show up at her doorstep with a new car for her ("I actually am quite wealthy, and can afford this: thanks!"). The retributivists must rest on this sort of insight into what is fitting if they are to provide an account of what punishments should be assigned to different crimes. (More on the possibility of this sort of insight below.)

Having briefly discussed the retributivist accounts of when to criminalize and at what levels punishment should be fixed, let us turn to the question of the point of punishing. Here the backward-looking character of retributivism is its basic liability. Everyone can see why the utilitarian rationale is plausible: our practical lives are tremendously future-directed; we characteristically deliberate in terms of the future benefits and burdens promised by the various courses of action available to us. Why, then, should we focus on the past? Why should we not treat what occurs in the past as a bygone, and turn our attention (as the utilitarian suggests) to the future consequences of punishing or failing to punish?

There are different retributivist responses available. But it is characteristic of retributivist defenses to begin with a "softening up" maneuver. The softening up maneuver is to point out that backward-looking action is not at all an unusual feature of our practical lives. We return the $50 because we *promised* to do so. We give someone a ride home because they *gave* us a ride home last week. We attend a funeral because a friend *died*. These are all actions that are on their faces oriented to some *past event*: a promise, a good deed, a friend's death. One could try to come up with forward-looking rationales for them: perhaps one will not be trusted again if one breaks the promise, or one will not receive good turns in the future if one shows oneself to be an ingrate (or one will discourage others from doing good turns if their kindness is not requited), or going to a funeral is a way to ease suffering and sorrow by being in the company of others. Retributivists suggest that these explanations are often false (sometimes the good consequences will not follow, and can be seen not to follow, without eliminating the reason we have to act in these ways) and even oftener strained (even when the consequences do follow, they seem rather awkward accounts of why we ought to keep our promises, act gratefully, or attend memorial services).

To say that backward-looking action can be reasonable is not to say that *this* backward-looking action, that of punishing transgressions, is reasonable. Punishment is subject to challenge not only because it is backward-looking but because it involves the infliction of harm. Kant, defender of classic philosophical retributivism, wholly rejects utilitarian defenses of the practice: "Woe to him who crawls through the windings of eudaemonism" in order to mold punishment for social purposes,[15] he writes, and as we saw above, his retributivism is striking for its unwillingness to be tempered by considerations of other social goods. His view is that the imposition of punishment is a strict matter of justice, a basic requirement of political right, "so that each has done to him what his deeds deserve."[16]

The retributivist might see the principle that wrongdoers ought to suffer for their deeds as a fundamental principle of right. This contrasts with the utilitarian view, which treats punishment as an implication of more fundamental principles concerning the promotion of good consequences. But it is not necessarily the worse for that: some principles have to be fundamental, on pain of a vicious regress in the derivation of principles. The question is, then, how we can offer evidence for the correctness of this fundamental principle to those who would doubt it.

There are a number of ways to try to do this. One is simply to appeal to the sorts of cases that I used above in discussing worries about utilitarianism: is it not clear in these cases that even where further good consequences are not to be had, punishment is a worthwhile thing to do? Here the suggestion is that affirming the retributivist principle explains and systematizes our concrete, considered reflections about cases of justified punishment. Another important way to support the retributivist principle has been suggested by Michael Moore. Imagine that *you* have committed a terrible deed. How would you view yourself in retrospect? Would you not think of yourself as responsible for your crime and *guilty, worthy of punishment*, for it? If you do think of yourself in this way, why would you not extend your judgment of guilt to all similarly situated people who commit such crimes?[17]

So one way for the retributivist to answer the question about the point of punishment is to say that the imposition of harm in response to moral wrongdoing is itself a fundamental demand of justice, not derived from other, more fundamental moral principles. Even if we grant the retributivists this view, they must still explain why they are so concerned to act to implement a fundamental demand of justice.

After all, if the retributivist is right, there can be a point to punishing even if it does not thereby improve overall social well-being. Is it really the role of a legal system to attempt to implement "cosmic justice," even when so doing will not improve the lives of the citizens living under it?[18] It seems to me that this is yet another point where the discussions of the last chapter on the aims of law take center stage. If the law's aims are restricted to promoting the welfare of its subjects, then even if the retributivist's basic principle is correct, it is not part of the appropriate aims of law to realize retributive justice as such. On the other hand, if the common good of the political community can include what I called "ideals" (3.4) – objectives worth pursuing even apart from their promoting people's well-being – then it seems plausible that *realizing the demands of retributive justice* could be an ideal worth pursuing by law.

There are other ways to defend the retributivist principle other than treating retribution as a basic demand of justice. Another way to defend it is by making a distinction between action that aims to *promote* a good and action that aims to *express the value of* some good. To provide a sick friend with medicine is to promote a good: it is to act to bring about the friend's good health. To mourn after a friend's death is to express the value of a good: it is to express the value of what one, and the world, lost when the friend died. One might claim that acts of gratitude are expressive: their justification comes not from the aim of making others willing to continue to benefit one, or from the aim of making others willing to confer benefits more generally; rather, the point is to mark symbolically the value of the gift and of one's relationship to the giver.

If one accepts that there is a category of action that is expressive of the good (and which is not reducible without remainder to action that promotes the good), then one might defend retributive accounts of punishment by reference to that category. When a justifiable legal duty is in place, it dictates what subjects must do in order to do their share with respect to the common good. But subjects sometimes flout these duties, and thus in some way fail with respect to the common good. Legal punishment could be justified as a way of expressing the value of the common good by setting outside the common good to some extent those that do not act responsibly toward it. To those who flout their duties with respect to the common good it is fitting that they are deprived of some share in that good – either by losing some of their wealth, or some of their liberty, or their citizenship, or their very lives.[19] Note that whether one accepts the traditional principle of desert or the expressive view as the basis for retributivism, one is arguing that punishment is important because of the common good: either because punishment realizes justice, which is an aspect of the common good, or because punishment expresses the value of the common good by depriving criminals of some share in it.

The defense of the point of retribution is controversial in a way that defense of the point of promoting the social good is not, and it is thus clear that from the start the retributivist takes on an argumentative burden that the utilitarian does not. The retributivists' best hope, then, is that they can make the case for that principle in at least a minimally plausible way, and then show that retributivism better accounts for our considered judgments about punishment than utilitarianism does. Since many of the plausible criticisms of utilitarianism are built around the way that utilitarianism can endorse punishments out of step with the intuitive gravity of the criminal offense, it seems that retributivism can claim a victory on this score. But it must be noted that there are very pressing questions to be dealt with concerning our judgments of proportionality between crime and punishment.

We considered above the retributivist notion of proportionality, and how it is to be understood. But notice that we assumed at the outset that we could construct a scale of offenses from most to least grave and a scale of punishments from most to least severe. If there is a problem of incommensurability that rears its head in dealing with utilitarian calculation, there is such a problem here as well. For, first, punishments of different kinds -- deprivations of wealth, liberty, life; inflictions of pain or wounds -- would have to be assessed alongside each other, and it is unclear by what scale such assessments are to be made. Second, offenses must be placed on a common scale, but we are dealing with a tremendous variety of different factors. Of those crimes that cause harm, some cause physical, others emotional, others proprietary, others financial harm: how do these types of harm get weighed against each other in determining the gravity of the offense? Some crimes cause harm to others, some may be failures to fulfill obligations, some may involve unfairness, some may be straight immoralities: how do these various rationales weigh against each other in determining the gravity of the offense? Some crimes are not entirely excused but mitigated by factors like duress or inadequate deliberation: how far should these be factored in the determination of the gravity of the offense?

It might be pointed out that we *do* make such assessments, regardless of the theoretical problems that we might have in understanding how the various factors enter into these judgments. That is true, and it is possible that these judgments are well-founded. But there is no use pretending that there is not a deep mystery here. We lack much insight as to how we go about ranking the gravity of offenses when the various factors pull against each other; we lack much insight as to how we go about ranking the severity of punishments when they are of such different kinds; and we lack much insight as to how we go about pairing up any particular punishment with any particular criminal offense.

Retributivists charge utilitarians with relying on vague and uncertain estimates of the results of introducing various schemes of criminal law, whereas utilitarians charge retributivists with relying on mysterious intuitions to determine the assignment of punishments to crimes. It seems to me that they are both right. How punishment can be rationally assigned to crime is on either view a very puzzling matter indeed.

4.4 Justification and Excuse

Suppose that you are charged with having committed a crime, say, trespassing. Suppose that the criminal law forbids one from knowingly entering without permission onto another's property, and subjects those who violate this norm to a fine and/or imprisonment. Under what conditions should you be found guilty and punished for this crime? Under what conditions should you be found not guilty and remain unpunished?

Our discussion of *actus reus* and *mens rea* earlier in this chapter (4.2) provides a couple of clear guidelines by which one can show that one clearly should not be found guilty of this criminal offense. If your body never was on the other person's property, or if your body was on the other person's property, but you had permission to be there, then there was no *actus reus*: there was no criminal behavior. If your body was on the other person's property without permission, but you were carried and dumped there while asleep, or you sleepwalked there, or mad scientists forcibly fitted your muscles up with electrodes and marched you over there by remote control, then there was no *actus reus*: there was no voluntariness.

Another way to establish that you are not guilty is to show that you lack the guilty mind that is a necessary element of the crime in question. In the crime of criminal trespass, it is essential to the crime that one knowingly performs the *actus reus* – that is, one must know that the property belongs to another. Suppose, for example, that you have been walking down the road on a dark and foggy evening, and you come to a fence. It looks like the fence that surrounds your property, so you decide to climb the fence and take a shortcut to your home. It turns out, though, that you have climbed the neighbor's fence and entered onto the neighbor's property. You are not guilty of criminal trespass: for while you chose to enter onto property that was owned and fenced off by another, you did not choose *to enter onto another's property*. You made a simple mistake of fact, and since the *mens rea* element of criminal trespass requires that one knowingly enter another's property, you can sincerely claim to be not guilty of the offense.

The most straightforward ways to show that one is not guilty of a crime is to show that one of the constitutive features of the crime is absent. But this is not the only way. To show that there is a statute that defines the *actus reus* and *mens rea* for a given crime, and to show that a criminal defendant both possessed the defined *mens rea* and performed the defined *actus reus*, are not together sufficient to show that one is culpable for a given offense. For there are well-established so-called "affirmative defenses" that one can employ even in such situations. The idea is that there are cases in which one can satisfy the conditions that on their face establish one's deed as criminal but nevertheless be unworthy of, not deserving, legal punishment.

There are two sorts of affirmative defenses, justifications and excuses, and both of them present philosophical puzzles. "Justification" and "excuse" as used in this legal context actually track fairly closely our ordinary uses of those terms. To say that one's act is justified is to say that it was the right, or at least not a wrong, act. To say that one's act is excused is to say that even if it was a wrong act, the agent is not to blame (or at least not as much to blame) for performing it. Recall that it is essential to punishment that punishment condemns the agent as performer of the criminal act. It is clear why both justifications and excuses render one unfit for punishment: in justification, the claim is

133

that the act is not to be condemned; in excuse, the claim is that even if the act is to be condemned, the agent who performed it is not to be condemned.

The general structure of all justification in law appeals to necessity, or lesser evil.[20] The idea is that although one has violated the letter of the law, one nevertheless is right to do so because in the particular case at hand it would be a lesser evil to break the law than to adhere to it. Suppose, for example, that I am walking down a road with my daughter, who takes it in her head to climb the neighbor's fence and play on the neighbor's property. She promptly falls into a well. If I enter the property to save her, then I am technically in violation of the law of criminal trespass. I am voluntarily entering my neighbor's clearly fenced-in property, and I am clearly doing so knowingly and willingly. So, on its face, it seems that I am guilty of criminal trespass. But the defense of necessity is available to me: I can claim that even if my trespassing on my neighbor's land is an evil, it would be a greater evil for me to let my daughter drown in the well while I seek permission to enter.

The other commonly cited justification defense is that of self-defense, but self-defense is probably best understood simply as a relatively easily codifiable case of necessity. It is a lesser evil to inflict harm on an aggressor than to suffer evil at the hands of that aggressor. This seems plausible enough, though it should be noted that there are interesting questions as to how far the self-defense justification extends. Must one be required to retreat from the attacker if possible? (Even if one is on one's own land? Even if one thinks that one might stand a better chance by sticking and fighting?) What sort of constraints is one under with respect to the way that one responds in self-defense? (Must one proportion one's violence against the attacker to the level of harm that one anticipates from the attacker?) May one do harm to another only to defend one's own body, or also to defend one's own property? If so, of what sorts? (May one shoot a mugger who is demanding one's *Philosophy of Law* book? May one shoot a mugger who is escaping with one's *Philosophy of Law* book?)

The general structure of the justification defense is both tremendously commonsensical and tremendously puzzling. It is tremendously commonsensical in virtue of the fact that rules are always coarse-grained, and lawmakers would have a very difficult time writing into them all of the exceptions to them that they think justified and moreover, even if they were able to manage the task, the resulting rule would probably be so cumbersome that it would be not very helpful for purposes of day-to-day living. Better to have a simple rule of trespass to guide folks' conduct, recognizing that as a matter of necessity it may be right to violate the letter of the rule. It is, however, tremendously puzzling in that it seems that every conscientious would-be lawbreaker would see himself or herself as able to use the justification defense. If I think that a law is mistaken or overly restrictive, and I form the (conscientious) opinion that it is not for the best, then I may very well form the opinion that it is a lesser evil for me to break this law than to abide by it. There are many criminals, of course, who are simply unconcerned as to whether their conduct is justified in such a way. But it would seem strange that conscientious criminals ipso facto believe themselves to have a legal defense.

There are a couple of typical qualifications on the necessity defense that narrow its scope somewhat and lessen the worry of overly broad use of necessity. One qualification is sometimes put in terms of the imminence of the danger to be averted – that the evil to be avoided by lawbreaking is temporally very near. Better, I think, to put it in terms of the lack of availability to recourse within the law, whether by pursuing a legal means to avoiding the evil or by asking lawmakers to provide an exception to the rule or by asking someone else, who is able to prevent the evil legally, to do so. The other qualification is that, as the Model Penal Code puts it,[21] "a legislative purpose to exclude the justification claimed does not plainly appear."[22] This limits the defense further. The idea is that if it is clear that the legislature meant to disallow the defense in the sort of case in which one wishes to invoke it, the defense must fail. If the legislature lays down a rule "no use of marijuana," and it is plain that the activity that one wishes to undertake is a clear instance of what the legislature meant to rule out, then the defense must fail. Even if one's considered opinion is that overall it is better that one violates the law by smoking the joint than it would be for one to adhere to the law's dictate on the matter, one cannot use necessity, because it is just this sort of case on which the legislature expressed a clear view when it outlawed marijuana use.

How should we make sense of these qualifications, and of the necessity defense generally? The necessity defense was well-established even prior to its being codified in statute law, so we should not say simply that "this is the law," and there's little more to be said. Rather, we should be looking for an account of why we would expect a system of law – a set of rules for use by rational beings like us – to include a defense of that form.

There are a couple of possibilities. We might make sense of it by treating necessity as falling out of generally sound *interpretive* legal practice. Above (2.4) we noted that when one lays down a rule that another is to x one need not be interpreted to mean that, in every imaginable circumstance, one is to x. When I tell my child that she is to stop before crossing the street, I do not have in mind the case in which she is being chased by a pack of rabid dogs. My rule covers the normal cases, not necessarily the bizarre ones. When there is a strange case in which the rule I lay down clearly undercuts my very purposes in rule-making, then my child is a better interpreter of my will by recognizing that the rule is not meant to have her stop to be attacked by dogs than she would be by stupidly adhering to a literal reading of it. Understood along these lines, the necessity defense piggybacks on proper interpretation of legal norms: to claim necessity is to claim that, properly interpreted, the law does not in fact forbid the action that it might seem on its face to forbid.

There is another possibility. Recognition of the necessity defense might be seen as a necessary correlate to treating law as authoritative. If law aspires to be authoritative, then it must present itself as providing decisive reasons for compliance (0.2.2). But the point in necessity cases is that adherence to the letter of the law is not backed by decisive reasons, because there are such weighty evils that attend such adherence. In order for the law to maintain its general claim to authority, it must recognize that in cases in which there are very weighty evils that would attend compliance, exceptions must be allowed to its general norms. Otherwise the law is demanding that people do what it is obvious that they clearly lack adequate reason to do, and thus is making a mockery of its claim to authority.

When one offers an excuse for one's conduct, on the other hand, one does not claim that one's action was somehow not really wrong; one admits that it was wrong while claiming that nevertheless one is not to be blamed. So one allows that one performed the forbidden act with the requisite guilty state of mind, but one claims that nevertheless one should be excused as not really blameworthy.

The most famous excuse for criminal conduct is insanity, but it is only in a subset of cases where insanity is successful invoked that we must think of it as an excuse. The earliest formulation of the insanity rule, the M'Naghten rule (1843),[23] allows one to offer as a defense to a charge of criminal conduct that one was so incapacitated by a "defect of reason" or "disease of the mind" that one does not understand the nature of the act or the act's wrongfulness. So, if by virtue of a mental disease or defect one believes that one is chopping celery but one is in fact chopping up another human being, the M'Naghten rule allows for a verdict of not guilty. Or, if one believes that one is chopping up another human being but by virtue of a mental disease or defect believes that the act is perfectly permissible, then the M'Naghten rule allows for a verdict of not guilty.

A little reflection makes clear that the effect of the M'Naghten rule is simply to make clear that insanity can be used as a way of showing that one lacked the necessary *mens rea* to be guilty of a crime. The M'Naghten rule appeals to the cognitive deficits that can result from mental illness, and notes that those cognitive deficits can prevent the subject from being guilty at all of the offense in question. One who chops up a person thinking the person to be a large stalk of celery is no more guilty of intentional killing than one who accidentally shoots a person, thinking that person to be a deer; neither killer has the requisite *mens rea*. While the characteristic rule is that persons are presumed to know the law that binds them, the other branch of the M'Naghten rule allows as a defense the fact that the law might be unknown or unappreciated by the insane person. The point is that under the M'Naghten rule we should not say that the person who satisfies its conditions has committed a crime but has an excuse; we should say that such a person has committed no crime at all.

The M'Naghten rule focuses on cognitive deficits resulting from mental disease or defect. But mental illness can generate deficiencies that are *volitional* rather than cognitive, and it is here that there is the possibility for mental illness to count as an excuse to the commission of a crime. One might be aware that an act is a crime, and perform it, without being able to help performing it. Mental illness can impair one's capacity to choose what one knows to be the right thing to do. Thus the American Law Institute's proposed insanity rule, which was largely adopted in American jurisdictions in order to deal with the deficiencies of the M'Naghten rule, holds that one is not to be held responsible if "at the time of such conduct as a result of mental disease or defect he lacks substantial capacity either to appreciate the wrongfulness of his conduct or *to conform his conduct to the requirements of the law.*"[24]

It seems correct to think that the failure of a person to have substantial capacity to conform his or her conduct to the requirements of the law limits that person's blameworthiness, and thus should serve as an excuse for the commission of the crime. To lack substantial capacity cannot be simply to have no ability whatsoever to control one's ability to act. It is far from clear that any mental illness that still leaves one with the capacity to act voluntarily – remember that a voluntary act is essential to the *actus reus* requirement – leaves one utterly bereft of the capacity to control one's conduct. What lacking substantial capacity must be is to have terribly deficient or defective control over the way that one's desires translate into actions. This seems a likely result of certain mental illnesses, and performing a criminal act while in such a condition might be voluntary though not blameworthy.

Here is the rub. Lacking substantial capacity to conform one's conduct to the law seems also to be a condition that belongs to the very vicious. What makes people particularly vicious is that they lack substantial capacity to conform their conduct to correct standards; they are habituated to acting in ways that cause damage and suffering, and while we might grant that it is possible for them to act rightly, we would no more expect them to do so than we would expect the wolf to refrain from eating the lamb. So we have a puzzle. The insane are not to be punished because they lack substantial capacity to conform their conduct to the law. The very vicious also lack substantial capacity to conform their conduct to the law. But the very vicious are surely just those persons whose deeds most merit punishment. We do not want our basis for excluding the insane from punishment also to exclude the very bad. (In the Model Penal Code, the clause that offers the excuse of insanity is followed by a clause that notes that "the terms 'mental disease or defect' do not include an abnormality manifested only by repeated criminal or otherwise anti-social conduct."[25] It seems clear that the point of this restriction is to make certain that the sick are distinguished from the bad. But the question is by what rationale that distinction is to be made.)

There are a number of other excuses that can be offered against criminal culpability. Immaturity is one excuse (four-year-olds cannot be expected to control their conduct to fit the law's demands). Duress – that one has reasons to violate the law that, though not justifying the action, ordinary folks would not be able to resist – can serve as an excuse as well. In the cases of insanity, immaturity, and duress, it is worthwhile to note the similarity that all of these sources of excuse are, so to speak, *internal* to the agent – it is a fact about the agent that makes the agent less worthy of punishment, whether completely or partially. The agent is too young to control his or her conduct; the agent is too sick to control his or her conduct; the agent is under too much pressure to control his or her conduct.

These internal sources of excuse make some sense on both a retributivist and a utilitarian conception of punishment. For, after all, on retributivism the whole point of punishment is to respond to blameworthiness: and it is clear how these internal factors can remove or lessen blameworthiness. On the utilitarian point of view, the main aim of the criminal law is to deter wrongdoing: and these deficiencies make people unable to be deterred by stripping them of their capacity to regulate their own conduct. We can conclude our discussion of excuses, and of the criminal law, by asking whether something *external* to the agent can count as an excuse – in particular, whether the agent was unsuccessful in realizing his or her criminal objective.

It is a common feature of systems of criminal law that attempts are punished less severely than successful crimes. In constructing a system of criminal law, the fact that a crime was attempted but was unsuccessful is not treated as an excuse, whether complete or partial. But the effect is precisely the same. To treat attempts as systematically less worthy of punishment is to treat a failure to succeed in bringing about one's criminal objective as mitigating one's blameworthiness. But it is extremely difficult to see why such failure mitigates blameworthiness.

Consider the following scenario. There is a very unpopular politician giving an address in a public square, and (independently) a half-dozen would-be assassins have converged on the area in order to kill her. Each plans to do the deed at precisely 12 noon. One of the assassins, Ms Badluck, is an excellent shot, but as she fires, there is a particularly strong gust of wind and the bullet misses its target by no more than a few inches. Another of the assassins, Mr Badaim, is a terrible shot; he sets up with a rifle, fires, and misses by 20 yards. Another of the assassins, Ms Badgun, sets up with a rifle and pulls the trigger, but the gun jams. Its firing mechanism had not been properly cleaned; it was pretty much inevitable that in its grimy condition it was going to jam when the trigger was squeezed. Ms Badgun attempts to clean the firing mechanism, but does not manage to do so. Another of the assassins, Mr Forgetful, sets up with an unloaded rifle, having forgotten to load it. Mr Forgetful aims and pulls the trigger; upon hearing the disappointing "click," he sets himself to the task of loading the weapon, but does not do so in time. Another of the assassins, Ms Clueless, sets up with an unloaded rifle, because she does not know that a rifle requires bullets; she thinks that rifles work a bit like ray guns in science fiction movies. (She has never seen a bullet come out of a gun, after all; she just hears a bang and then sees the effect on its target.) So she takes aim, preparing to kill the politician, and pulls the trigger. Upon hearing the disappointing "click," she sets up again and pulls the trigger; nothing happens. Another of the assassins, Mr Thoughtrays, is of the opinion that he is able to produce deadly thought rays by looking intently at a victim and directing lethal thoughts toward him or her. (Once he had visited a very sick aunt in the hospital, and the aunt had been rude, and Mr Thoughtrays had had such thoughts; the aunt died the next day. So he had, he thought, *evidence* that he could do this.) At the noon hour he looked directly at the politician, and sent a stream of death-dealing thoughts directly at her, sure that this would be sufficient to end her life.

By 12.02 p.m. all six of the aforementioned would-be assassins have tried and failed to kill the politician. At 12.03 p.m. Ms Efficient, a seventh would-be assassin, fires at the politician and kills her.

Two questions: first, should all six of the failed assassins receive a punishment equal to that of Ms Efficient, whose act was successful? And, second, if one distinguishes between the failures and the success, should all of the failed assassins be punished equally?

The Model Penal Code says no to both questions. On its view, a failed attempt to commit a capital crime or felony of the *first* degree counts as a felony of the *second* degree – failure amounts to an automatic lessening of the seriousness of the crime. And among attempts:

> If the particular conduct charged to constitute a criminal attempt ... is so inherently unlikely to result or culminate in the commission of a crime that neither such conduct nor the actor presents a public danger warranting the grading of such offense ... the Court shall exercise its power ... to enter judgment and impose sentence for a crime of lower grade or degree or, in extreme cases, may dismiss the prosecution.[26]

Failure to succeed automatically reduces the grade of this homicide attempt from first to second degree, and if the attempt was itself tremendously lacking in dangerousness, the judge has the discretion to lower its grade even further or even to dismiss the charges. So while Ms Efficient is guilty of first-degree murder, the other six can be guilty of no more than a felony of the second degree; and among those six, if any of their conduct seems particularly lacking in dangerousness – Mr Thoughtrays's conduct comes to mind – then the Code allows discretion to lessen or (more likely) even eliminate the charges against him.

The law generally treats unsuccessful attempts as less worth punishing, and the Model Penal Code does not depart from this common treatment. But it is not at all obvious that this differential treatment is justifiable. What distinguishes Ms Efficient from the other would-be assassins is just that she was successful and they were not. But this seems to be relevant neither from a retributivist nor a utilitarian point of view. If one is a retributivist, the relevant question is whether an agent is more morally blameworthy for a successful attempt than for a failed one; and it seems that the answer to this question is no. All seven of the would-be assassins constructed a plan whose outcome was the death of the politician. Each, acting with the beliefs available to him or her, selected a way of proceeding that was likely to be effective in ending the politician's life, and that way of proceeding was selected just because it would end the politician's life. None is morally less blameworthy in his or her action than Ms Efficient is. If one is a utilitarian, the relevant question is whether it serves deterrence to treat successful attempts more severely than unsuccessful ones; and it seems that the answer to this question is no. While one might like to be able to focus one's deterrent efforts on preventing successful crimes (who cares about unsuccessful ones?), the obvious point is that from the would-be criminal's point of view, the criminal is set on making the act a successful one: the criminal never faces a choice of the form "Well, let's see: I am set on committing a murder . . . should I commit a successful one or an unsuccessful one?"

The law generally treats goofy or utterly ineffective attempts as less worthy of punishment than more probably effective attempts, and the Model Penal Code does not depart from this common treatment. But, again, it is not at all obvious that this differential treatment is justifiable. From a retributivist point of view, again, it seems to make no difference to the blameworthiness of the actors that Mr Thoughtrays has made a very bad mistake about the effectiveness of mental death rays or that Ms Clueless is deeply confused about the killing power of an unloaded rifle; each is just as set on killing as Ms Badluck and Mr Badaim were, and similarly carried out the steps of their plan to kill. From a utilitarian point of view, it might seem more important to deter dangerous attempts over nondangerous attempts. While one might like to be able to focus one's deterrent efforts on preventing dangerous attempts (who cares about innocuous ones?), the obvious point is that from the would-be criminal's point of view, the criminal is set on making the act a dangerous one: the criminal never faces a choice of the form "Well, let's see: I am set on committing a murder . . . should I use dangerous or nondangerous means?"

Indeed, the very appeal to the notion that the conduct of an attempt must present a danger is rife with puzzles based on how the attempt is described. If the dangerousness of an act is determined by the level of risk associated with acts of that kind, then we have to face the fact that attempts can be described at different levels of generality, and each may have a different level of risk associated with it. So, for example, how shall we describe Mr Thoughtrays's act: as "using thoughtrays to bring about another's death" or "attempting to bring about another's death"? Surely he was doing both: but while the former act is not very risky, the latter act may well be. (A pretty high percentage of acts that are attempts to bring about another's death cause danger; a vanishingly low percentage of acts that are attempts to use thoughtrays to bring about another's death cause danger.) Again, for example, how shall we describe Ms Badgun's act: as "using a rifle with a jammed firing mechanism to bring about another's death" or as "using a rifle to bring about another's death" or "attempting to bring about another's death"? The first has a vanishingly low probability of causing harm; the second has a very high probability of causing harm; the third a probability in between. It matters which level of description one uses, but we lack criteria to determine which level of description counts.

For Further Reading

Joel Feinberg's "The Expressive Function of Punishment" is a very important account of how the notion of punishment is to be analyzed; it appears in his *Doing and Deserving* (Princeton, NJ: Princeton University

Press, 1970), pp. 95–118, and also in a useful collection of philosophical, legal, and sociological work on punishment, R. A. Duff's and David Garland's *A Reader on Punishment* (Oxford: Oxford University Press, 1994). For a defense of a utilitarian account of punishment, see Richard Brandt, "The Utilitarian Theory of Criminal Justice," in *Ethical Theory* (Englewood Cliffs, NJ: Prentice-Hall, 1959), pp. 489–96, and for a related economic justification, see Richard Posner, *Economic Analysis of Law*, 6th edn (New York: Aspen, 2003 [first published 1973]), Chapter 7. For an extended defense of a retributivist account, see Michael S. Moore, *Placing Blame* (Oxford: Clarendon Press, 1997). There are accounts of punishment that do not fit easily in the retributivist/utilitarian framework: see, for example, Warren Quinn's classic "The Right to Threaten and the Right to Punish," *Philosophy & Public Affairs* 14 (1985), pp. 327–73, which argues that the right to punish is grounded in a prior right to threaten with evil those who are proposing to violate one's rights.

For an exploration of the central ideas of criminal law, see George Fletcher's *Rethinking Criminal Law* (Boston, MA: Little, Brown, 1978) and his *Basic Concepts of Criminal Law* (New York: Oxford University Press, 1998). For an attempt to provide a more systematic account of the various forms of *mens rea*, see Larry Alexander's "Insufficient Concern: A Unified Conception of Criminal Culpability," *California Law Review* 88 (2000), pp. 931–64; for his account of the difficulties surrounding the necessity defense, see his "Lesser Evils: A Closer Look at the Paradigmatic Justification," *Law and Philosophy* 24 (2005), pp. 611–43. R. A. Duff offers a treatment of the problem of attempts in his *Criminal Attempts* (Oxford: Clarendon Press, 1996). Further overviews of the state of the philosophy of criminal law can be found in Larry Alexander, "The Philosophy of Criminal Law," in Jules Coleman and Scott Shapiro (eds.), *Oxford Handbook of Jurisprudence and Philosophy of Law* (Oxford: Oxford University Press, 2002), pp. 815–67, and Douglas Husak, "Criminal Law Theory," in Martin P. Golding and William A. Edmundson (eds.), *The Blackwell Guide to Philosophy of Law and Legal Theory* (Malden, MA: Blackwell, 2005), pp. 107–21.

Notes

1 There are some, and I mean a very few, crimes that do not include a *mens rea* element. For example, some jurisdictions define a crime of selling alcohol to a minor in such a way that one is guilty for doing so even if one has taken reasonable steps to ensure that the purchaser is of age. But

there is nevertheless a *mens* element, even if the *mens* need not be *rea*, to these crimes: the agent must be shown to have intentionally sold the alcohol, even if the agent need not be shown to have done so with knowledge that (or in the absence of reasonable care to find out whether) the purchaser is a minor. As is clear, these crimes of strict liability are aberrations, and they should probably be understood as deviant cases of crimes.

2 See H. L. A. Hart, *Punishment and Responsibility* (Oxford: Oxford University Press, 1968), pp. 4–5.

3 363 U.S. 603 (1960).

4 Joel Feinberg, "The Expressive Function of Punishment," in *Doing and Deserving* (Princeton, NJ: Princeton University Press, 1970), pp. 95–118. Feinberg himself rejects the Court's argument in *Flemming v. Nestor*, though; he thinks that the law's punitive intent was clear.

5 Jeremy Bentham, *Introduction to the Principles of Morals and Legislation* (Buffalo, NY: Prometheus Books, 1988 [first published 1781]).

6 Bentham, *Introduction*, Chapter XIII, p. 170.

7 Ibid.

8 Ibid, p. 171.

9 See John Rawls, "Two Concepts of Rules," *Philosophical Review* 64 (1955), pp. 3–32.

10 501 U.S. 957 (1991).

11 For a critical discussion of recent arguments for such a deterrent effect, see Richard Berk, "New Claims about Execution and General Deterrence: Déjà Vu All Over Again?," *Journal of Empirical Legal Studies* 2 (2005), pp. 303–30.

12 See the highly amusing and persuasive article by Robert Bartels, "Capital Punishment: The Unexamined Issue of Special Deterrence," *Iowa Law Review* 68 (1983), pp. 601–7.

13 In Andrew von Hirsch, Anthony Bottoms, Elizabeth Burney, and P. O. Wikström, *Criminal Deterrence and Sentence Severity* (Oxford: Hart Publishing, 1999), von Hirsch and his co-authors suggest that current research indicates that while the increases in the certainty that a certain crime will be met with punishment generates deterrence, it is far from clear what deterrent effects are generated by making punishments more severe. It is impossible to read this account without being struck by how little we have to go on if we want to proceed in matters of punishment as strict utilitarians.

14 Immanuel Kant, *The Metaphysics of Morals*, trans. Mary Gregor (Cambridge, UK: Cambridge University Press, 1996 [first published 1797]), pp. 104–9.

15 Ibid., p. 105.

16 Ibid., p. 106.
17 Michael S. Moore, *Placing Blame* (Oxford: Clarendon Press, 1997), pp. 144–9.
18 See, for example, Russ Shafer-Landau, "The Failure of Retributivism," *Philosophical Studies* 82 (1996), pp. 289–316, particularly pp. 294–8.
19 See Mark C. Murphy, *Natural Law in Jurisprudence and Politics* (New York: Cambridge University Press, 2006), pp. 152–62.
20 For a helpful discussion, see Larry A. Alexander, "Lesser Evils: A Closer Look at the Paradigmatic Justification," *Law and Philosophy* 24 (2005), pp. 611–43.
21 The Model Penal Code is a suggested reformulation of the criminal law constructed by the American Law Institute. It was completed in 1962. It has no binding legal force on its own, but has been influential in the drafting of statutes by state legislatures and in courts' restatements of legal rules.
22 Model Penal Code, §3.02.
23 So called because it arose in a British case involving one Daniel M'Naghten, who killed the Prime Minister's private secretary (by mistake, in the belief that he was killing Robert Peel, the Prime Minister) because M'Naghten's mental illness led him to believe that Peel was conspiring against him. The House of Lords thus had occasion to offer a ruling on the conditions under which persons "afflicted with an insane delusion" were criminally responsible for their acts.
24 Model Penal Code, §4.01, italics added.
25 Ibid., §4.01.
26 Ibid., §5.05.

Chapter 5

The Nature and Aims
of Tort Law

5.1 Torts and Crimes

The previous chapter was concerned with crimes, violations of authoritative legal standards for which punishment is an authorized response. This chapter is concerned with torts. To commit a tort is also to violate a legal standard, but the authorized response to a tort is (typically) the payment of damages:[1] victims of torts are authorized to seek recompense from the violator of the standard (the "tortfeasor") in compensation for the injury suffered by the victim.

Torts can be distinguished into three types: intentional torts, torts of negligence, and torts of strict liability. The world of torts revolves around torts of negligence, and I will take this type as the paradigm for discussion, returning to intentional torts and torts of strict liability at the end of the chapter.

5.2 Torts and Damages

Torts are to damages what crimes are to punishment: just as no violation of an authoritative legal standard counts as a crime unless there is punishment authorized for it, no violation of an authoritative legal standard counts as a tort unless damages are authorized for it.

The elements of a tort – of a tort of negligence, that is – are four, and these elements must be related to one another in a very specific way.[2] Torts are always relations between parties: A commits a tort against B. (While one can argue about whether there ought to be victimless crimes, there is no incoherence in the very idea of a victimless crime;

a victimless tort, on the other hand, is a contradiction in terms.) The first of the elements that is necessary for a tort, the element of *duty*, is that A has a duty of care with respect to B: that is, A is under some legal duty to show due care with respect to B's interests. The second element that is necessary for a tort, the element of *breach*, is that A did not live up to this duty: A somehow failed to show due care with respect to B's interests. The third element, that of *loss*, is that B must have suffered an injury, some setback to B's interests. The fourth element, that of *cause*, is that (in the relevant sense) A's failure to perform A's duty of due care with respect to B caused B's loss.

All of these elements must be present in order for there to be a tort of negligence. If A has no duty to show care for B's interests, then even if A's failure to look out for B causes harm to B, A has committed no tort and thus B cannot recover damages. If A has a duty to show care for B's interests and does not fail in that care, then even if A's actions cause B to suffer injury, A has committed no tort and thus B cannot recover damages. If A has a duty to show care for B's interests and fails in that care, and B ends up suffering a loss, A has committed no tort unless A's failure caused the loss to B. (If A is reckless with respect to B's safety – suppose that A drives at 100 miles per hour up and down the sidewalk in front of B's house – and B purely coincidentally slips on a banana peel and falls on the sidewalk and fractures his or her skull, A has committed no tort against B: even if A is negligent with respect to B, A's negligence did not cause B's loss.) And there can be no tort if B suffers no loss: there is no such thing as a tort without injury.

Damages are the payments that courts can require tortfeasors to pay to victims on account of their torts. Damages are characteristically sums of money. So if you have a duty to take reasonable care not to injure me, but you nevertheless drive too fast up and down my sidewalk, striking me and breaking my legs, I can file a complaint against you for having negligently injured me; the court, finding that your breach of a duty of due care toward me caused my injury, will require you to pay me a sum of money as damages.

We will proceed with a discussion of the philosophy of tort law in much the same way that we proceeded with a discussion of the philosophy of criminal law. We can first consider the very point of tort law: why require those that injure others through their negligence to pay damages? The answers, perhaps unsurprisingly, divide themselves in a way similar to the way that the classic answers to the problem of punishment divide themselves: some are forward-looking, emphasizing the way that the common good is better furthered by a tort regime, and some are backward-looking, suggesting that the common good includes in part intrinsically appropriate responses to injustice. We will then turn to a discussion of the various elements of the negligence tort – duty, breach, cause, and loss – and how our accounts of them should be shaped by our views on the point of tort law. We will conclude by considering intentional torts and torts of strict liability, considering how these are distinct from negligence torts and how their distinctive features are to be justified.

5.3 Economic and Justice Accounts of Negligence Torts

The basic structure of the negligence tort is that those who injure others through their negligence can be required by the courts to pay compensation for the losses caused by that negligence. As in the case of the criminal law, the most straightforward way to ask about the overall point or justification of such a scheme is to imagine it away and to ask how the common good is more poorly served by its absence. Why have such a system in place?

The central suggested answers to this question fall, like the central suggested answers to the question of punishment, into forward-looking and backward-looking camps. On one view, the point of the establishment of a tort system, and of the more specific rules within a particular tort system, is that the overall well-being is best promoted by the existence of those rules. On another view, the point of the establishment of a tort system, and of the more specific rules within a particular tort system, is that such rules express what justice and fairness require in response to the actions of tortfeasors and the corresponding losses of victims.

Begin with the forward-looking view. Here is one way of thinking about the justification for tort law. The tort of negligence is concerned not with intentional harm but with unintentional, but preventable, harm – accidents. Accidents are instances in which human well-being is set back, is lost. Either property is destroyed, or financial losses are sustained, or personal injuries incurred, or reputations sullied, or pain and suffering experienced – and all because someone failed to take care to prevent that setback from occurring. Accidents are thus, from the point of view of the common good, setbacks. Any scheme of rules that has the virtue of lessening the losses from accidents is, on its face, a good thing, to be adopted unless there are reasons to the contrary.

But there is a plausible argument to be made that in the absence of something like the negligence regime, there will be more accidents, and this will be costly with respect to the common good. Suppose, for example, that the owners of a factory know fully well that unless they take care not to dump pollutants from their factory into the river, the inhabitants of a village downstream are likely to suffer health problems. Disposing of the pollutants in an alternative way may be costly, though. And so long as the factory owners are for the most part motivated by their own economic advantage, they have reason to dump pollutants into the river rather than to dispose of them in the costlier but safer way. They have reason, that is, to *externalize* the costs of factory production, to impose those costs on others. This can cause grave setbacks to the common good. For it may be that the damage that these pollutants do to others will far outstrip the savings that the owners reap from dumping pollutants in the river. Given the dominance of self-interest as a motivation and the ability to externalize the costs of one's activities, one can see the beginnings of an argument for tort liability. If the factory owners were subject to paying compensation for all of the people whose health is damaged by their pollutant dumping, then they would have an incentive to take the extra measures to dispose of those pollutants safely. Tort law can thus be viewed as a mechanism to motivate otherwise undermotivated parties to prevent those accidents whose effect is to set back the common good.

While the idea that the internalization of costs provides some justification for tort law may be sound, the foregoing line of reasoning was profoundly challenged by the work of Ronald Coase, who argued that at least under certain ideal conditions (in particular, absence of transaction costs – we will discuss this below) there is no loss to efficiency by choosing to make the factory owners or the downstream inhabitants liable for paying the costs.[3] Suppose that we make the factory owners liable for the damages caused by that activity. Now, if the costs of not polluting are less than the costs of paying the downstream residents, then the factory owners will refrain from polluting, using an alternative means to dispose of the waste; if, however, the costs of paying the downstream residents for their loss of health is less than the cost of finding an alternative means of getting rid of the pollution, the factory owners will simply go on polluting and compensate the downstream residents for their health troubles. Suppose, on the other hand, that we simply let the costs fall on the downstream residents. If the cost to their health is greater than the cost of preventing the loss, the downstream residents will pay the factory owners to dispose of the pollution in an alternative way – will, in effect, strike a deal with the factory owners not to pollute. If the cost to their health is less than the cost of preventing the loss through not polluting, then the downstream residents will simply accept the loss. Under any of these scenarios, the outcome most favorable to the common good is reached.

To make this more concrete: suppose that polluting is free, whereas the alternative disposal method costs $1 million; if pollution occurs, then the 500 downstream residents will suffer $10,000 of health costs each. If the factory owners are liable for the costs of the pollution, then they will stop polluting and invest in the alternative method of waste disposal. If, on the other hand, the downstream residents must bear the costs, then they will pay the costs for the factory owners to install the alternative waste-disposal technology. On the other hand, suppose that polluting is free, whereas the alternative method costs $1 million; if the pollution occurs, then the 500 downstream residents will suffer $1,000 of health costs each. If the factory owners are liable for the costs of the pollution, then they will go on polluting, and compensate the downstream residents for their health troubles. If the downstream residents must bear the costs, then they will swallow those costs, it not being worth it to them to pay the factory owners to install the technology.

The interesting point of this story is this: under these idealized conditions, *if it is worth it to prevent the accident, then the accident will be prevented.* This might seem to kick the feet out from under the forward-looking argument for the tort system, which was predicated on the notion that imposing liability for negligent imposition of costs on others was the way to make sure that the level of accidents was lowered to its optimal level. And this would indeed be so, if our world were one in which the ideal conditions were realized: for these ideal conditions, the argument goes, guarantee efficient accident prevention. But that is not our world, for these ideal conditions are not realized. That does not mean that Coase's point about the irrelevance of liability rules from an efficiency standpoint is no longer of interest.

Rather, we can use Coase's point to guide the development of a system of tort rules whose outcome mimics the results that would occur under ideal conditions.[4]

What makes our usual conditions less than ideal, so that we can be pretty confident that our choice of liability rules will be relevant to the extent to which accidents are efficiently prevented? One difference is the existence of transaction costs. It is not as if the downstream residents must be one collective body that can simply write a check to the factory in order to get the pollution-prevention technology installed. There are costs involved in getting together, coming to an agreement, dividing up the payments, and so forth. And it is not as if the agreement between the factory owners and the residents will itself be an obviously costless process: for the factory owners will want to secure as high a payment as possible for installing the technology, while the residents will want to make as low a payment as possible. The factory owners will accept no less than the cost of the technology; the residents will pay no more than what they would have to pay in terms of health costs. In the space in between these two, there is room to bargain, and the process of bargaining may be costly. Another difference concerns information: the factory owners may have information about how to control pollution, and at what costs, that the residents do not have. The result of these idealization failures may well be that it does make a difference from the point of view of efficiency who initially is bound to deal with the accident costs. It may not be worth it for the residents to bear the costs of getting together to figure out what to do and to enter into a bargain with the factory owners, and thus the factory owners may go on polluting even if the costs of polluting overall are higher than the costs of installing the waste-disposal technology. The guarantee of an efficient accident-prevention outcome holds only if the parties involved are well-informed, rational, and are unburdened by transaction costs.

Given the departure from this ideal in everyday life, the forward-looking view suggests that tort liability be imposed in a way that enables the most efficient accident prevention – that is, it imposes liability for the cost of accidents in such a way that those who are in a better position to prevent those accidents efficiently have an incentive to do so.[5] If it seems unrealistic that the downstream residents will be able to get their act together sufficiently to reach a bargain with the factory owner in terms of pollution control, then it makes sense to impose liability for accidents on the factory owners: the factory owners, we might think, are in a better position to assess the relevant costs of accident occurrence or prevention and to decide whether to take steps to prevent the accident or to compensate the victims should an accident occur.

This way of looking at the justification of tort law is the hallmark of the law and economics movement, which has aimed both to understand the development of and to offer recommendations for the reform of tort law in economic terms. As Oliver Wendell Holmes wrote in 1897, "For the rational study of the law the black-letter man may be the man of the present, but the man of the future is the man of statistics and the master of economics."[6] It bears an obvious resemblance to utilitarianism as an account of punishment: the aim of punishment rules, like the aim of tort rules, is to provide a certain set of incentives for conduct that promotes the overall social well-being; the law-and-economics spin on this in the case of tort law is that the measure of the good is wealth, understood as willingness to pay – wealth, it is assumed, can serve as a measure of social value, and thus something worth maximizing.[7]

The major alternative to the economic account of tort law appeals to a notion of justice – that the point of tort law is to rectify an injustice that exists because of a party's tortious act. Instead of looking at the result of torts starting from a social point of view – what are the overall costs of accidents, and accident prevention, and what way of imposing these costs best serves overall social well-being – we should instead look to the nature of the interaction between the two parties in question, the tortfeasor and the victim.[8]

Begin with this basic idea: every one of us has a moral right not to have his or her interests set back through the carelessness of others. (This idea will require later some amplification and perhaps qualification, but the main point is clear enough.) This is a right that I have against you, and every other individual who might affect my interests; this is a right that you have against me, and every other individual who might affect your interests. Corresponding to this moral right is a duty on each and every other person not to set back my, or your, interests through their carelessness.

Suppose that this is true: it seems plausible enough. It seems plausible enough that if you are injured as a result of an action of mine that is careless toward you, then I have failed in my duty, and have wronged you. Suppose that I do injure you in this way: I drive carelessly through your neighborhood, and while you are crossing the street (you are crossing at the corner, having looked both ways) I come blazing around the corner at a high speed and strike you. You are badly injured, your interests set back.

I may at this point offer an argument. "Look, it is true that you are injured," I concede, looking at your broken bones. "And it is true that your injuries are the result of my carelessness. It is true that an injustice has been done. But that is no reason for *me* to have to pay for it. Why don't you have insurance against misadventures of this sort? Why don't you ask the government to pass laws granting relief to accident victims, at least when it is the result of an injustice?"

It might seem that this is a remarkably obtuse response for me to make. But as a philosophical matter it is reasonable to ask why it is so obtuse for me to make this response. The basic structure of tort law is *personal* – it requires the person, the tortfeasor, to pay compensation to another person, a victim. It does not shove the costs of accident onto insurers, or to general government schemes for compensation. These are in fact alternatives to tort law, and have been taken up in some places as at least partial replacements of it. So our question is: why does it follow from the fact that A has a *prospective* right against B not to be injured by B's carelessness that A has a *retrospective* right to be compensated by B when A is in fact injured by B's carelessness? Why does it follow from the fact that B has a duty to A not to injure A by B's carelessness that B has a duty to compensate A when B injures A by B's carelessness?

As Stephen Perry points out, the answer to these questions cannot be of the form *because A has suffered a wrongful loss* or *because B has acted wrongly*.[9] If the reason is simply that A has suffered a wrongful loss, that does not explain why we should prefer a scheme of tort law to a scheme in which those who suffer wrongful losses are compensated from some governmentally administered compensation fund. If the reason is simply that B has acted wrongly, that does not explain why we should make B pay compensation, as opposed to being punished or criticized. We need an account that explains how the connection between A's right to be free of loss caused by B's carelessness and B's duty not to cause loss to A out of carelessness yields an after-the-fact right to compensation.

Perry's explanation is, in effect, that we do not have here two different reasons – a reason not to injure, and a reason to compensate – that require some ingenious philosophical argument to connect them. Rather, the reason not to injure and the reason to compensate are *one and the same reason*, seen from two different perspectives – the forward-looking perspective, and the backward-looking perspective. I have a reason to take care so that in the future I do not do you injury through my carelessness. If I do not injure you through my carelessness – either I am adequately careful, or my carelessness luckily does not result in injury to you – then I have satisfied that reason. But if I do you injury, that reason is unsatisfied. The only way to satisfy it is to, in effect, "undo" the injury – to make it so that you are not worse off from my careless action. Correspondingly, you have a right not to be made worse off through my carelessness. If I do not injure you this way, then you have what you are entitled to. If I do injure you this way, then you do not have that to which you are entitled. The only way to give you what you have a right to is to undo the injury, to make it the case that you are not worse off through being injured by me. This undoing of injury is the ideal aim of compensation in tort actions.

The justice interpretation of tort law has the longer history – it reflects the views of the majority of the judges responsible for its development in court cases – but it is the economic interpretation that has exploded over the last half-century. Both views, however, are subject to fairly predictable difficulties. The economic interpretation of tort law, both as a description of past and present practice and as a recommendation for future reform, surely has in its favor the common interest in deterring accidents at acceptable cost, which points the way toward the sort of information that would be needed to determine who should be held liable for injuries in negligence cases. Like the utilitarian theory of punishment discussed in Chapter 4, the point of accident prevention and overall efficiency needs little explanation to make sense, and it is on its face an attractive feature of the view that it makes the outcome of these cases depend not on deeply controversial moral or political argument but on the findings of the social sciences. Again, like the utilitarian view of punishment, its greatest strengths lead into its greatest weaknesses: while no one can deny that accident prevention and overall efficiency is a worthwhile aim, one can wonder about whether it is the exclusive aim that tort law ought to pursue or whether tort law is really the best tool for realizing these aims; and while it is always nice to solve problems by appeal to a set of plain findings of empirical fact rather than by appeal to the ever disputable conclusions of moral and political argument, it is unclear whether the judges or the legislators able to direct the transformations within tort law have access to the information that is needed in any more than a rough and ready way, with the result that it is not clear whether economic analysis gives us a clearer decision procedure than the moral reasoning that the economic view means to supplant. The justice interpretation, by contrast, seems more in tune with the initial intuitions that we have in thinking through the requirements of harm and compensation; but it is subject to all of the difficulties that we are familiar with from trying to think through matters of political morality. As we will see below in thinking through the various elements of negligence torts, the justice interpretation raises hard moral issues at every turn. It is no surprise that one would be tempted to turn to economic theory as an alternative to the moral questions that the justice interpretation invites.

5.4 Elements of the Negligence Tort

As we noted above, there are four interrelated elements of a negligence tort: duty, breach, cause, and loss. Each of these raise questions that have to be settled in order to determine the extent to which one party is responsible for losses suffered by another, and while some of these questions have been and can be settled by legislation, for the most part these questions are settled by judges whose reasoning is often nearly indistinguishable from philosophical argument.

5.4.1 Duty

In order for one to be held liable for losses suffered by another due to one's careless conduct, it must be the case that one had a duty to show due care toward another. It might sound paradoxical to hold that one *ever* fails to have a duty to show due care toward another: would it not be strange to concede that I did not show due care toward you, but nevertheless deny that I violated any duty? To put the point another way: doesn't "due care" just *mean*, at least in part, "the care that one owes to another as a matter of duty"? If this were the case, then the elements of duty and breach would collapse into one element. But we need not hold this. We might say that the notion of duty is a strictly legal notion: we are asking what *legal* duty one has to show the *morally requisite* care for another. There is nothing absurd about holding that while one has a moral duty of care with respect to another, one lacks a legal duty to do so. So one might hold that the legal duty of care is narrower than the moral duty that one owes.

What generates the most interesting cases in tort law are just those cases in which the legal duty of care and the moral duty of care seem to pull apart: we might ask whether they should pull apart, and if so, to what extent. While the distinction has been qualified to some extent in recent years, it is a well-established doctrine that as a matter of tort law one does not owe an *affirmative* legal duty of care to others as such; one owes only a *negative* duty of care. Tort law distinguishes between *nonfeasance*, the nonperformance of actions exhibiting care toward others, and *misfeasance*, performance of actions that fail to exhibit adequate care toward others, and it imposes a duty not to commit misfeasance while not concerning itself with nonfeasance. If we are both at a party, and I see that you have bees on your burger, I am not liable for damages to you by failing to warn you that your burger is buzzing with danger. If we are both at a party, and I have brought my pet bees, which subsequently escape and sting you, I am liable for damages for negligently failing to control my bees.[10] If you are a partygoer aboard my private yacht, and I take you to an area where the water is very shallow and fail to warn you of the danger, then if you dive in, break your neck, and are paralyzed, I am not liable for damages. If I invite you aboard my boat, take too sharp a turn, and you fall into shallow water, break your neck, and are paralyzed, then I am liable for damages. In the former instance of each pair of cases, because I have merely *failed to act* toward you in a way that exhibits due care for your well-being, I have not violated a legal duty to you; in the latter instance of each pair of cases, because I have *acted* toward you in a way that fails to exhibit due care for your well-being, I have violated a legal duty to you.

Why am I not bound by an affirmative legal duty of care to you in these cases? The costs to me are low: it requires very little effort to shoo the bees away or to give a quick warning. Yet the consequences to the bee-burger eater or the shallow-water diver are catastrophic. One explanation/justification for the absence of a positive legal duty of care in these cases is that there is no affirmative moral duty of care in these cases: I am morally free to ignore the bees on the burger and the shallowness of water, and the threats that they pose to my fellows. One might defend this view by holding an egoistic view on which there are generally no moral duties owed to others, but this has not been the preferred strategy. The preferred strategy has been to hold that the difficulty with holding a positive moral duty in these cases is that such duties will rapidly multiply, given the number of cases in which small sacrifices by oneself will generate large benefits for others. If the rationale for the moral duty in this case is just that a small self-sacrifice generates much larger benefits for others, then one will find oneself emptying one's wallet for the hungry, devoting all of one's free time to worthy causes, relentlessly pursuing a greater overall good.[11]

This worry about positive moral duties to others is on its face persuasive, but it can be answered successfully by distinguishing two kinds of case in which one might find oneself in a situation in which one's small sacrifice can prevent a much greater loss for another. There is an important difference between telling the fellow partygoer that there are bees on the burger and giving all of one's money to the homeless. Call an *emergency* a case in which the danger posed to someone cannot be equitably distributed among all those who have reason to prevent it; any other cases are *nonemergencies*. The needs of the homeless are nonemergencies:[12] their plight is such that it is possible for there to be collective action concerning how their needs are to be met, collective action whose burdens can be distributed justly among those called upon to contribute. The cases of the person about to take the bite of the bee-burger and about to dive into the shallow water do not allow for collective action and distribution of responsibility. If the danger is to be averted, it must be averted *now*, and by whoever is *now* in a position to intervene.

The point of the distinction is that whatever might be said against holding that there are positive duties of care in nonemergency cases – perhaps there is no more than a duty to do one's share in a just cooperative endeavor to deal with the danger, or the equivalent in individual sacrifice toward easing the dangers – there is much less to be said against holding that there are positive duties of care in emergency cases. It is thus difficult to morally justify a failure to say "Watch out for the bees on that burger."

Perhaps instead the justification for rejecting a general positive duty of care is to be found in the gap between moral and legal duties: even allowing for the existence of a positive moral duty of care in emergencies, there may be reasons to refrain from taking that moral duty up into the law. It may be too difficult to specify what counts as an emergency, or it may be that some people's lives come into contact with so much more emergency than others that it would be unfair to impose a legal duty upon them. Even if they are in fact morally bound to render aid in emergencies, we might think that it would go beyond the dutifulness that most of us expect from our fellow human beings to impose the legal burdens of compensation upon them. But the question is far from settled: it is in fact a live issue whether the courts, or legislatures, should go further in enforcing a positive duty to show due care.[13]

While tort law generally rejects a full positive duty to show due care, it nevertheless recognizes some pockets of positive duties of one person toward another, those classes of cases in which one party is in a "special relationship" with another. In some cases, special relationships with corresponding duties are generated by a contract – if, for example, you contract with me to be my bodyguard, you are under a legal duty to show positive care, not just to refrain from damaging me – but these are, unsurprisingly, duties enforced in contract law rather than tort law. Tort law recognizes some positive duties in cases that fall short of a contract but in which nevertheless there seems to be a certain role-relationship between parties that establishes a legal duty. People who undertake a joint, dangerous venture – think of adventurers traveling together up a treacherous mountain – can be held to be in a special relationship with one another so that positive duties of care exist. Some courts have held that friends who are simply "companions on a social venture" owe positive duties of care to one another.[14] Once the ball is rolling on "special relationships" as a source of positive duties, there are other ways that one might extend it: one might claim that a special relationship between two parties can generate duties with respect to a third party. For example: a psychiatrist is in a special relationship with a patient, and thus has positive duties of care with respect to him or her; but in an influential California case,[15] the court held that this special relationship places the psychiatrist under a duty to protect third parties who, in the psychiatrist's professional opinion, are endangered by the patient.

It seems pretty plain why we see in these cases a back-and-forth between the rejection of a general positive duty of care and an expansion of the notion of special relationships within which there are positive duties of care. The general positive duty of care is rejected on the basis of worries about its seeming relentlessness; but the implications of this general rejection seem unjust and inefficient, and so certain domains are carved out in which positive duties have a place (doctor–patient, innkeeper–customer, property owner–invitee); but once such domains are carved out, it becomes unclear by what rationale these special relationships are defined and limited. The special relationships with which tort law is concerned are not contractual. They can be defined by reference to social roles; they can be defined by reference to social expectations; they can be defined by reference to individual expectations; they can be defined directly by reference to moral or political argument. How one decides questions of liability in these cases will depend on what one counts as the relevant special relationships, and it is unclear by what criteria relationships are to be classified *special* or *relevant*.

While there is a general negative duty of care toward others, there is no general positive duty of care; rather, positive duties exist only where there is a special relationship. The pattern here, then, is that while each of us owes this general negative duty of care to everyone else, there are additional duties owed over and above these as a result of our special relationships. Interestingly, though, there is some tradition in tort law of certain special relationships actually making one *less* liable for injuries caused by one's negligence, less liable, that is, than if one caused those injuries in precisely the same way to strangers. Tort law generally used not to recognize, for example, a right of action by one spouse against another: the idea was that the relationship between husband and wife was so special, so tight, that for one spouse to sue the other would be as absurd as a person suing himself or herself. In the United States there was also a doctrine of parental immunity, on which parents could not be sued by their children for either intentionally or negligently caused injury. While these immunities have given way – spousal immunity entirely so, parental immunity in the case of intentional harm and now, in a number of jurisdictions, in the case of negligent harm as well – it is worth thinking through why the notion that special relationships might lessen liability in tort is not an obviously crazy idea. If we accept that not all moral duties are strictly replicated in legal duties, and that there might be good reason not to make every wrongful harm compensable as a matter of tort law, we might ask whether there are good reasons to leave certain relationships free from regulation by tort law. (That does not mean that they would not be regulated by law at all: they might be regulated by criminal law, for example.)

5.4.2 Breach

Suppose that it is established that one has a duty of care with respect to another. In what cases is that duty of care violated? What is the standard that must be followed in order to be free from fault, and thus free from liability with respect to any accidents that occur as a result of one's conduct?

The answer is rather brief: all that is truly settled with respect to the question of due care is that due care is that care that would be shown by a reasonable person in the circumstances at hand. There have been a few attempts to make this standard of care more specific, more concrete – we will turn to the most famous of these in a moment – but for the most part the question of whether an alleged tortfeasor has violated a duty of due care is a matter of fact for the jury to decide. This stands in contrast with the question of whether there is a duty of care in the first place. Whether there is a duty of care is what is called a question of law, and it is decided by judges, not by juries. Whether the duty of due care has been violated by someone is a question of fact, to be decided by the jury.

Here is what we can say positively about what constitutes a breach of the duty to show due, or reasonable care. First, it is an *objective* standard. To say that one showed, or failed to show, due care is determined by reference to the decisions that would be made by a hypothetical person, *the reasonable person*, in the circumstances that obtained. The circumstances here include the context of one's action and, importantly, the condition of one's body. So what counts as due care in a given case is fixed by the "external" arena of action (what is the condition of the roads, how heavy is the traffic, how fast is it moving, are there pedestrians about?) as well as by the physical (as contrasted to mental) condition of the agent (is the agent strong, healthy, sick, vision-impaired, etc?). In order to determine whether an actual person violated a duty of care, the question to ask is: might a reasonable person in that physical condition and in that external context have acted in that way? If a reasonable person would not have acted in that way, then there is a breach of due care.

What is *not* relevant to a determination of the actual agent's reasonableness are the various mental conditions of the agent that might impair his or her capacity to act well. That an agent is stupid, or massively poorly informed, or prone to lapses of judgment, or impulsive, is irrelevant in determining the reasonableness of his or her conduct. Rather, the standard is: did the agent do as well as a reasonable person – one who lacks such mental shortcomings – would have done? It is pretty clear why one needs to affirm this difference. One can use the reasonable person standard sensibly to ask about how physical deficiencies should modify the agent's choice: of a blind person we can ask "Did he or she act as a reasonable blind person would have acted?"; we cannot, by contrast, ask of an impulsive person "Did he or she act as a reasonable impulsive person would have acted?" For an impulsive person is, by that very fact, not a reasonable person.

Here is how Oliver Wendell Holmes characterized the objectivity of the tort standard:

> The standards of [tort] law are standards of general application. The law takes no account of the infinite varieties of temperament, intellect, and education which make the internal character of a given act so different in different men. It does not attempt to see men as God sees them... A more satisfactory explanation [for this feature of tort law] is that, when men live in society, a certain average of conduct, a sacrifice of individual peculiarities going beyond a certain point, is necessary to the general welfare. If, for instance, a man is born hasty and awkward, is always having accidents and hurting himself or his neighbors, no doubt his congenital defects will be allowed for in the courts of Heaven, but his slips are no less troublesome to his neighbors than if they sprang from guilty neglect. His neighbors accordingly require him, at his proper peril, to come up to their standard, and the courts which they establish decline to take his personal equation into account.[16]

Holmes supposes that it is for the general welfare that personal eccentricities that make it more difficult for one to adhere to the common standard of care are not taken into consideration in determining whether one is liable for damages. But this need not be understood simply in terms of promotion of the general welfare – even if, indeed, Holmes's argument is successful on that score. Arthur Ripstein argues that there is nothing unfair about holding even those less able to comply with the objective tort standard to the terms set by that standard – corrective justice requires that folks be held to an equal and impartial norm; the fact that impulsive people have trouble controlling their impulsive conduct makes it no less the case that they ought not to injure me through their impulsiveness. Ripstein notes that this willingness to assign liability even when folks have done their best to take care is common in contract law: if you contract with me to pay me $100 for a bicycle, and I deliver the bicycle but somehow you find yourself, through no fault of your own, unable to pay, you do not get to keep the bike; you must pay the $100 or return the bicycle. I have a right not to be made worse off by your not keeping your part of the agreement, and so you must either return the bike or pay the money. I have a right not to be made worse off through your unreasonable conduct, and so you must either refrain from acting toward me in a way that does not show reasonable care or you must compensate me for having made me worse off.[17]

Here is the second point concerning the standard of reasonable care. The model of conduct is that of the reasonable person: this hypothetical reasonable person is, however, an interesting combination of the ideal and the actual. The reasonable person is an ideal in the following sense: the reasonable person always takes perfectly adequate care with respect to those to whom a duty of care is owed. It surely is the case that there is no one in any community who actually takes the high level of care that the hypothetical reasonable person takes: "He is not to be identified with any ordinary individual, who might occasionally do unreasonable things; he is a prudent and careful person; he is always up to standard."[18] The standard to which the reasonable person always lives up, though, is a community standard, the actual standard for conduct accepted as correct within the community. The idea is that of the notions of reasonable conduct accepted by the community, the reasonable person scrupulously and faithfully honors these demands of reasonableness.

To what might we look to determine what counts as a community's standards of reasonable conduct? Legislators can take it upon themselves to specify legal duties and back them up with damage awards, but for the most part development of tort law has been left for the development of the courts, where notions of reasonableness get worked out case by case. We might look at criminal or regulatory statutes: we might take cases in which lawmakers have laid down rules as to how persons are to treat one another as laying down an account of the minimal requirements of reasonable conduct. We might look at prevailing customs within the community. But there has been a general reluctance by courts simply to say that the failure to adhere to a statute requiring a certain sort of conduct with respect to another in and of itself counts as a breach of due care or that failure to comply with a general custom constitutes due care. Juries are generally told to treat violations of the letter of statutes or failure to adhere to prevailing customs as *evidence* for findings of breach of duty of due care, or even *presumptions* of failures of due care, but are not decisive of the issue.

The one serious attempt to impose a clear definition on the notion of breach of duty came in a decision rendered by the great judge Learned Hand in the 1947 case *United States v. Carroll Towing*.[19] In this case, the employees of the Carroll Towing Company were adjusting the lines holding a barge, belonging to Conners Marine Co. Inc., in place. They did so poorly, and the barge broke free of its lines and did severe damage. Carroll Towing argued that even if it was negligent in the way that it fastened the ropes, Conners was also negligent in not having someone aboard to deal with such occurrences. The case is complicated by rules concerning the law of contributory negligence, with which we will not concern ourselves here, but the significance of the case is that in it Judge Hand attempted to articulate a more definite guideline for determining whether a failure of care counts as negligence. Here is Hand's comment on the specific case:

> The [barge] owner's duty...to provide against...injuries [resulting from the barge breaking away from moorings] is a function of three variables: (1) The probability that she will break away; (2) the gravity of the resulting injury, if she does; (3) the burden of adequate precautions. Possibly it serves to bring this notion into relief to state it in algebraic terms: if the probability be called P; the injury, L; and the burden, B; liability depends on whether B is less than L multiplied by P: i.e., whether $B < PL$.

Richard Posner thinks that we should not view this as Hand attempting a judicial intervention that will replace the old reasonable care standard: rather, the idea is that Hand's formulation is "an attempt to make explicit the standard that the courts had long applied."[20]

The idea is that the standard of reasonable care is an efficiency standard: Hand's rule tells us that one is negligent in failing to do what is necessary to prevent an accident if the expected costs of preventing the accident are lower than the expected costs of the accident.[21] The expected costs of preventing the accident are Hand's B: the costs of keeping a worker on board the barge, the costs of a pollution control device, the costs of driving more slowly. Most accidents are not certain to occur if one fails to take precautions; we can only estimate the probability that they will occur if one does not take precautions; this accident probability is Hand's P. The cost of the accident can be, more or less, estimated in advance: this is Hand's L. If we treat the plaintiff's losses and the defendant's losses as of equal importance, in themselves – that is, a dollar's worth of value lost by the plaintiff is no more valuable than a dollar's worth of value lost by the defendant – then we should say that what it is reasonable to do is to act in a way so that the expected loss is least. And so, if the expected cost of taking precautions is lower than what we should expect the accident costs to be – the probability of an accident multiplied by the cost if it occurs – it is unreasonable not to take those precautions.

It is clear that use of the Hand formula has some nontrivial presuppositions. It supposes, for example, that the cost of preventing accidents can be commensurated with the cost of the accidents themselves: that the cost of installing safety equipment can be measured in the same terms as the cost of sickness or injury. (We will turn to a similar question in more detail below, in thinking through the idea of damages.) It supposes that as a practical matter we can get a clear sense of the probabilities of loss and of the costs of prevention and loss. It supposes that in assessing reasonableness of conduct the losses that accrue to the agent should be treated as equivalent to the losses that accrue to the victim – that is, that in deciding what constitutes due care I should give no more weight to the loss that I might impose on you as to the loss that I might impose on myself. All these are interesting and contentious suppositions.

The Hand formula is quite obviously at home within the law-and-economics interpretation of tort law: as Posner notes, if one were to set a negligence rule in which one is liable to pay damages even if the cost of preventing the accident is higher than the expected costs of the accident itself, then a self-interested actor should be willing to risk the accidents and simply pay the damages.[22] But we should keep in mind that there is nothing about the Hand rule that necessitates its being employed only within a law-and-economics account. One might argue that the Hand formula provides a helpful account of the reasonable care that is owed as a matter of duty with respect to others; its assumption that dollars lost in accident prevention by the agent count for no more and no less than the dollars lost in accidents by the victim might be interpreted as simply an instance of the impartiality that all true moral principles must embody.

5.4.3 Cause

For one to be liable for damages in a tort action, it is not sufficient that one violate a duty of care, and that someone else suffer an injury. It is not even enough that one violate a duty of care and that one cause someone else to suffer an injury. It has to be the case that the violation of the duty of care *caused* the injury to occur. For example: suppose that I am driving my car at night with my lights off, and I strike you and injure you. Am I liable for your injury? Not necessarily: for it has to be determined whether my failure of care – the fact that I was driving with my lights off – caused your injury. It might very well be the case that the fact that my lights were off had nothing whatsoever to do with the fact that I struck and injured you. You might have stepped out between two parked cars, not even checking to see whether anyone was coming; I would have struck you with my car regardless of whether my lights were on or off. In such a case you would not be able to recover damages from me, for my negligence was not the cause of your injury.

It is customary to distinguish between two factors, both of which must be satisfied if one's negligent conduct is held to satisfy the causal element.[23] The first is that the negligent conduct must be a *"but for"* cause, or a *cause in fact*. The requirement here is that the accident would not have occurred but for the negligence. In the case I described in the previous paragraph, the "but for" test is not passed: the accident would have occurred even if I had turned my lights on. There are some philosophical questions that arise with respect to this feature of the causation element, but they are in no sense special to law: they are simply the general worries that philosophers have about the causation itself. Consider, for example, a case in which two people independently park their cars negligently; both cars roll down a hill and strike a third person, killing him. Either car alone would have been sufficient to kill the third person, though. Does this mean that *neither* person's

165

negligence caused the injury? For even if the first person were not negligent, the third person would have died; even if the second person were not negligent, the third person would have died. But it is absurd to say that neither caused the accident: were it not for negligence – and the first and second person are the only parties whose negligence affected the third party – the third party would not have been killed. This is a general philosophical problem about the proper description of causation for events that are overdetermined, and indicates that in certain cases the "but for" test is inadequate, requiring supplementation from some additional account.

The second factor is that the negligent conduct must be the *proximate* cause of the injury. The rationale for including this additional factor on top of cause in fact is straightforward: once "but for" causation is satisfied, there is nothing that prevents this sort of causation from stretching indefinitely into the future. For want of a nail the shoe was lost; for want of a shoe the horse was lost; for want of a horse the rider was lost; for want of a rider the battle was lost; for want of a battle the kingdom was lost; now, if the nail was lacking because of a clerk's negligence, do we therefore want to say that the clerk owes the equivalent of the kingdom in damages? Tort law has been firm in its aim to provide some limit to the extent to which one is burdened by liability for one's negligence.

A couple of kinds of theory of proximate cause dominate, one of which is centered on the natural relationship between the negligent conduct and the harms that result, and the other of which is centered on the extent to which the harms are a foreseeable effect of the negligent conduct. An example of the former view is that offered by H. L. A. Hart and A. M. Honoré.[24] The picture of proximate causation that they offer begins by setting human agency against the background of the course of nature, where nature is governed by causal regularities. Into the natural events governed by causal regularities is a human intervention: on Hart's and Honoré's view, whatever happens from the conjunction of that intervention and the laws of nature is caused by that intervention. Two kinds of event set a natural limit to the causal consequences of an agent's intervention: first, other human interventions, and second, freak occurrences, that is, events that occur outside of the normal course of nature. So, Hart and Honoré argue, if one throws a lighted cigarette into the brush, the brush catches on fire, and the forest burns down, one is the cause of the forest's burning down. But if, when the fire is about to go out, another person pours gasoline on the flames, this intervention breaks the chain and makes it the case that the one who dropped the cigarette is not the cause of the subsequent burning. Similarly, if the cigarette is about to go out when a freak burst of flammable mist fizzes up from the earth, this is sufficiently outside of the ordinary course of nature that one cannot be held to be the cause of the forest's burning down. In sum, Hart's and Honoré's view is that the proximate causes of one's action are those effects that follow from one's action in the ordinary course of nature.

The important question to ask Hart and Honoré is how this view of causation answers to the need to limit liability in an intelligible way. Why should we take other human interventions to cut off liability? Why should we take freak occurrences of nature to cut off liability? One straightforward answer to this question suggests the alternative general conception of proximate cause, that of foreseeability. If one can foresee that the unfortunate effects of one's negligent action will be perpetuated by another agent's action, then one should not be freed of liability for it, one might say; and the reason that one's liability of negligently caused harm should be limited if the effects of that negligence are sustained or strengthened by freak occurrences is just that one cannot foresee such occurrences. (If one were an expert geologist who knew that the freak belching of flammable gas were about to occur, would that not clearly be a case in which one should be treated as the cause of the forest fire that follows on one's careless cigarette disposal?)

These thoughts motivate the alternative foreseeability account of proximate cause, on which one is treated as proximate cause of the results of one's negligent conduct if one can foresee the results of that conduct. The foreseeability test has an obvious appeal. But it is subject to obvious difficulties as well. The first is that of giving a tolerably clear understanding of what counts as foreseeability. If we put the test very loosely – would the reasonable person acknowledge that this particular injury is a possible outcome of this negligent conduct? – it is pretty clear that foreseeability is no screening test at all. In every case in which this test will be employed, an accident has occurred, and the negligent conduct is a "but for" cause. If we ask "Would the reasonable person have foreseen that this accident is a possible outcome of the negligent conduct?," surely the answer will always be "Yes"; seeing mere *possibilities* is easy for almost everybody, and will surely be within the ken of the hypothetical reasonable person. But surely the answer is not "Would the reasonable person think that this result is *more likely than not* going to occur if this negligent conduct is performed?"; negligently caused injuries often do not have nearly a 50 percent chance of following the negligent action. (The vast, vast majority of drunk driving does not result in accidents; do we want to say that causing an accident is not a foreseeable result of drunk driving, and thus one's drunk driving is not a proximate cause of car accidents?[25])

The second difficulty, when first stated, may have the appearance of sophistry, but it is in fact a serious point. One of the plainest features of human life is that it is foreseeable that our actions have unforeseeable results. If we are reasonable, we recognize that whatever action we take may very well generate costly results for somebody. When one decides upon a career, one ends up with a lot of unforeseeable results, and one is responsible for dealing with them: we characteristically do not think that we are socially bound to provide full compensation to people for the unforeseeable effects on them of their career choices. We think it perfectly acceptable to define a sphere of responsibility in which people must bear the costs of their own choices, even when, despite exercising all the foresight that one could reasonably exercise, they suffer fairly large losses. (Prudent investment decisions can go very, very bad.) With this in mind, we might ask again why it is unacceptable to hold people liable for the injuries their negligence in fact causes, even when those injuries could not be foreseen. Why should we not say, echoing Elizabeth Anscombe, that if one does one's duty to others one is not responsible for the bad consequences that follow, but if one fails to do one's duty, one is responsible for bad consequences, be they foreseen or not?[26] One might, of course, still want some limitation on liability for injuries that one's negligence causes while nevertheless rejecting the view that foreseeability is the right test. One might simply declare that as a matter of public policy tort law must limit the extent to which it forces tortfeasors to pay damages for losses caused by negligence, without offering anything like a theory of proximate causation.[27]

It is worth noting that the very notion of causation in tort has been subject to challenge, even within the case law itself. In one case,[28] two hunters negligently discharged their shotguns, and the pellets from one (and only one) of the shotguns struck another hunter. It was impossible to determine from whose shotgun the pellets came. The court held both of the negligent hunters liable, even though it could not be shown which of the hunters caused the damage, and the result was that it was a matter of practical certainty that someone who had not caused the injuries was held liable for them. One might say: why does this matter, since both hunters were negligent? But remember that just being negligent is not enough to make one liable for damages; you will probably be negligent half-a-dozen times today, but unless your negligence harms someone you would certainly resent being made to pay compensation for someone's injury. In another case, drug manufacturers marketed virtually indistinguishable drugs to expectant mothers, which caused harm to their children; while the victims could be sure that they were harmed by the drug that their mothers took, and that one of these manufacturers had produced it, none of the victims could identify which particular drug company actually caused their injuries.[29] The court held all of the drug manufacturers liable for the injuries, and in proportion to their market share (i.e., those that held 15% of the market share were bound to pay 15% of the total damages, and so forth). Again, causation is pushed to the side. It is worth asking whether there is a way to treat these cases as a natural extension of the causation element, or whether these cases are the thin end of the wedge that, if taken seriously, will likely subvert the causation element altogether.[30]

5.4.4   Loss

There are no torts without losses. In order to claim damages from someone else, one must have been injured by the other's tortious conduct. The key question within tort law and the theory of tort law is what sorts of losses count.

It is undisputed and uncontroversial that damage to one's body or to one's property counts as a loss for the purposes of a tort action. If you break my leg by negligently hitting me with your car, I have suffered a loss for which I may recover; the same holds if through your negligent driving your car damages my house. The interests in the integrity of one's body and the security of one's property are obvious, and damage to either is easily observable and thus easily provable in a tort action. (Their measurement for the purposes of determining damages can be a harder matter, as we will see below.) What is less obvious is the extent to which other sorts of undesirable effects on one's life should also count as losses for the purposes of tort law.

What are these other undesirable effects whose status as losses are more controversial? For one, there is the pain and suffering that accompany bodily injury. When one is injured in an automobile accident, there is not only the cost of medical expenses and lost wages; there is also the pain of the injury sustained and the suffering that comes with a protracted recovery time. A further sort of undesirable effect on one's life that can result from other's negligence is emotional: the result of an accident (one can be traumatized by being struck by a car), or even a near-accident (one can be traumatized by the panic that precedes a near-miss, or the recognition that one was just involved in a near-miss), or even an accident to a loved one (one can be traumatized by seeing a loved one injured or killed in an accident), is emotional distress. A third is a sort of social loss: negligence can deprive one of the companionship ("consortium") of another person with whom one has an intimate relationship, thus damaging one's well-being (imagine a negligent act causing the death of a spouse or child).

Worries about counting these as losses for the purposes of tort law are in part worries about proof: that one is suffering emotional trauma is not so obvious in contrast to one's having a broken leg, and thus it can be argued that for the sake of avoidance of massive fraud in the tort system we must (regrettably, perhaps) limit recovery for these sorts of losses. Another argument appeals to the fact that we seem to make a distinction in advance between losses to property and person and losses of these other kinds: we tend to insure against property losses and bodily injury, but we do not tend to insure against emotional distress, pain and suffering, or losses of consortium.[31] Standing in contrast to these rationales is the general principle of tort law that "presumptively there should be recourse for a definite injury to a legitimate interest due to a lack of prudence or appropriate care to that occasion."[32] And, in fact, as tort law has developed, losses of all of these kinds have been, within limits, recognized as proper bases for tort claims.

5.5 Damages

The general principle embraced by tort law for determining the damages that the tortfeasor must provide to the victim is captured in a simple metaphor: the tortfeasor must make the victim *whole*. Prior to the negligent act, the victim was, from the limited point of view taken by tort law, *complete*; after the negligent act, the victim is *incomplete*; the handing over of damages should *recomplete* the victim. The ideal is to leave the victim as well off as he or she was before the accident took place.

Now, if what one has lost because of another's negligence is something like payment for medical bills, there is really no difficulty. The victim's bank account had $X; the victim paid the medical bill of $Y for treatment for injuries suffered because of the tortfeasor's negligence, and so ended up with a bank account with $X−Y; the tortfeasor is ordered to pay the victim $Y, restoring the victim's bank account to $X. If the victim's property is damaged, and must be repaired or replaced, compensation is needed to restore that property to its previous condition or to replace it; if the victim loses three weeks' wages because the injury made him or her unable to work, compensation is needed to replace those wages. There is an unproblematic sense in these cases in which the victim is made whole: after compensation, the victim is no worse off (in these respects) than he or she would have been had the accident never taken place.

The difficulty concerns those losses that are not easily translatable into economic terms: loss of life or bodily integrity, emotional distress, pain and suffering, loss of consortium, and the like. The problem can be put in the form of a dilemma. It seems bizarre to compensate for (e.g.) pain and suffering with money. It seems bizarre not to compensate for (e.g.) pain and suffering with money. It seems that both options lead to strange results.

The reason why it is bizarre to compensate for pain and suffering with money is that pain and suffering are not commensurable with money. The ideal of damages is that the damages paid by the tortfeasor equal the loss suffered by the victim. But when two things are held to be equal to one another, there must be some common measure by which they are assessed. And it is not clear that there is any such measure with respect to money on one side and pain and suffering on the other. We can assess pain and suffering in terms of more or less, but we do not have a unit of measure for emotional trauma, and much less is that unit of measure the dollar, pound, or euro.

The reason why it is bizarre *not* to compensate pain and suffering with money is that money seems the most feasible object by which compensation can be given and it would be extremely objectionable not to compensate at all. The most salient effect of an injury might be the pain and suffering that it causes rather than any economic effects that it generates (medical bills, lost wages, etc.); how could we justify a system requiring tortfeasors to compensate for the injuries they cause while refusing to compensate some of the most important losses that they impose?

In the absence of the sort of clear commensuration between loss imposed and damages to be paid, it is plausible to suggest a more subjective approach – what we might call an *indifference measure* for tort damages. Here the idea would be that the way to determine the compensation that is due is for the tortfeasor to pay the victim a sufficient amount for the tortfeasor to be indifferent between his or her condition prior to the accident and his or her condition after the accident in conjunction with payment from the tortfeasor. So, if I am indifferent between my life without the pain caused by an accident and my life with the pain plus an extra $X in my bank account (or, better, with whatever I could best use that $X for), then $X counts as a sufficient damage payment to make the victim whole.

One way to make this indifference test vivid is to use a hypothetical offer test: imagine receiving an offer from someone for a payment in exchange for your undergoing this loss; the least amount that you would accept must satisfy the indifference test. But it seems to me that this is a bad test. First, the test must be taken either by someone with the relevant injuries or by those who do not have such injuries. On the one hand, those who do not will likely lack an adequate representation of what it is like to have those injuries, either through lack of experience or lack of vividness, and thus will be prone to form a preference in the absence of good information about what they are agreeing to. What's more, there is a relevant difference between suffering that one has agreed to undertake and suffering that one has not agreed to undertake; the hypothetical test necessarily concerns the former, while the situation in a tort case concerns the latter. On the other hand, those who have the injury, and are being asked what it would take to make them indifferent, have every reason to form preferences that raise the price of the injury. (Since it is not a real market situation, after all, they have no reason to keep their asking price down.) In either case, the fact that the test is hypothetical is a burden: people are generally lax about their spending of hypothetical money, and may be trusted to be generally lax about their willingness to suffer hypothetical injuries.

Second, the hypothetical test is bound to be burdened by the fact that in the case of certain types of losses it is distasteful or perhaps simply morally wrong even to entertain the question, much less to answer it. If someone were to ask me how much I would be willing to accept in order to lose the companionship of my wife, I should find the question obnoxious. If I were somehow forced to answer it, I hope that no one would find my answer a reliable assessment of my preferences on the value that I place on spousal consortium.

The indifference notion is poorly implemented by the hypothetical choice test. And the very idea of the indifference test has problems. Again, the indifference test in general can be given a before-the-injury and after-the-injury reading. Suppose it is read to hold that, before the injury, one is indifferent between remaining uninjured or being injured and having what an extra $X can buy for one. This makes the tort damages susceptible to inadequate information, lack of vivid representation, failure of adequate consideration, and so forth. Suppose it is read to hold that, after the injury, one is indifferent between having remained uninjured and now being injured and having what an extra $X can buy for one. This test cannot be used in cases in which the effect of the injury itself is to markedly change the victim's preferences, especially when the effect is to make the party injured indifferent between his or her previous uninjured condition and his or her present injured condition. The clearest case is that in which one has none of the relevant preferences at all after the accident: one is in a coma, or has become so damaged by the accident that one lacks the capacity to make meaningful distinctions between conditions that normally functioning human beings would find meaningful. (Imagine an injury that makes a person a quadriplegic but also causes sufficient brain damage to make the person unable to distinguish cognitively between quadriplegia and normal physical mobility.)

The problem of compensation is hard to escape, and the economics and the corrective justice approaches to torts both find themselves caught up in it to some degree. The economic approach surely must embrace some sort of strong commensurability claims: defenders of this view are committed to treating the dominant goal of the tort system as efficiency, which is assessed in terms of wealth, and they are committed to thinking of negligence along the lines of the Hand formula, which presupposes that the cost of preventing an accident and the cost of the accident are to be measured in the same units. The justice view, while not embracing the economic interpretation of tort law, is committed to the view that what explains the tortfeasor's requirement to pay is the requirement that he or she not make the victim any worse off as a result of the tortfeasor's negligence; and so the defender of the corrective justice account must provide some sense to the idea that compensation for these multifarious injuries is possible.

It seems that a direct comparison of these individual noneconomic losses with sums of money is hard to make intelligible and an appeal to agent indifference is itself an unreliable and eccentric measure. Perhaps instead what is needed is an appeal to more holistic forms of assessment based on less eccentric measures of value.[33] It may be useful to think in terms of *patterns of human lives as wholes* rather than in terms of the *individual goods and evils* that appear in those lives. We are accustomed to making judgments about agents' well-being over whole lives, or significant stretches of their lives, and these judgments are not formed wholly by reference to those agent's preferences (we often say that people don't know or appreciate how well-off they are, after all), and these judgments are not formed simply by summing up the goods and bads in those lives. When shown a person's life up to a certain point, we could, if we wished, describe a number of ways that that life could go on from there that are, so far as our views of characteristic human life are concerned, on a par. I am sure that you can imagine an indefinite number of ways your life could go on from this point forward that are no worse than each other, each with its own distinctive goods and bads, indeed, in some of which the bads are very bad indeed.

The suggestion, then, is that the assignment of damages should be made by comparing the rough picture of how the victim's life would have gone on in the absence of the injury in comparison to the various ways that the victim's life could go on in the presence of the injury. This is a third person matter, done from the point of view of a characteristic human life rather than from one's own personal point of view or even from the point of view of the victim. There are then three relevant questions. Are there any ways that the victim's life could go on in the presence of the injury that are no worse than the ways that the victim's life would have gone on in its absence?[34] If so, could the means necessary for the victim to have that life be provided by money? If so, how much money? If the answer to the first two questions are "Yes," the answer to the third question determines the damages owed by the tortfeasor to the victim.[35]

The answer to the first question or the second question may, however, be "No." It may be the case that there is nothing, or nothing that money can buy, that can be sufficient for the victim to be able to make a life for himself or herself that is as good as the life he or she would have had in the absence of the injury. Compensation in such cases will be impossible, but that does not mean that the tortfeasor should be free of liability: in such cases the payment required serves a symbolic function – the payment is a gesture toward compensation when compensation is strictly impossible. Determining reasonably what sort of award is properly expressive of the noncompensable harm done is a vexed question, as is the question of symbolic conduct generally. But it is hard to see anywhere else to turn to account for the sort of liability that is called for when an injury demands compensation but it is impossible for the injured to be made whole.

5.6 Intentional Torts and Torts of Strict Liability

Our discussion has focused on negligence torts, which form the bulk of tort actions. But in addition to negligence torts there are intentional torts and torts of strict liability. Intentional torts share with negligence torts the notion of fault – that is, that it is in virtue of some fault in the action of the tortfeasor that he or she is liable for damages. Intentional torts differ from negligence torts in that in an intentional tort the harm to the victim is either the tortfeasor's goal – he or she was aiming at doing harm to the victim – or at least an outcome that the tortfeasor was substantially certain would occur as a result of his or her action. Torts of strict liability are similar to torts of negligence in that the tortfeasor need not foresee the loss to the victim that results from the action. They differ from negligence torts, though, in that there is no claim made that the tortfeasor's act was an unreasonable one.

Intentional torts (including, for example, assault, battery, conversion of property, intentional infliction of emotional distress) are, if anything, less philosophically problematic than negligence torts. Problems concerning what counts as a loss and how damages are to be determined are no different with respect to intentional and negligence torts, since the aim in both cases is compensation for legally acknowledged losses. The problems of determining the nature of reasonableness and the scope of legal duty are less difficult, since it seems fairly clear that there are strong reasons generally to prohibit intentionally inflicted losses and to demand that those who inflict such losses compensate their victims. The most serious philosophical question that arises within intentional tort doctrine that goes beyond those problems that arise with respect to negligence torts concerns the causation element: it seems to be accepted as a matter of law that the tortfeasor's responsibility for the harms caused by his or her intentional act extend further as a causal matter than the tortfeasor's responsibility for the harms caused by his or her negligent act.

Consider the famous case of *Palsgraf v. Long Island Railroad*.[36] Two men were running to catch a train that was pulling away. One of the men made it aboard without incident. The other, while being, in effect, hurled onto the train by railroad guards, dropped a package that he was carrying: it turned out that the perfectly plain package contained fireworks, which landed on the tracks and exploded. As a result of the explosion, a scale on the other side of the platform fell and struck Helen Palsgraf, injuring her. She sued the railroad company, claiming that the railroad employees had been negligent in the careless way that they pushed the late passenger aboard, and claiming damages for her loss. The court found against Mrs Palsgraf: even if the hurrying passenger might have had a cause of action for negligence (e.g., for the loss of the fireworks caused by the rough treatment by the railroad guards), she had none, for "The conduct of the . . . guard, if a wrong in relation to the holder of the package, was not a wrong in its relation to [Mrs Palsgraf]." Justice Benjamin Cardozo argued that the railroad workers failed in no duty of care to her, and thus the railroad company was not liable for injuries to her. The case could have very easily gone the other way, though, if the railroad workers' actions were intentional: if they were irritated by the late passenger's tardiness and purposefully swatted the package out of his hands to be destroyed on the tracks, it is more likely that the causal consequences of that intentional harm – that is, the injury to Mrs Palsgraf – would have been attributed to the railroad worker. Above we noted Elizabeth Anscombe's remark that one who acts wrongly is responsible for the negative consequences of his or her action, foreseen or not. Is this, broadly speaking, right? And if so, is it also true that the more wrongful one's action, the further one's responsibility for the consequences extends?

The causation issue notwithstanding, intentional torts seem to generate less difficulty than negligence torts, but torts of strict liability have been thought especially puzzling, at least from a point of view that takes corrective justice to be the (or a) central justifying point of tort law. As matters stand, there are pockets of strict liability in tort law for certain sorts of activities. Manufacturers and sellers of consumer goods are strictly liable for the harms caused by the defects in their products or for inadequacy in warnings of the dangers of those products. (So if one can show that a product is in itself defective or lacks sufficient warning labels, and that these inadequacies caused harm to the victim, it is no defense for the manufacturer or seller to hold that it did everything it reasonably could to make sure that the product was well-designed, well-produced, and well-labeled.) Those who engage in ultrahazardous activities – blasting with dynamite, for example – are strictly liable for the harm that they do to others. Those who own and keep animals that are abnormally dangerous or destructive are liable for damages when those animals get loose and cause harm, even if the owners of those animals have done all that they reasonably can to prevent them from getting loose.

From the economic point of view, explaining strict liability is not tremendously problematic (though, of course, there can be arguments about which activities should be subject to strict liability). One can argue simply that it turns out to be best from an efficiency point of view for those who engage in very dangerous activities, or who have exclusive and one-sided control over the production of a potentially dangerous object, to be burdened by the costs of those activities when they damage others. From a corrective justice point of view, matters might appear less straightforward. For intentional and negligence torts include a fault condition, and one might think that it is the fact that someone is at fault for harming another that makes it so clear that he or she is bound to assume liability for the harms caused. But in strict liability there is no fault involved: it is not necessary that the tortfeasor acted unreasonably in using dynamite, or in running a zoo, or in manufacturing mousetraps, even though the tortfeasor will be held liable if debris from the blast kills someone on the highway, or a tiger escapes and mauls someone, or someone who uses the mousetrap according to instructions ends up not with a dead mouse but with a broken thumb.

It is useful to compare strict liability torts with a defense against negligence torts, that of assumption of risk. (This comparison is characteristically forwarded by those sympathetic to the economic reading of torts, but it is equally available for those who favor the justice view.)

Suppose that I am negligently driving while very tired. You are in the car with me. I have an accident, and you are injured as a result. It is a defense open to me to note that, as you got into the car, I said to you: "Look, I'm extremely tired. I've been up all night; I can barely keep my eyes open. Are you sure you want a ride?" If you accept the ride knowing these facts, it is open to me to defend against your claim for damages that you assumed the risk: knowing fully well what the risks of riding with me were, you chose to go ahead and do so anyway. If my defense succeeds, the result is that the costs of the accident fall on you, even though no fault is imputed to you. You must bear the costs of the accident even though it was I, not you, who was at fault in causing them. The suggestion, then, is that strict liability torts are parallel to assumption of risk. Instead of the potential victim assuming the risk of damages from an accident, even without fault, one who engages in certain activities assumes the risk of losses to others resulting from an accident, even without fault.

This pushes the inquiry back one step, though. Why should certain activities be burdened by strict liability, even when we do not forbid entirely the activity or deny that it can be carried out in a reasonable way? Perhaps the answer is to be found in the *one-sidedness* of the activities to which strict liability is attached: they are activities that are both risky and not mutually engaged in by the tortfeasor and victim.[37] While some have argued that automobile driving should be handled with strict liability, the basic reason for rejecting that in favor of the current negligence regime is that the risks of driving are (for the most part) mutually imposed and mutually enjoyed. The world is not such, however, that most are dynamiters, and mutually impose and benefit from the risks of dynamiting; nor is it such that most are zookeepers, and mutually impose and benefit from the risks of keeping dangerous animals; nor is it such that most are manufacturers, and mutually impose and benefit from the risks of manufacturing products whose safety is taken for granted by consumers.

Torts are not crimes, and compensation is not punishment; so there is no reason to think that wrongdoing is essential to torts in the way that it is essential to crimes. The law of torts specifies the ways that one may not harm others: one may not make others worse off through acts that aim to harm them; one may not make others worse off through acts that negligently harm them. Similarly, one may not make others worse off through engaging in ultrahazardous activities, or producing defective consumer goods, or through harboring dangerous beasts.[38] In none of these cases is the aim of tort law to condemn those who make others worse off in one of these ways, so it does not seem an obvious objection to strict liability regimes that they require compensation in the absence of fault. What an argument that strict liability is unjust would require is the claim that it is unjust to make folks pay for the results of their dynamiting, if they wish to dynamite, and that is it unjust to make folks pay for the results of their tiger-keeping, if they wish to keep tigers. It is far from clear how such an argument would go.

For Further Reading

For applications of the economic account of tort law, see Richard A. Posner, *Economic Analysis of Law*, 6th edn (New York: Aspen, 2003 [first published 1973]), Chapter 6, and Guido Calabresi, *The Costs of Accidents* (New Haven, CT: Yale University Press, 1970). Several useful papers on the economic analysis of tort law, both pro and con, are collected in Mark Kuperberg and Charles Beitz (eds.), *Law, Economics, and Philosophy* (Totowa, NJ: Rowan and Allanheld, 1984); included are Ronald Coase's classic (and surprisingly accessible) "The Problem of Social Cost" and George Fletcher's "Fairness and Utility in Tort Theory." Stephen Perry's writings constitute an extensive working through of the justice approach; see his "The Moral Foundations of Tort Law," *Iowa Law Review* 77 (1992), pp. 449–514 and "Responsibility for Outcomes and the Law of Torts," in Gerald J. Postema (ed.), *Philosophy and the Law of Torts* (Cambridge, UK: Cambridge University Press, 2001), pp. 72–130. (Postema's collection generally contains a number of cutting-edge articles on tort theory.) For alternative formulations of the justice view, see Ernest Weinrib, "Toward a Moral Theory of Negligence Law," *Law and Philosophy* 2 (1983), pp. 37–62, and (from a point of view very different from both Perry's and Weinrib's) Jules L. Coleman, *The Practice of Principle* (Oxford: Oxford University Press, 2001), Part One. Excellent overviews of the philosophy of tort law can be found in Arthur Ripstein, "The Philosophy of Tort Law," in Jules Coleman and Scott Shapiro (eds.), *The Oxford Handbook of Jurisprudence and Philosophy of Law* (Oxford: Oxford University Press, 2002), pp. 656–86, as well as Benjamin Zipursky, "Philosophy of Tort Law," in Martin P. Golding and William A. Edmundson (eds.), *The Blackwell Guide to Philosophy of Law and Legal Theory* (Malden, MA: Blackwell, 2005), pp. 122–37.

Notes

1 One might also seek injunctive relief, asking that the party committing the tortious action be ordered to cease doing so. If, for example, a factory down the street is spewing pollution into one's neighborhood – committing the tort of nuisance – one might seek a court injunction requiring the factory to cut it out.

2 See W. Page Keeton, *Prosser and Keeton on Torts*, 5th edn (St Paul, MN: West Publishing, 1984), §30.

3 Ronald Coase, "The Problem of Social Cost," *Journal of Law and Economics* 3 (1960), pp. 1–44.

4 Richard Posner, *Economic Analysis of Law*, 6th edn (New York: Aspen, 2003 [first published 1973]), p. 16.

5 See Guido Calabresi, *The Costs of Accidents* (New Haven, CT: Yale University Press, 1970), p. 135.

6 Oliver Wendell Holmes, "The Path of the Law," *Harvard Law Review* 10 (1897), pp. 457–78, quotation p. 469.

7 For an important challenge to this assumption, see Ronald Dworkin, "Is Wealth a Value?," *Journal of Legal Studies* 9 (1980), pp. 191–222.

8 In presenting the justice view as I do, I inevitably run together several versions of the justice account that are distinctive (and thus have distinctive strengths and distinctive weaknesses). For a disentangling of them, see Stephen Perry, "The Moral Foundations of Tort Law," *Iowa Law Review* 77 (1992), pp. 449–514.

9 Stephen Perry, "Loss, Agency, and Responsibility for Outcomes: Three Conceptions of Corrective Justice," in Kenneth D. Cooper-Stephenson and Elaine Gibson (eds.), *Tort Theory* (York, ON: Captus University Press, 1993), pp. 24–47.

10 Indeed, I would almost certainly be liable as a matter of strict liability; see 5.6.

11 See Richard A. Epstein, "A Theory of Strict Liability," *Journal of Legal Studies* 2 (1973), pp. 151–204, particularly pp. 197–9.

12 Keep in mind that to say this is not to cast doubt on the severity of the plight faced by the homeless: it calls attention only to the fact of the possibility of dealing with the problem through a common plan in which the burdens of assistance are justly distributed.

13 For an argument in favor of such positive duties, see Ernest Weinrib, "The Case for a Duty to Rescue," *Yale Law Journal* 90 (1980), pp. 247–93.

14 *Farwell v. Keaton*, 240 N.W.2d 217 (Mich. 1976).

15 *Tarasoff v. Regents of the University of California*, 551 P.2d 334 (Cal. 1976).

16 Oliver Wendell Holmes, *The Common Law* (Boston, MA: Little, Brown, 1881), pp. 109–10.
17 Arthur Ripstein, "The Philosophy of Tort Law," in Jules Coleman and Scott Shapiro (eds.), *The Oxford Handbook of Jurisprudence and Philosophy of Law* (Oxford: Oxford University Press, 2002), pp. 656–86, particularly p. 671.
18 Keeton, *Prosser and Keeton on Torts*, §32.
19 *United States v. Carroll Towing Company*, 159 F.2d 169 (2d. Cir. 1947).
20 Richard Posner, "A Theory of Negligence," *Journal of Legal Studies* 1 (1972), pp. 29–76, quotation p. 32.
21 Strictly speaking, Hand should have put the formula in terms of a comparison between the marginal benefit of additional accident prevention measures and their marginal costs rather than in terms of a comparison between the overall costs and benefits of these measures.
22 Posner, "A Theory of Negligence," pp. 32–3.
23 Keeton, *Prosser and Keeton on Torts*, §§41–2.
24 Hart and Honoré, *Causation in the Law*, 2nd edn (Oxford: Clarendon Press, 1985 [first published 1959]), pp. 68–81; for the applications of Hart's and Honoré's views as principles of proximate causation in tort, see pp. 136 and 162.
25 The chance of having an accident while driving drunk is .0045; the chance of being involved in a fatal accident while driving drunk is about one per 600,000 miles. See H. Laurence Ross, *Confronting Drunk Driving* (New Haven, CT: Yale University Press, 1992), p. 47, cited in Douglas Husak, "Is Drunk Driving a Serious Offense?," *Philosophy & Public Affairs* 23 (1994), pp. 52–73, particularly p. 63.
26 G. E. M. Anscombe, "Modern Moral Philosophy," *Philosophy* 33 (1958), pp. 1–19, particularly p. 12.
27 This frank appeal to policy is favored by the dissenting Judge Andrews in the famous *Palsgraf v. Long Island Railroad*, 162 N.E. 99 (N.Y. 1928), which is discussed briefly below. Judge Andrews there writes that "What we do mean by the word 'proximate' is, that because of convenience, of public policy, of a rough sense of justice, the law arbitrary declines to trace a series of events beyond a particular point. This is not logic. It is practical politics."
28 *Summers v. Tice*, 199 P.2d 1 (Cal. 1948).
29 *Hymowitz v. Eli Lilly & Company*, 539 N.E. 2d 1069 (N.Y. 1989).
30 See, for an attempt to make these market-share liability rules compatible with the centrality of the causal element, Arthur Ripstein and Benjamin Zipursky, "Corrective Justice in an Age of Mass Torts," in Gerald J. Postema (ed.), *Philosophy and the Law of Torts* (New York: Cambridge University Press, 2001), pp. 214–49. See also the interesting defense of the import-

ance of causation in Judith Jarvis Thomson, "The Decline of Cause," *Georgetown Law Journal* 137 (1987), pp. 137–50.

31 See, for example, Paul H. Rubin, *Tort Reform by Contract* (Washington, DC: AEI Press, 1993).

32 *Diaz v. Eli Lilly & Company*, 302 N.E.2d 555 (Mass. 1973).

33 For thoughts along similar lines see Heidi Li Feldman, "Harm and Money: Against the Insurance Theory of Tort Compensation," *Texas Law Review* 75 (1997), pp. 1567–1603.

34 One might object that this does not take into account the fact that the victim has had the course of his or her life changed without his or her own choice. This is not so. For (within limits) determining the course of one's own life is part of the good of a characteristic human life, and so one thing that would be taken into consideration in assessing what lives would be on a par with the victim's imagined uninjured future is that all of the injured lives involve changes that the victim did not choose for himself or herself.

35 One might object that this way of viewing damages has the unfortunate effect that the tortfeasor's responsibility is lessened by the ability of the victim to make the best of a bad situation, to take steps that can make his or her life better. But this is not a good objection. It is a sensible extension of tort law's doctrine of "avoidable consequences," that victims must take steps to mitigate losses caused by tortfeasors' negligence.

36 162 N.E. 99 (N.Y. 1928).

37 See George Fletcher, "Fairness and Utility in Tort Theory," *Harvard Law Review* 85 (1972), pp. 537–64, particularly p. 542. Ripstein expresses a similar idea when he holds that fundamental to tort law is the notion that one party may not set terms of interaction unilaterally; see Ripstein, "Philosophy of Tort Law," p. 661.

38 As Ripstein emphasizes. See "Philosophy of Tort Law," pp. 685–6.

Chapter 6

Challenging the Law

6.1 Putting Legal Roles to the Question

In the past five chapters we have been concerned to provide an account of law that satisfies our commonplaces about law – that law is a matter of social fact, that law is authoritative, and that law is for the common good. While it is pretty clear that law's existence is a matter of social facts about rule acceptance and use, it is also pretty clear that law, in order to be nondefective, must be genuinely authoritative and genuinely for the common good (Chapter 1), and we saw that law's aspiration to authority and to the common good shape the character and binding force of fundamental legal roles (Chapter 2). We have considered how one might approach the question of the aims of law (Chapter 3) as well as how one's view of those aims can brought to bear on both criminal law (Chapter 4) and tort law (Chapter 5).

The approach to the commonplaces that I have employed throughout this book has been a constructive one. I have been trying, that is, to review the contributions that have been offered toward justifying and elaborating our commonplaces about law and, to a lesser extent, to evaluate the successes and failures of these contributions. But it would be a mistake to think that the tasks of the philosophy of law must be carried out in this way, or with this aim. As I mentioned in the Introduction (0.1), there is no reason for us to think in advance that our commonplaces about any subject matter are in good order, that they are fundamentally sound and simply in need of deeper philosophical investigation in order to achieve a more satisfactory understanding. Rather, it may very well be that our commonplaces are in some ways incoherent, or false, or massively misleading, and to proceed without taking this prospect seriously is to blind oneself to the possibilities of error.

We can conclude our investigation into the commonplaces about law by considering a variety of challenges that have been made to them. It will help to focus our discussion to frame them as challenges to the fundamental legal roles. Since these roles are at the heart of legal systems, a rejection of the practicability or justification of these roles is a rejection of the practicability or justification of law as understood in terms of our commonplaces. It is hard to imagine what more fundamental criticisms would be like.

6.2 Against the Role of Subject: Philosophical Anarchism

The role of the subject within a legal system is, as we have seen (2.2), that of obedience to authoritatively interpreted legal norms. In our discussion of this role we considered, and criticized, a number of accounts of why those occupying this role are genuinely bound to comply with its demands, and ultimately I argued for an account based on the requirement to do one's share for the common good. But it has been argued that the subordination to authority that is central to the life of a subject is morally unjustifiable; and even if this charge turns out to be false, it has been argued that there is no genuinely successful account of why subjects are morally bound to obedience. Both of these views – that law necessarily lacks legitimate authority over subjects, or that as a matter of fact law fails to have genuine authority over subjects – go by the label "philosophical anarchism." (*Philosophical* anarchism contrasts with *political* anarchism, which we will consider below.)

The stronger version of the philosophical anarchist position has been defended by Robert Paul Wolff.[1] In an influential book that spurred a great deal of discussion over the justification and limits of legal authority, he argues that there is a fundamental incompatibility between *authority* and *autonomy*. For one to have authority over another, one's dictates must bind that other to compliance. But for one to be autonomous is for one to take responsibility for one's actions, where to take responsibility for one's actions is for one's actions to be the product of one's own deliberation and decision about what is to be done. When one acts autonomously, there is no "passing the buck" – if there is a question of who is to be praised or blamed for the action, the object of praise or blame must be the agent himself or herself, for it was that person who determined that this action was the thing to do. These characterizations of authority and autonomy are sufficient to show, Wolff thinks, that authority and autonomy are incompatible. For the person who acts under authority goes along with what the authority demands. If one is told to do something, and then deliberates about what to do, then one is not acting as someone under authority, even if one ends up doing just what the authority told one to do. (If I tell my daughter to clean her room, and she thinks about how messy her room is, and why now is a good time to do it, and then decides to go ahead and do it, she is not acting as someone under my authority – she is just making up her own mind that, on the merits, cleaning her room is the thing to do.) We have a choice: we can do what we are told to do or we can act on the merits of the case. To act in the former way is to act under authority; to act in the latter way is to act under autonomy.

So far, all Wolff has told us is that there is a conflict between authority and autonomy. He has not told us why we should opt for autonomy. His answer is that we have a moral duty to be and remain autonomous.[2] This capacity is what is most valuable about us, for it is what makes us rational beings. It is thus a morally subpar state of affairs to yield one's autonomy in order to subject oneself to authority.

Wolff's argument is subject to criticism at a number of points. One might argue, first, that there is simply no incompatibility between authority and autonomy as Wolff describes them. To be autonomous is to deliberate for oneself on the basis of the reasons that are available to one. But to be under authority is for another's dictates to be strong reasons for one to act. An autonomous agent could, therefore, deliberating for himself or herself, correctly treat an authority's dictates as reasons for action. If I am in authority over my daughter, and tell her to clean her room, she might reason thus: "Well, the room does not seem all that messy to me . . . But my dad told me to, so I suppose that I'll do it." She may very well be acting autonomously in the sense that she makes her decision based on reasons: she need not be responding blindly, or out of habit. (You can imagine two different scenarios: one in which she chooses to clean her room based on the reason of my authoritative dictate, and another in which she mindlessly goes along with what I tell her to do.) But surely she is acting on the basis of my authority: it is because I told her to clean her room that she decides it is worthwhile to do it. If there is a problem about authority and our nature as moral agents, it is not that seeing oneself as under authority precludes one from acting on the basis of the reasons that one judges to apply to oneself.

Perhaps the problem is to be understood as the sort of reasons that are involved in authority: that, for example, reasons of authority are of the sort *because A told me to*. One might claim that it is reasons of that sort that are unfitting for autonomous agents to act on. The difficulty, then, is not that authority precludes one from acting on the basis of one's deliberate response to reasons, but that authority precludes one from acting on the basis of one's deliberate response to reasons of the right kind. An autonomous being should not, it might be claimed, have his or her course of action determined by another's will. But this objection is surely far too strong. Suppose that you and I are deciding what movie to go to see. We cannot agree, so you suggest a compromise: "We'll go to see the movie you want to see this time; and next week, I can decide which movie we will go to see." If I agree, I have made myself subject to your will: next week, I will have reason to go to see whatever movie you decide. Have I yielded my autonomy? Perhaps, to a degree. But there is nothing objectionable about my course of action. I have yielded some decision-making power for good reasons, for the sake of an agreeable accommodation between friends.

Wolff has given us no reason to think that to be under authority is itself an objectionable condition for rational beings like us. One might, however, concede these claims while nevertheless offering a Wolff-inspired line of argument. Perhaps the problem for autonomy is not authority in general, but legal authority in particular. Legal authority is tremendously vast in scope, or at least claims to be. To be under the authority of law is not like making a one-off agreement with a friend to defer to each other's movie choices. It is to be under a system where any number of authoritative standards might be imposed upon a subject, and the subject is expected to comply. It is that condition, the Wolff-inspired critic might suggest, that is an objectionable intrusion on autonomy. To be a faithful subject simply asks too much sacrifice of one's autonomy to be a role worth fulfilling.

There is something right and something wrong in this objection. What is right in the objection is that if faithfully occupying the role of subject means being prepared to obey any rule laid down by legal authorities, then that is too much deference for beings like us to tolerate. We should not be willing to obey rules that are grossly unjust, for example. What is wrong in the objection, though, is that one can defend a very robust account of the extent to which people ought to adhere to the demands of the role of subject without being an absolutist about it. In the account I suggested earlier (2.2), for example, I argued that one should adhere to the law insofar as the law specifies one's share of the burdens for the common good. This means that one need not be prepared to do the law's bidding no matter what: if the law places deeply disproportionate burdens on one, or requires one to commit injustice, then one might refuse to comply. But unless law violates these constraints one should obey, because there needs to be a common standard to divide up the responsibilities to promote the common good, and law is the best candidate to fill this role. This involves some loss of decision-making power – I can no longer decide for myself what I must do for the common good – but it is worth it, given the need to divide up our common duties with my fellow citizens.

The account of the moral requirement to honor the role *subject* offered above (2.2) is immune, I think, to Wolff's and Wolff-inspired objections. But there is a line of argument against the moral requirement to honor the role *subject* that is less ambitious than Wolff's but which has been more successful and even more influential. Defenders of this view do not claim that it is impossible, or even necessarily morally undesirable, for there to be a moral requirement for subjects to adhere to the demands of that role. What they claim, rather, is simply that in present circumstances there is no such moral requirement.

How do they argue for this claim? In two stages. First, these philosophical anarchists – M. B. E. Smith, A. John Simmons, Joseph Raz, and Leslie Green, to mention the four most prominent elaborators of the view[3] – argue that all of the present accounts of the moral requirement to obey the law are failures. The path that they follow is very much like the path of our earlier discussion (2.2) – there we considered several arguments for this moral requirement and how each of them is wanting in an important respect. How the philosophical anarchists differ is that they think that no positive account has been offered. If they were to criticize the account in terms of the requirement to do one's share for the common good (2.2), they would likely argue that this requirement itself calls for explanation. Why do I have a special moral requirement to promote the common good of this particular community that I happen to live in? Is it a brute fact that, wherever one is located, one is bound to promote the common good of that community? (So, if I were to travel to Spain, I would have the exact same obligations to the common good of Spain that I have toward the common good of the United States, the country of which I am a citizen? Is that right?) If it is not a brute fact, how is it to be explained? (It can't be consent, or fair play, or anything like that – as we saw, we do not generally perform the requisite voluntary acts.) The philosophical anarchists would also likely criticize the claim that the law's status as a clear standard to divide up the responsibilities to the common good binds people to act in accordance with it. Why is that? (Again, the answer cannot be one of agreement – but, then, how do we explain the moral relevance of the law's being a salient standard?)[4]

So the first stage of the philosophical anarchists' argument is to show that no existing theory of the moral requirement to obey the law is in fact successful. That might be interpreted as showing that there is no such moral requirement; or it might be interpreted as showing that philosophers of law have not been clever enough in constructing arguments. The second stage of the philosophical anarchists' argument is to provide a stronger basis for accepting the first interpretation. The way that they do this is to give reasons to think that it is not a massively counterintuitive conclusion to think that there is no moral requirement to obey the law. If one were to suppose that, if there were no moral requirement to obey the law, then people would have license to do all sorts of seemingly morally bad things, then we might think that philosophers simply need to work a little harder on their arguments, rather than that there is no moral requirement to obey the law. Here is an analogy. If I were able to show you that all philosophical arguments against murder were bad arguments, you would not conclude that it is morally permissible to murder; you would decide that philosophers are just not very clever. The reason is that it is clear to you that if there were no moral requirement against murder, then there would be some actions – for example, killing one's aunt for an inheritance – that would not count as wrong, but which you know fully well to be wrong. What the philosophical anarchists want to show is that the alleged moral requirement to obey the law is not like the moral requirement against murder – although you cannot dismiss the latter without counterintuitive results, you can dismiss the former without counterintuitive results.

The philosophical anarchists note, for example, that much of what the law forbids is wrong on other grounds: one does not need to believe in moral requirement to obey the law against murder in order to believe that one ought not to murder; one does not need to believe in a moral requirement to obey the law against rape in order to believe that one ought not to rape; and so forth. There are many acts that the law forbids that are "*mala in se*" – wrong in themselves – and so are acts that we ought not to perform even if the law were silent on these topics, or even if the law, though forbidding these actions, is not something that we are bound to heed. Even for those acts that are not wrong in themselves, it is often the case that the law establishes patterns of coordination that it would be wrong (and even deeply imprudent) to frustrate: traffic patterns (stoplights, right of way, proper side) should be complied with, even if there is no obligation to obey the law, because now that these patterns of coordination are in place it endangers self and others to violate them.[5]

The philosophical anarchists argue, then, that even if there is no moral obligation to obey the law, no reason to honor the demands of the role *subject*, there are other moral requirements that cover much of the same ground. Suppose that you came to believe that the fact that the law requires some action is not a moral reason for performing it: how would it change your behavior? To what extent is your actual judgment of the moral obligations that you are under influenced by a belief that you are genuinely bound to adhere to the law's demands?

Again, there is something right and something wrong about these arguments. It is true that there are a number of reasons that would require one to act in conformity with the typical demands of law, even if we came to believe that the law is not genuinely authoritative over subjects. But it seems to me that there is a wide swath of cases that do not neatly fit into the *mala in se*/patterns of coordination dichotomy that the philosophical anarchists employ to cover the ground that might be left uncovered by the absence of a moral requirement of obedience to law. An extraordinarily important role that law has is that of regulating the demands that we can make on each other. I should be able to demand of you that you not endanger me through drunk driving. You should be able to demand of me that I not endanger you through drunk driving. (Indeed, our law enforces this demand both through the criminal law and through tort law.) But, as Aquinas notes in his discussion of determinations (see 1.6.2), this is a *vague* demand: what constitutes the drunk driving that we should be able to bind each other to not performing? Is it to be measured by amount consumed? By actual impairment? By blood alcohol level? If the first, what amount? If the second, what level of impairment? If the third, by what percentage? If law is not authoritative, then we will in fact lack a common standard to apply to one another. If you want to hold me to a demand that I not drive after having drunk four beers, and I want to be held to the demand of not driving with a blood alcohol level over 0.10 percent, nothing can settle this between us: the standard "no drunk driving" is too vague to resolve the disagreement in either of our favors. So much of law concerns making more precise these standards of justice among subjects that it is hard to believe that no important practical consequences fall out of philosophical anarchism.

Philosophical anarchism is a thesis concerning the nonexistence of genuine authority of the law over its subjects. It is not to be confused with *political* anarchism, which is a claim about the undesirability of the state, or about the desirability of taking action to dismantle the state. One might hold one of these views without the other. Contemporary philosophical anarchists tend not to be political anarchists: they hold that while there is no moral obligation to obey the law, the existence of a state is overall a desirable thing. One might also be a political anarchist while not a philosophical anarchist: one might hold that there is indeed a moral requirement to obey the law of one's state, but that this is an unfortunate state of affairs; it would be better if there were no states at all.

Why might one affirm political anarchism? Given the need for a state to provide for defense, look after the needs of the less well-off, and so forth, why might one be tempted to the view that the existence of the state is overall an undesirable thing? The political anarchist's challenge typically comes from two directions: first, the political anarchist points out all of the dangers, real and actual, posed by states; second, the political anarchist argues that the state is itself in large measure the source rather than the remedy to the harms it is supposed to guard against. First, the state exhibits a hierarchical structure, ruling through authority and coercion. While one might find the notion of authority as considered in the Introduction rather benign, in practice authority in modern legal systems is wielded for the most part by elites of power and wealth, and the result is that subjects are oppressed by the rule of law. Second, the dangers of internal violence (crime) and external violence (war) are themselves largely the product of political structures. This is clear enough in the case of wars, which are state actions. In the case of crime, the anarchist claim is that states have the effect of dividing subjects from each other, and oppressing some for others' benefit (more on this below); it is this oppression and lack of solidarity that is a major source of criminality. As criminality increases, states assume more power to combat it; the increased level of insularity and oppression breeds more criminality; states assume more power to combat it; and so forth. Better to break the cycle through alternative ways of organizing (or refusing to organize) social life. While there are of course significant differences among political anarchists in terms of moral viewpoint and the extent to which they envision the particular character of life alternative to that under a state, these twin themes – that state authority is in some way ipso facto oppressive and that social ills, the handling of which is supposed to justify the state, are instead caused by it – are common to the political anarchisms of William Godwin, Pierre Proudhon, Mikhail Bakunin, Peter Kropotkin, Emma Goldman, and others.[6]

I will not attempt to assess here the political anarchist's criticisms of the structure of the modern state. I want just to note that the criticism of the *state* is not necessarily a criticism of *law*. If we were right to reject in Chapters 1 and 2 a conception of law in which law is essentially tied to sanctions, and we were right to reject in Chapter 2 any particular account of how the role *legislator* is occupied, it does not seem at all obvious that what political anarchists take to be the deeply objectionable features of the modern state – its hierarchical structure and oppressively coercive character – would have to be realized in every society that has law. In order to make that claim, the political anarchists would have to hold that any society that creates and applies rules through the role-differentiation essential to legal systems must harden into hierarchical structures in which persons hold power over, and thus oppress, others. But it seems that we could imagine schemes in which lawmaking is a formalized, though communal, activity and judging a task that rotates among members of the community rather than being an office that can be occupied only by social and economic elites. One can be antistate without being antilaw.

6.3 Against the Role of Legislator: Marxism, Feminist Legal Theory, Critical Race Theory

The anarchist challenge to law attacks the claim that people can be, or in fact are, morally bound by the role of subject. I want to consider now a challenge to the role of legislator, that is, whether that role can be successfully exercised. One of these challenges is easy to present once we recall the conditions for the successful exercise of that role and the way that the anarchist challenge bears on it. The other challenge, that rooted in Marxist thinking on law, politics, and class, is not standardly framed in terms of a challenge to a legal role. But, again, once we bring back to mind the conditions for the successful exercise of that role, we will see the clear relevance to that topic of the Marxist interpretations of social and political life.

Recall that the performance rule for the role *legislator* is that legislators are to make nondefective law, where nondefective law is law that is both authoritative and for the common good (2.3). Given this understanding of the role of legislator, it is clear that the question of the correctness of philosophical anarchism is relevant to the question of whether it is possible for legislators to carry out their role. Legislators can be successful in discharging their role only if the law that they make will be authoritative over the subjects to whom it applies; but if the philosophical anarchists are right, then legislators are doomed to fail in that role. So philosophical anarchism challenges not only the binding character of the role *subject*, it challenges the possibility of successful exercise of the role *legislator*.

The other line of challenge against the role of legislator is extensively developed in Marxist thought. Although an adequate development of Marxist ideas is impossible here, the following will suffice to bring out the source of difficulty for success in legislation brought to light by this line of thought. Marx's view is that the history of political and social life is a history of class struggle, in which an economically dominant class has power over an economically subordinated class.[7] While Marx did not affirm the view that every detail of social life is determined by the economic features of society, it is clear that he did hold that the economic features of a society generate constraints on the noneconomic possibilities within that society – constraints on what politics can be practiced, what social relationships are in place, what ideas can be thought and expressed – and that in the long haul the non-economic features of social life are ultimately determined by these economic features.[8]

These views – that societies are divided into classes in conflict, and that the noneconomic is broadly and ultimately determined by the economic – have important implications for our understanding of law. On Marx's view, the economic class to which one belongs will largely determine the conception of morality and value that one adopts: this is an implication of the broad determination of the noneconomic by the economic. Because these classes are not in harmony with each other but rather are in conflict with one another, it is fairly clear that these ideologies will be in conflict with one another as well. The conceptions of the good affirmed by the lord differ from and are in opposition to those affirmed by the serf; the conceptions of the good affirmed by the owner differ from and are in opposition to those affirmed by the wage-laborer.

Furthermore, it is inevitable that over the long haul the political and legal results of one class economically dominating another will be reflected in politics and law itself. Principles that might appear to be neutral on their face will turn out to be favorable to those in power. This bias can have a number of sources: it might simply be that those in economic power ultimately control the making and applying of law; it might be that those who are qualified (by facially neutral criteria, of course) to serve as lawmakers and judges are drawn from the economically dominant classes, with the result that the ideology of the dominant class is reflected in the made and applied law; it might be that, even without being traceable to any individuals' decisions, the legal order will be unable to sustain norms that go too contrary to the prevailing economic relationships.

Consider as an example of this effect the condition of working people in the United States in the early 1900s. The conditions of industrialization at that time were such that injuries to working people were dreadfully common. In theory, working folks could sue their employers to exact compensation for injuries suffered on the job as a result of negligently maintained working conditions. One can easily imagine a state of affairs in which employees were able to win such lawsuits, deterring factory owners from negligently maintaining their factories and requiring that justice be done to the workers whose labor generated the manufactured products. But as a matter of fact this is not the way things worked out. What arose in the courts is what is now sometimes called "the unholy trinity" – a trio of defenses to negligence claims that factory owners relied upon to block lawsuits and to ensure that injured workers could not recover. Sometimes the "fellow servant" rule was invoked: under this rule, one could not recover for injuries suffered on the job if the injuries were traceable at all to the negligence of a fellow worker. Sometimes the contributory negligence rule was invoked: under this rule, one could not recover for injuries suffered on account of another's negligence if one was in any way, and to even the slightest degree, negligent oneself. If all else failed, the assumption of risk doctrine could be invoked: it could be claimed that the worker knew what he or she was getting into, and so the losses must fall on the worker rather than on the employer.[9]

The Marxist view is sometimes invoked in order to bring out the point that what is held to be a rule of law that applies neutrally and impartially to subjects really is nothing like that. The rules of the negligence tort turned out to be a tool for the rejection of worker claims rather than that by which workers could be compensated for their unjustly suffered losses. The rules of property are not neutral but tools by which the economically advantaged can continue to accumulate wealth and thereby power over the economically less advantaged. The structure of free speech law is not neutral but enables those who are wealthy to have a much louder and influential voice in the crafting of law and policy than those who are poor.[10] The test of neutrality is not the appearance of the words of a legal text but the real effects within the network of social and economic relationships that actually holds sway.

This point about nonneutrality is not just a contingent feature of legal practice, something that well-meaning legislators could work their way around through conscientious reasoning and refusal to succumb to political and economic pressures. If Marx is right, it is inevitable that in societies constituted by classes in conflict the law will favor the economically powerful. But to say this is not to say that on *each and every occasion* in which law might favor the economically stronger class, it will do so. Rather, it points to an inevitable *trend* in favor of the economically stronger and to limits on law imposed by the demands of these economic relationships. Return to the case of industrialization in the United States, and to the unholy trinity: the result of this refusal to grant recovery was an increasing level of protest by workers about the inability to recover, and the eventual results of this was the advent of worker's compensation as an alternative to tort recovery. This might seem like a setback to the economically dominant owners. But in fact it was a concession that blocked the path to fuller reform: by establishing a schedule of payments for injury that did not attempt to cover all losses (it excludes compensation for pain and suffering, for example) and that capped recoveries, employers continued to be able to pay out far less than full compensation for on-the-job injuries.

Part of the explanation for the inability to achieve impartiality in legal norms is that, on Marx's view, legal norms are constrained by existing economic relationships, which are themselves one-sided. But part of the explanation is also that the impartiality itself is bound to be chimerical. To be impartial in making law is to apply a notion of justice and the common good equally to the interests of the subjects that will be governed by that law. But Marx's point is that there is no such neutral conception of justice and the good available: class status shapes members' conceptions of justice and the common good as well.

As I said, these Marxist ideas are woefully inadequately developed here. But, inadequate as they are, it should be clear how their correctness would generate serious difficulties for the performance of the role of legislator as we have formulated it. In addition to the demand that laws made by the legislator must be authoritative, we have also said that laws made by the legislator must be for the common good. But these Marxist ideas call into question that possibility. For if Marx is right, the inevitable long-term trend in law is not toward the common good but toward the interests of one class, that is, the economically dominant one; and, since the interests of this class are opposed to the interests of the economically subordinate class, there is no genuine long-term prospect of law being for the common good. (This is compatible with individual laws managing to promote the interests of the economically subordinate class: Marx's thesis concerns the ultimate determination of law by economic power, not the impossibility of there being any laws that are contrary to the interests of the economically dominant class.)

Further, it is hard to see how legislative deliberation for the common good would be possible on a Marxist understanding of ideology. If legislative deliberation must be done from the perspective of the common good, then that must be a perspective that it is possible for a member of a classes-in-conflict society to take up. But if the conceptions of interests taken up by the distinct classes are not only different but opposed, it is hard to see what it would be like to legislate for the *common* good. On Marx's view, there can be no hope for law that is for the common good until society no longer consists of classes in conflict: until revolution abolishes economic class distinctions and thus the power relations that are sustained by those distinctions, law will inevitably fail to be for the common good, and thus the task of the legislator is doomed to failure.[11]

Marx's views on economics, law, and politics are formulated as they are because of Marx's position that economic relationships are the ultimate determining ground for other sorts of relationships that constitute a social life. But one might reject Marx's views about economics as the ultimate determining ground while nevertheless affirming his views on power and how differences in power preclude neutrality in law, constrain law's potentials as a reforming force, and shape the conceptions of justice and the common good belonging to the oppressors and the oppressed. We might call those who affirm these views *pluralists* about power – they take the sources of power to be various, though the ways that these power relationships limit law-making and preclude a genuinely common good are the same.

A movement in legal theory begun in the 1970s called "critical legal studies," about which I will speak in a little more detail in 6.4, has affirmed something like this Marxist take on law with this pluralist spin. Suffice it to say here that adherents of critical legal studies were deeply concerned to call into question any lazy assumptions that law operates in a neutral or formal way; rather, it is constantly taking a substantive stand on matters of justice and the common good that is biased in favor of the interests of dominant groups. Unlike under standard Marxism, the dominant groups need not be characterized primarily in economic terms. The offshoots of this general program in critical legal studies include feminist legal theory and critical race studies.

The point of departure of feminist legal theory is that men hold a socially and economically dominant position over women, and thus it is to be expected that the law, even that which on its face appears to be neutral between men and women, should exhibit a bias in favor of men. So it is unsurprising that when feminist social theorist Andrea Dworkin and feminist legal theorist Catharine MacKinnon drafted antipornography statutes adopted by the city of Indianapolis, those statutes were struck down as unconstitutional restrictions on free speech.[12] The harm to women that pornography causes, MacKinnon claims, is invisible from the point of view of the allegedly neutral free speech jurisprudence.[13] The point of departure of critical race studies is that whites hold a socially and economically dominant position over members of other races, and thus it is to be expected that the law, even that which on its face appears to be neutral among members of different racial groups, should exhibit a bias in favor of whites. So it is unsurprising that when a statute is passed that forbids hate speech, that statute is struck down as an unconstitutional abridgement of free speech.[14] The harm to racial minorities caused by such speech is invisible from the point of view of free speech jurisprudence.

Feminist legal theorists and critical race theorists have been perfectly willing to offer legislative proposals that will ease the burdens of injustice against women and minority groups. This is perfectly consistent with the view that, until the power relationships between members of the different sexes and races are abolished, it is inevitable both that the law will tend to favor the white and the male and that the distinctive interests of these social groups preclude legislators from genuinely deliberating about law from the point of view of the common good.

Even taking for granted the view that distinct and opposed social groups tend to have distinct and opposed conceptions of the good, it does not quite follow that the legislative task is an impossible one. What is impossible is for the legislator to carry out the legislative task in a representative way (see 2.3), representing the perspective of society at large in coming to a judgment about what laws should be adopted, revised, or abolished. If one is to represent in a society constituted by classes in conflict, then one will represent one of these groups or another. On the other hand, it may well be possible for legislators to carry out their task if they may proceed from the perspective of objective benevolence, asking what laws and policies would best serve the actual interests of the parties in their care. For while different groups may have different conceptions of their interests, that does not mean that their interests are in fact simply opposed; for one's conceptions of one's interests may well fail to line up with what one's interests actually are. One might object, of course, that this ignores the Marxist belief that one's view of justice and the common good is fixed by one's class; but that puts the point too strongly – the most Marx can say is that the broad tendency is for members of a social class to share a common conception of justice and the common good. It is consistent with Marx's view that there be extraordinary individuals who can see – better than others, though not of course perfectly – the ways in which ideologies blind us to our common human nature and common human goods shared by members of rival social groups.[15] It may be conceded that until these rival groups are no longer dominating and dominated, the trend will remain toward bias and oppression. But there is always the possibility that intelligent and extraordinary lawmaking can selectively undermine the conditions of dominance or, at least, pave the way for more massive and revolutionary forms of social change.

6.4 Against the Role of Judge: American Legal Realism, Critical Legal Studies

The distinction between the legislator and the judge is the distinction between rule-maker and rule-applier. The legislator crafts a variety of rules to guide the conduct of citizens; the judge applies rules to particular cases. Now, we have seen already that this is in many ways a misleading picture of the way that judging works. We have to keep in mind that legislators do not supply all of the rules that judges must apply to cases: not even all of what Hart calls the duty-imposing rules (see 1.4) are the products of legislation. Some such rules might be taken up into the norms of a legal system by the judiciary's acceptance of customary norms, for example. And judges characteristically take one of their tenets of rule-interpretation and rule-application to include deference to judges' decisions in earlier cases – this is the doctrine of *stare decisis*, that is, that the (earlier) decisions should stand. (Most of tort law is developed by this appeal to custom and precedent, built up by judges in what is called the "common law.")

There is no trouble describing the role of the judge so that it includes more than just the application of rules created by legislators: the role of the judge is to apply the law – understood in the broad sense as whatever falls under the rule of recognition – to cases. Trouble begins to brew, though, when one considers the presuppositions of the notion of "application" and the extent to which the sources of law available to judges enables them to engage in this task.

What is it to *apply* a rule or set of rules to an individual case? If I am called upon to make a decision in a particular situation – say, I have to decide whether the defendant is bound to pay damages to the plaintiff, or whether instead the defendant is free of liability – what would make it true that my decision was the result of an application of a set of rules to the case at hand? Surely it is not that I have a book of rules on my desk, look at it earnestly, and then come to a decision. My looking at the rules may have nothing to do with my decision – I might not even understand them. Even if I understand the rules, the rules might not be the source of my decision – I might just like the looks of the plaintiff, while I find the defendant irritating. It is not even enough that the rules *cause* me to make the decision that I make. If my reading and understanding the rules causes me to be disgusted at the very idea of bringing lawsuits, and thus to decide against the plaintiff, no one would say that my decision was the result of my applying the rules to the case at hand. To be caused to make a particular decision by the rules is not the same as to apply the rules in making that decision. Rather, to apply the rules to a case is *to take those rules as one's guide* in reaching the decision in the case. Applying rules is like using a map: to use a map is to take it as a guide to determining locations, or to finding one's way on a real or imagined trip; to apply rules is to take them as a guide to determining the result of a real or hypothetical case.

The role of judges is to take the law as their guide to determining the decisions in cases before them; the good judge is one who is well guided by the law, who correctly follows the course that the law has set for him or her. As we saw above, though, there are cases in which it seems that the law runs out. In such cases, to some extent the judge's decision is not fixed by rule-application; the judge will have to make the decision in a way that goes beyond what is mandated by rule-application.

The interesting and important questions are, first, how pervasive this phenomenon is, and second, to what extent this calls into question the role of the judge as one who renders decisions according to law. A school of thought that has been massively influential in bringing out the extent to which law fails to yield determinate decisions in cases is that of *American legal realism*. The legal realists were early twentieth-century philosophers, lawyers, and judges who, while holding different views on political issues of the day, were united by the perspective that students of the law need to take a less idealistic and more realistic view of how decisions are reached. On their view, such a realistic appraisal leads to the thesis that law is massively *indeterminate*: there is a huge variety of fact-patterns in which law fails to yield a determinate verdict, and so any judges' decisions in these cases must go beyond what could possible be reached on the simple basis of rule-application.

The notion that there is a huge variety of fact-patterns in which law fails to yield a determinate verdict is unhelpfully vague, but that description can be supplemented so that the realists' view is an informative one. As Brian Leiter describes their collective view, the point emphasized by the realists is not that in run-of-the-mill lower court cases there are no legally right answers; characteristically, there will be.[16] What the realists wanted to claim was that once we move beyond these mundane cases to those cases that make their way to appeals courts, indeterminacy prevails. At the level of appeals, in which open questions of law are brought to and argued before judges, there is no decision that is determined by the legal materials at hand.

What is the basis for this view? Why the skepticism about the extent to which law yields determinate answers when there is a question about whether one owes a duty of care to warn a partygoer about shallow water; or about whether bringing in an Anglican clergyman counts as importing labor; or about whether the death penalty counts as cruel and unusual punishment? The skepticism does not arise simply from the fact that some lawyers might be of one opinion on the question, and some lawyers are of another. That there are folks with different opinions might be explained simply by the fact that some people are less legally skilled than others, or have not considered the issues at hand carefully enough. The skepticism arises, rather, from an account of what legal resources would be sufficient to produce legal determinacy, and an argument that these legal resources are lacking.

What would be sufficient to produce legal determinacy would be something like this. To the extent that one is drawing legal rules from earlier decisions to decide a present case, one would need rules of interpretation that prescribe unambiguously how to extract those legal rules from those cases. But we lack such rules: it is characteristic to proceed on the basis of analogy, noting similarities between past and present cases; but it is unclear by what legal standard certain similarities are judged relevant and others not. Nor is there any legal consensus about whether the rules extracted from precedents should be extracted narrowly (thus holding tightly to the facts of the case, which is the honorable practice of trying to confine a decision to the facts) or broadly (thus formulating a more abstract rule, which is the honorable practice of trying to articulate a general principle that will govern future cases).[17] To the extent that one is drawing legal rules from statutes, we face (as we noted in 2.4) questions about how the inevitable vagueness in language is to be handled: there are legally honorable traditions of speaker's meaning, hearer's meaning, community meaning, and so forth that can be employed to reach a decision. And of course one will also have to face questions about the extent to which seemingly conflicting precedents should be handled, and how statutes should be read against precedents, and against each other.

The realist point is that the sources of law are not self-interpreting, and the interpretive standards that are treated as within the pale inside legal practice are not sufficient to decide the real disputes that arise on appeal. Law is thus to that extent indeterminate: legal resources are not sufficient to decide legal questions. If judges think that their decisions in these cases are fixed by law, then they are mistaken. The fact that judges' decisions are largely predictable cannot be explained by the fact of the law's determinacy, but from some other set of facts: these explanations could be sociological, having to do with general truths about judges and the tendencies of the social classes to which they usually belong; or they could be individual psychological explanations, having to do with individual judges' preferences and predilections; or they could be normative explanations, having to do with the moral rightness of certain decisions and how judges, being generally morally decent folk, will be drawn to these decisions in the absence of determinate legal solutions.

We will examine below how we ought to respond to the realists' claims, if those claims are true. But note for the moment how these claims are subversive of our understanding of the role of the judge. I argued above that the role of the judge is to apply the law; to the extent that the judge's decisions are not the result of the application of the law, the person occupying the role of judge is not making decisions in accordance with that role. If the realists are right, no appellate court judge is rendering decisions determined by his or her role as judge. Appellate court judges are rendering decisions based on their social status, or political sympathies, or moral views, or religious convictions.

American legal realism had its heyday in the earlier half of the twentieth century. But there was a revival of realist themes in the last few decades of that century under the title "critical legal studies." Critical legal studies was, as is obvious, a *critical* movement, calling into question a variety of presuppositions of the practice and teaching of law. Important here for our purposes is the way that it took up and carried further the realist assault on legal determinacy. We can think about the contrast in the following way. The legal realists were content to carry out their critique within the domain of the appellate courts. On their view, that is where the action is, the hard cases of law whose solution judges claim to be able to provide through specifically legal techniques but whose solution must come instead from extralegal sources. Advocates of critical legal studies – the "crits" – took their critique further, holding that even in the everyday workings of the lower courts the law is rife with indeterminacy.

One might think that this is a plainly implausible hypothesis. For if it is the fact of disagreement at the appellate level that gives the first suggestion that perhaps at that level legal determinacy is not to be had, it is the fact of by-and-large agreement at the trial court level that suggests that at that level there is a large measure of legal determinacy. The strategy of the crits, though, is to argue that the by-and-large agreement at that level is not the result of the determinacy of legal sources, but is explained in some other way. For all of the sources of indeterminacy that appear at the appellate level appear at the trial court level: we have precedents from which a number of competing principles can be extracted; we have analogies that can be made or refused without a legally nonarbitrary way of selecting among them; we have statutes that can be read from various perspectives and with various interests in mind; and so forth. So it is not obvious why indeterminacy should not be rife even at this level. How, then, do we explain the by-and-large agreement? Not through the determinacy of the legal sources: through the fact that judges have shared, substantive, *extralegal* understandings – shared moral/political views on the priority of social stability; on the authoritative character of their own rulings; on the inviolability of property; on the proper relationships between husband and wife, parent and child, stranger and stranger; and so forth.[18] For those who share these extralegal understandings, the law can seem crystal clear. But to those who do not share those understandings – to those who wish to call into question the shared understandings as unjustifiable, misguided, or oppressive – it will be far less clear that law requires these outcomes; judges' decisions will appear as imports of extralegal values into the law, clearly the product of a choice rather than a matter fixed by the law itself.[19]

The crits took their views to lead to a conclusion summarized by the slogan "law is politics," and which we can frame in terms of the roles of legislator and judge. On the crits' view, there is no clear line between the lawmaking role of legislators (politics) and the law-applying role of judges (law). In both cases the decisions made may be unconstrained by prior rules and can be simply the product of the legislator's/judge's own value commitments. As we conceded above (2.4), the existence of gaps in the law require those who occupy the role of judge to make determinate what is not yet settled by law in order to resolve a dispute that requires resolution. But if the crits are right, this is the typical rather than the atypical case: judges are constantly imposing their moral and political vision, whether idiosyncratic or shared with like-minded judges, in settling disputes. Legislators and judges are not, respectively, lawmakers and law-appliers, but rather both lawmakers operating in different contexts and under different social constraints.

Both the realists and the crits share this view: if judges are not self-deceived, then they will recognize that they are not discovering what is hidden in law or making explicit what is already there implicitly. They are, instead, going beyond what is already there. Suppose that this is true. How should we think of the role of the judge?

One way of responding to the realists'/crits' claims about legal indeterminacy and its implications for the role of judging is to say that judges should just go on doing, self-consciously and publicly, what they must have been doing all along anyway: deciding cases on extra-legal grounds. Judges should, that is, acknowledge the extent to which extralegal considerations must be drawn upon in reaching their decisions, and argue for the way that they treat certain of these extra-legal considerations as being relevant and ultimately decisive.[20] Two features of this recommendation merit comment. The first is that judges will, on this view, no longer be able to claim that they are only doing what the law requires when rendering decisions that serve only to perpetuate oppressive social relationships. The second is that judges will be making public, bringing out into the open, the genuinely determining grounds of their decisions, so that they can be scrutinized and criticized on their proper bases: moral and political, rather than narrowly legal.

Challenging the Law

The "do-publicly-and-openly-what-you've-been-doing-privately-and-secretly" solution to the problem of judging under conditions of legal indeterminacy admits of its own problems. The most obvious question to raise with respect to it is that of the extent to which subjects should be willing to accept judicial decisions as authoritative if those decisions are in fact not fixed by prior law but are the product of wide-reaching judicial discretion. There is of course nothing in principle that precludes two levels of rule-making, one context for which is that associated with legislators and one context for which is that associated with judges. The problem is that of asking what features of the practice of judging have been developed under the assumption of legal determinacy, and figuring out to what extent these other practices would also have to be revised in order to make sense of the authority of this revised conception of the judicial role.

For example: legislators, it is often thought, ought to be elected by the people, whether the conception of lawmaking that is adopted is that of objective benevolence or representation (2.3). Judges are, however, characteristically not elected but appointed, and often not for fixed terms but for life. One can make sense out of this if one conceives the role of the judge to be that of an expert technical reasoner – an expert, that is, in the technique of legal reasoning. Experts tend not to lose their expertise from electoral cycle to electoral cycle, and to be freed from election pressures is to preserve the law-applier from moral and political pressures that are irrelevant to determining what the law is. But if one rejects the view that judging is by and large an exercise in technical legal reasoning isolated from broader moral and political thinking, then it is hard to see why we would accept judicial rule-making when the judges are appointed for life. If we think legislators should not be immune to the moral and political pressures of the day, then why shouldn't judges be subject to those same pressures?

One might suggest that the relevant comparison here is not to legislators but to bureaucrats – those government officials who staff administrative agencies and develop detailed policy under the responsibilities delegated to them by elected officials. These bureaucrats have expertise in their fields that could justify their exercising limited legislative authority, even if unelected. But the cases are dissimilar. Judges' expertise is, if anything, expertise in the law. Some judges have expertise in other areas: economics, perhaps, or political science, or history, or philosophy. But there is no expertise that judges have *as a class* that goes beyond whatever legal abilities are presumably typical of them. There is no reason at all to think that judges are in some way expert in moral or political reasoning that would justify their ruling as philosopher-kings within their zones of discretion.

The most powerful claim that can be made on behalf of the judicial claim to authority under conditions of legal indeterminacy is simply one of *need*: we *need* to have binding decisions when there is a dispute between two parties; relying on the parties themselves to work it out may be fruitless; and so we should defer to those who have expertise in the law so far as it is relevant and can exercise discretion to rule in cases where the law yields no determinate result. This argument may hold good in many cases. But its force depends entirely on how pressing the need for a resolution is and whether there are alternative sources of resolution to which we would be more inclined to grant deference than a judge's resolution. So it may be true that in a contract dispute in which both sides cannot agree to an arbitrator, we should recognize that a judge has and should have the authority to render a binding decision in the case, even if the decision involves exercise of judicial discretion of a substantial sort. But it may not be true that in, say, some weighty constitutional matter – at least when the decision would be binding not only on the parties to the case but on legislators and subjects generally – exercise of judicial discretion is the way to go. There may be massive costs in not allowing the dispute to be carried out in a more inclusive manner, for by rendering a binding decision, judges cut off the possibility of deliberation by citizens and legislators about how to make the law more determinate. Insofar as common deliberation about the course of a political society's common life is a good thing, this sort of exercise of judicial discretion would be on its face suspicious. The point, then, is that a one-size-fits-all response to legal indeterminacy is not obviously correct: it may be that different sorts of law call for different sorts of responsible judging in the face of legal indeterminacy.

We should also keep in mind that it is not clear how damaging even the most wide-ranging crit attack on legal determinacy is. The crit attack turns on two claims: first, that legal sources plus canonical modes of legal interpretation leave an enormous measure of indeterminacy in law; and, second, that to the extent that this indeterminacy does not generate unpredictability it is only because of the shared moral and political understandings of judges. But one can simply point out that the canonical modes of legal interpretation may very well take for granted at least some subset of judges' shared moral and political understandings. *It is almost never morally justifiable intentionally to kill another* is a shared moral understanding that is unlikely to yield anytime soon, no matter how pervasive the critique of law one might offer; it is part of judges' shared understanding, and influences the way that the law of homicide is understood and justifications for killing vetted, because it is true and easily known. If there are general truths about human good, and what we basically owe to one another, that are in fact generally shared because true and easily known, then one might simply take the crits' point that, in the absence of an acceptance of these truths, the law of murder would be deeply indeterminate to be very much like the claim that, if human beings had exoskeletons like insects, the law of battery would be very different. What the crits would have to imagine away is something very central to the human condition, and it is unclear why we would take reflection on the legal world of humans with insect bodies, or humans who do not know that murder is wrong, to be of relevance in our attempt to understand *our* legal world.

For Further Reading

A. John Simmons's *Moral Principles and Political Obligations* (Princeton, NJ: Princeton University Press, 1979) is one of the most important works defending philosophical anarchism, and is both accessible and philosophically rigorous. William A. Edmundson's *Three Anarchical Fallacies* (New York: Cambridge University Press, 1997), while accepting much of the force of Simmons's argument, calls into question some of the alleged implications of philosophical anarchism. For an overview of anarchist arguments, see Richard Sylvan's excellent article "Anarchism," in Robert E. Goodin and Philip Pettit (eds.), *A Companion to Contemporary Political Philosophy* (Oxford: Blackwell, 1993), pp. 215–43. Accounts of a number of important anarchist figures can be found in Paul Avrich, *Anarchist Portraits* (Princeton, NJ: Princeton University Press, 1990).

The quantity of Marx's writings is hard to fathom: a judicious selection can be found in *Selected Writings*, ed. David McLellan, 2nd edn (New York: Oxford University Press, 2000). An excellent brief guidebook to Marx's thought is Jonathan Wolff's *Why Read Marx Today?* (Oxford:

Oxford University Press, 2002). Alan Hunt offers an overview of Marx's views as applied to law in "Marxist Theory of Law," in Dennis Patterson (ed.), *A Companion to Philosophy of Law and Legal Theory* (Malden, MA: Blackwell Publishers, 1996), pp. 355–66. For readings on critical race theory, see Kimberle Crenshaw, Neil Gotanda, Garry Peller, and Kendall Thomas (eds.), *Critical Race Theory: The Key Writings That Formed the Movement* (New York: New Press, 1995), and Richard Delgado and Jean Stefancic (eds.), *Critical Race Theory: The Cutting Edge* (Philadelphia, PA: Temple University Press, 1999); for an overview of the movement, see Richard Delgado and Jean Stefancic, *Critical Race Theory: An Introduction* (New York: New York University Press, 2001). For readings on feminist legal theory, see Katharine Bartlett and Rosanne Kennedy (eds.), *Feminist Legal Theory* (Boulder, CO: Westview, 1991) and Patricia Smith (ed.), *Feminist Jurisprudence* (New York: Oxford University Press, 1993); for an article-length overview of several themes of feminist legal thought, see Patricia Smith, "Four Themes in Feminist Legal Theory: Difference, Dominance, Domesticity, and Denial," in Martin P. Golding and William A. Edmundson (eds.), *The Blackwell Guide to Philosophy of Law and Legal Theory* (Malden, MA: Blackwell, 2005), pp. 90–104.

For a wide-ranging collection of writings of American legal realists, see William W. Fisher III, Morton J. Horwitz, and Thomas Reed (eds.), *American Legal Realism* (New York: Oxford University Press, 1993). Brian Leiter's work expounding and defending legal realism is highly recommended: see his "Legal Realism and Legal Positivism Reconsidered," *Ethics* 111 (2001), pp. 278–301 and "American Legal Realism," in Martin P. Golding and William A. Edmundson (eds.), *The Blackwell Guide to Philosophy of Law and Legal Theory* (Malden, MA: Blackwell, 2005), pp. 50–66. For formulations and defenses of crit positions on adjudication, see Roberto Unger, *The Critical Legal Studies Movement* (Cambridge, MA: Harvard University Press, 1986) and Duncan Kennedy, *A Critique of Adjudication* (Cambridge, MA: Harvard University Press, 1997); Andrew Altman's *Critical Legal Studies: A Liberal Critique* (Princeton, NJ: Princeton University Press, 1990) offers a sympathetic exposition and a forceful rejoinder to the crits' distinctive claims.

Notes

1 Robert Paul Wolff, *In Defense of Anarchism*, 2nd edn (Berkeley: University of California Press, 1998 [first published 1970]), pp. 3–19.
2 Ibid., p. 13.

3 M. B. E. Smith, "Is There a Prima Facie Obligation to Obey the Law?" *Yale Law Journal* 82 (1973), pp. 950–76; A. John Simmons, *Moral Principles and Political Obligations* (Princeton, NJ: Princeton University Press, 1979); Joseph Raz, *The Authority of Law* (Oxford: Clarendon Press, 1979); Leslie Green, *The Authority of the State* (Oxford: Clarendon Press, 1990).

4 Both of these are genuinely difficult questions. For one response to them, see John Finnis, *Natural Law and Natural Rights* (Oxford: Clarendon Press, 1980), pp. 245–52; for another, see Mark C. Murphy, *Natural Law in Jurisprudence and Politics* (New York: Cambridge University Press, 2006), pp. 109–32.

5 See, for one employment of this argument, Raz, *Authority of Law*, pp. 247–8.

6 See, for representative works, William Godwin, *An Enquiry Concerning Political Justice* (New York: Penguin, 1985 [first published 1793]); Pierre-Joseph Proudhon, *Selected Writings*, ed. Stewart Edwards, trans. Elizabeth Fraser (Garden City, NJ: Anchor, 1969); Mikhail Bakunin, *Bakunin on Anarchy*, ed. Sam Dolgoff (New York: Knopf, 1972); Peter Kropotkin, *Selected Writings on Anarchism and Revolution*, ed. Martin A. Miller (Cambridge, MA: MIT Press, 1970); and Emma Goldman, *Anarchism and Other Essays* (New York: Dover, 1969).

7 Karl Marx and Friedrich Engels, *The Communist Manifesto*, in *Selected Writings*, ed. David McLellan, 2nd edn (New York: Oxford University Press, 2000), p. 246.

8 Marx, "Preface to *A Critique of Political Economy*," in *Selected Writings*, p. 425.

9 See W. Page Keeton, *Prosser and Keeton on Torts*, 5th edn (St Paul, MN: West Publishing, 1984), §80.

10 Note, for example, that in *Buckley v. Valeo* (424 U.S. 1 (1976)) the United States Supreme Court rejected certain limits on campaign contributions by individuals, holding that such restrictions were tantamount to restrictions on free speech and thus unconstitutional. One might plausibly claim that the effects of this allegedly neutral ruling on the requirements of freedom of speech are obviously far from neutral: the less well-off are even more deprived of influence over the political process as a result.

11 Marx, like the political anarchists, is antistate. But Marx's criticisms of the state, as I understand them, are criticisms of its hierarchical structure, operating in a top-down way, which is sure to sustain the domination of one class over another. After the revolution, the state will eventually be dissolved (*Communist Manifesto*, in *Selected Writings*, p. 262) but that does not mean that law will be absent: there may be ways of establishing norms that are recognizably legal but which do not proceed from a coercive apparatus of class domination.

12 *American Booksellers Association v. Hudnut*, 771 F.2d 323 (7th Cir. 1985); affirmed (by memorandum) 475 U.S. 1001 (1986).
13 Catharine MacKinnon, "Francis Biddle's Sister: Pornography, Civil Rights, and Speech" and "The Sexual Politics of the First Amendment," in *Feminism Unmodified* (Cambridge, MA: Harvard University Press, 1987), pp. 163–97 and 206–14.
14 *R. A. V. v. City of St. Paul*, 505 U.S. 377 (1991).
15 Marx, "Moralizing Criticism and Critical Morality," in *Selected Writings*, p. 234. Indeed, Marx may have seen himself as one such, given his confident assertions about the nature of human "species-being," that is, what is necessary for us to reach our fulfillment not simply as bourgeoisie or proletarian, but as human; see *Economic and Political Manuscripts*, in *Selected Writings*, pp. 89–91.
16 Brian Leiter, "Legal Realism and Legal Positivism Reconsidered," *Ethics* 111 (2001), pp. 278–301, particularly p. 298.
17 Karl Llewelyn, *The Bramble Bush* (Dobbs Ferry, NY: Oceana, 1973 [first published 1930]), pp. 66–9.
18 See David Kairys, "Legal Reasoning," in David Kairys (ed.), *The Politics of Law* (New York: Pantheon, 1982), p. 15:

The shared backgrounds, socialization, and experience of our judges, which include law school and usually law practice, yield definite patterns in the ways they categorize, approach, and resolve social and political conflicts. Moreover, some rules and results are relatively uncontroversial and predictable in a particular historical context, not based on *stare decisis* or any other legal principle but because of widely shared social and political assumptions characteristic of that context.

19 See, for one among many examples, Duncan Kennedy, "Freedom and Constraint in Adjudication," *Journal of Legal Education* 36 (1986), pp. 518–62.
20 Holmes, "The Path of the Law," *Harvard Law Review* 10 (1897), pp. 457–78, particularly p. 467; other approaches are distinguished and discussed by Brian Leiter in "American Legal Realism," in Martin P. Golding and William A. Edmundson (eds.), *The Blackwell Guide to Philosophy of Law and Legal Theory* (Malden, MA: Blackwell, 2005), pp. 50–66, particularly pp. 58–9.

Index

actus reus 113
affirmative defenses 133, *see also*
  excuses; justifications
aims of law
  distinguished from common
    good 81–3
  Mill's account of 83–8, *see also*
    Mill, John Stuart
  moralist accounts of 101–8
  paternalist accounts of 93–7
American legal realism
see legal realism, American
analysis, conceptual 14–16
  and commonplaces 14–15
  and clear cases 15–16
  importance of 16
anarchism, philosophical
  184–90
anarchism, political 184, 190–1,
  208n11
Anscombe, G. E. M. 168
Aquinas, Thomas 38–44
  on definition of law 38
  on determinations of general
    principles 40
  on law as rational
    standard 38–40
  on morals legislation 100
Aristotle 1
Armstrong, Lance 5
assumption of risk 177–8
attempts, criminal 139–42
Austin, John 17–26, 42
  on commands 17–18, 21
  on law's authority 19, 22–3

on law's orientation to the
    common good, 19–20, 23–5
  on law's sociality 17–18, 25
  on obligations 18
  on sanctions 18
  on sovereignty 18–19, 21–2
authority
  alleged conflict with
    autonomy 184–7
  de facto 8
  genuine 8
  practical 7–9
  theoretical 7
authority commonplace 6–9
autonomy, good of 87, 95–7
  alleged conflict with
    authority 184–7

Bakhunin, Mikhail 191
Bix, Brian 42
Buckley v. Valeo 208n10

Cardozo, Benjamin 176
cause, in tort
  "but for" (cause in fact)
    165–6
  proximate 166–9
*Church of the Holy Trinity v. United
    States* 71–2
clear cases, and conceptual
    analysis 15–16
Coase, Ronald 149–51
common good
  critical race theory challenge
    to 197

Index

harm-to-others principle 83–90, 91–2
  as appealing to what is due to others 83–4
  and conduct 84–7
  and nature of harm 88–9
  qualifications to 92–4
  and speech 84, 91–2
Hart, H. L. A.
  on causation 166–7
  on judicial discretion 75
  on law's authority 30–1
  on law's orientation to the common good 31
  on law's sociality 26–30
  on morals legislation 102–13
  on the nature of law 26–31, 33–4
  on the rule of recognition 29
  on social rules 26–8
Holmes, Oliver Wendell 152, 161–2
Honoré, A. M. 166–7
Hymowitz v. Eli Lilly 169

incapacitation 118
inclusive legal positivism
see soft positivism
injunctive relief 180n1
insanity defense 136–8
  American Legal Institute rule for 137–9
  M'Naghten rule for 137
intentional torts 175–6
interpretation, legal 70–5

judges, basic legal role of 50, 69–79
  American legal realist challenge to 199–201
  critical legal studies challenge to 201–3
  and interpretation of legal materials 70–5
  occupancy rules for 69–70

performance rules for 70–1, 198–9
  and problem of legal indeterminacy 75–7
justifications 134–6

Kant, Immanuel 123–4, 129
knowledge, analysis of 14–15
Kropotkin, Peter 191

lawyer, role of 50–1
legal indeterminacy 75–7, 200–1
legal positivism
  Austin's version of 17–26
  defined 25–6
  hard 34–5, 36
  Hart's version of 26–31
  soft 32–4, 36
legal realism, American 77, 199–201
legislator, basic legal role of 50, 63–9
  anarchist challenge to 192
  critical race theory challenge to 197
  feminist legal theory challenge to 196–7
  Marxist challenge to 192–6, 197–8
  and objective benevolence 65–7
  occupancy rules for 63
  performance rules for 63–5
  reasons to adhere to demands of 68–9
  and representation 66–7
Leiter, Brian 200
lex talionis 124–5

MacKinnon, Catharine 196–7
mala in se violations of law 189
Marmor, Andrei 42–3
Marxism 192–6

212

Index

mens rea 113
Mill, John Stuart
  on the harm-to-others
    principle 83–90, 91–2, *see also*
    harm–to–others principle
  as a utilitarian 85
M'Naghten rule 137, 145n23
morality, critical/positive distinction
  concerning 101, 105–6
morals legislation 98–108
  coherence of 98–9
  Devlin's defense of 101–3
  idealist defense of 106–8
  neo-Devlinian defense of 105–6
  paternalist defense of 103–5
Moore, Michael 129

natural law theory
  Aquinas's substantive version
    of 38–43, *see also* Aquinas,
    Thomas
  defined 36
  Fuller's procedural version
    of 36–8, *see also* Fuller, Lon
  as a label 47n27
necessity, as a criminal defense
  134–6
negligence torts
  breach element of 147, 160–5
  cause element of 147, 165–9
  duty element of 147, 155–60
  loss element of 147, 169–70

objective benevolence, as account of
  legislative role 65–8
obligation to obey the law
  consent account of 55–7
  consequentialist account of
    57–8
  fairness account of 59–62
  survey argument against
    187–8

  as unnecessary to explain our
    moral intuitions 188–90
offensive conduct 89–92

Palsgraf v. Long Island Railroad 176
paternalism 93–7
Perry, Stephen 153–4
philosophical anarchism *see*
  anarchism, philosophical
pluralism, about sources of political
  power 196
police officer, role of 50–1
political anarchism *see* anarchism,
  political
Posner, Richard 151, 163–4
prison warden, role of 50–1
Proudhon, Pierre 191
proportionality, between crime and
  punishment 125–8
punishment
  analysis of 113–5
  basic problem of 116–17
  problem about amount of 117
  problem about target of 117
  see also retributivist account of
    punishment; utilitarian account
    of punishment

Rawls, John 59–60, 61
Raz, Joseph 34–5, 187
reasonable person standard 161–5
  Hand formula for 163–5
rehabilitation 118
representation, as account of
  legislative role 66–8
retributivist account of
  punishment 122–32
  criticisms of 131–2
  and desert 129–30
  on excuses 139
  and expressing the value of the
    common good 130–1

213

Made in the USA
Middletown, DE
11 September 2022

10197299R00128